The Last Years of Karl Marx

THE LAST YEARS OF
KARL MARX, 1881–1883

AN INTELLECTUAL BIOGRAPHY

Marcello Musto

Translated by Patrick Camiller

Stanford University Press
Stanford, California

STANFORD UNIVERSITY PRESS
Stanford, California

English translation ©2020 by the Board of Trustees of the Leland Stanford Junior University. All rights reserved.

The Last Years of Karl Marx: An Intellectual Biography was originally published in Italian in 2016 under the title *L'ultimo Marx, 1881–1883. Saggio di biografia intellettuale.* ©2016, Donzelli Editore.

No part of this book may be reproduced or transmitted in any form or by any means, electronic or mechanical, including photocopying and recording, or in any information storage or retrieval system without the prior written permission of Stanford University Press.

Printed in the United States of America on acid-free, archival-quality paper

Library of Congress Cataloging-in-Publication Data
Names: Musto, Marcello, author. | Camiller, Patrick, translator.
Title: The last years of Karl Marx, 1881–1883: an intellectual biography / Marcello Musto; translated by Patrick Camiller.
Other titles: L'ultimo Marx. English
Description: Stanford, California: Stanford University Press, 2020. | Translation of: L'ultimo Marx. | Includes bibliographical references and index.
Identifiers: LCCN 2019041945 (print) | LCCN 2019041946 (ebook) | ISBN 9781503610583 (cloth) | ISBN 9781503612525 (paperback) | ISBN 9781503612532 (epub)
Subjects: LCSH: Marx, Karl, 1818–1883. | Communists—Biography. | LCGFT: Biographies.
Classification: LCC HX39.5 .M9813 2020 (print) | LCC HX39.5 (ebook) | DDC 335.4092 [B]—dc23
LC record available at https://lccn.loc.gov/2019041945
LC ebook record available at https://lccn.loc.gov/2019041946

Cover photo: Karl Marx, 1882. Alamy.

Cover design: Rob Ehle

Text design: Kevin Barrett Kane

Typeset at Stanford University Press in 11/14 Minion Pro

Dedicated to Babak.

In the Foxhole, in the Clinique,
or wherever the next will be.
Come rain or come shine.

CONTENTS

NOTE ON SOURCES

Marx's writings have generally been quoted from the 50-volume *Karl Marx / Frederick Engels: Collected Works* (MECW), Moscow / London / New York: Progress Publishers / Lawrence and Wishart / International Publishers, 1975–2005. In a few cases, the reader is referred to single works translated into English but not included in MECW. When necessary, translations have been modified to conform more closely to the original German. Texts that have not yet been translated into English are referenced to the *Marx-Engels-Gesamtausgabe* (MEGA²), Berlin: Dietz / Akademie / De Gruyter, 1975– . . . , of which 67 of the originally planned 114 volumes have so far appeared in print.

In the notes and the bibliography, the references to Marx's writing have been given in German as well as English, drawn from the 44-volume *Marx-Engels-Werke* (MEW), Berlin: Dietz, 1956–1968, when available, otherwise from the *Marx-Engels-Gesamtausgabe* (MEGA²) or from individual works still not published in the latter.

Finally, Marx's still-unpublished manuscripts are indicated according to their location in either the International Institute of Social History (IISH) of Amsterdam or the Russian State Archive of Socio-Political History (RGASPI) of Moscow, where they are kept.

As regards the secondary literature, quotations from books and articles not published in English have been translated for the present volume. Sometimes the translations of English-language editions of books originally published in other languages have been modified to conform more closely to the original.

All the names of journals and newspapers have been given first in English, followed by the original in square brackets. The names of political parties and organizations have been treated in the same way. The birth and death dates of authors and historical figures have been provided the first time they are mentioned. A question mark between parenthesis (?) is used where such dates are unknown.

NOTE ON THE ENGLISH EDITION

First published in September 2016 by Donzelli Editore, Rome, with the title *L'ultimo Marx, 1881–1883. Saggio di biografia intellettuale*, this book aroused considerable interest among readers of Marx and is now being made available in English.

The original Italian edition, printed in 2,000 copies and complemented by an e-book, quickly sold out and was reprinted in January 2017. Subsequently, after another reprint, it appeared in the form of a print-on-demand option.

The first translations of the book came out shortly afterwards. In 2018, on the occasion of the bicentenary of Marx's birth, the present volume appeared in five languages. The first, with a print run of 1,000, was brought out in Tamil by the long-established Chennai publisher New Century Book House Private Limited. A few months later, Boitempo in Sao Paulo followed with a Portuguese edition in a print run of 4,000; and within a few weeks of that, Sanzini in Busan published a Korean edition of 1,000 copies—reprinted in 2019—and VSA in Hamburg a German edition of 2,000 copies. Before the end of 2018, the book had also been translated into Japanese by Horinouchi in Tokyo, in a 500-page volume, with a print run of 2,000 copies, that also contained a Japanese version of my recent *Another Marx: Early Manuscripts to the International* (London: Bloomsbury, 2018).

As of 2019, the volume had been translated into two more languages: Arabic, 1,000 copies, by Al Maraya in Cairo; and Farsi, initially 1,000 copies quickly followed by three reprints, by Cheshme in Tehran. At the beginning of 2020, four more editions were published: a Spanish edition from Siglo XXI, Mexico City, in 2,000 copies; a Hindi edition, by Samvad, New Delhi, in 1,000 copies; and a Portuguese edition, by Parsifal, Lisbon, in 1,500 copies. An Indonesian version—which, like the Japanese, also contains *Another Marx: Early Manuscripts to the International*—was published by Marjin Kiri in South Tangerang, Indonesia.

This English edition, which includes new sections and some changes from the original Italian, follows a long series of translations and reprintings. It also precedes the Turkish translation with Yordam Kitap, the Chinese translation with People's Publishing House, the Catalan translation with Tigre de Paper, a new Italian enlarged edition, as well as a French translation to appear soon.

In three years since its first publication, the book presented here to English-language readers has been reviewed in many newspapers and journals, in a considerable number of countries.

The author would like to thank Patrick Camiller for his excellent translation, Enrico Campo for his help in completing the references and bibliography, and Emma Willert for the preparation of the index.

Marcello Musto
NAPLES, JANUARY 2020

The Last Years of Karl Marx

INTRODUCTION

Perhaps one socialist in a thousand
has ever read any of Marx's economic writings,
and of a thousand anti-Marxists
not even one has read Marx.[1]

1. MARX'S FINAL LABORS AND
THEIR POLITICAL RELEVANCE TODAY

For more than a decade now, prestigious newspapers and journals with a wide readership have been describing Karl Marx as a far-sighted theorist whose topicality receives constant confirmation. Many authors with progressive views maintain that his ideas continue to be indispensable for anyone who believes it is necessary to build an alternative to capitalism. Almost everywhere, he is now the theme of university courses and international conferences. His writings, reprinted or brought out in new editions, have reappeared on bookshop shelves, and the study of his work, after twenty years or more of neglect, has gathered increasing momentum. The years 2017 and 2018 have brought further intensity to this "Marx revival," thanks to many initiatives around the world linked to the 150th anniversary of the publication of *Capital* and the bicentenary of Marx's birth.[2]

Of particular value for an overall reassessment of Marx's oeuvre was the resumed publication, in 1998, of the *Marx-Engels-Gesamtausgabe* (MEGA²), the historical-critical edition of the complete works of Karl Marx and Friedrich Engels. Twenty-seven more volumes have already appeared (forty were published between 1975 and 1989), and others are in the course of preparation. These include: (1) new versions of some of Marx's works (most notably *The German Ideology*); (2) all the preparatory manuscripts for *Capital* composed between 1857 and 1881; (3) a complete collection of the correspondence sent and

1

received by Marx and Engels; and (4) approximately two hundred notebooks. The latter contain excerpts from his reading and the reflections to which they gave rise. All of this together constitutes the workshop of his critical theory, opening up the complex itinerary he followed and the sources on which he drew in developing his ideas.

These priceless materials—many available only in German and therefore confined to small circles of researchers—show us an author very different from the one that numerous critics, or self-styled followers, presented for such a long time. Indeed, the new textual acquisitions in MEGA² make it possible to say that, of the classics of political, economic, and philosophical thought, Marx is the author whose profile has changed the most in the opening decades of the twenty-first century. The new political setting, following the implosion of the Soviet Union, has also contributed to this fresh perception. For the end of Marxism-Leninism finally freed Marx's work from the shackles of an ideology light years away from his conception of society.

After 1917, to be sure, Marx's writings enjoyed a significant diffusion in geographical zones and social classes from which they had, until then, been absent. But after the first impetus of the Russian Revolution was spent, the later Soviet orthodoxy imposed an inflexible monism that had perverse effects on Marxist theory. In the form of manuals put together at the Marx-Engels-Lenin Institute in Moscow, or "Marxist" anthologies on various topics, Marx's writings were often dismembered and remixed into sets of quotations designed to serve preordained purposes. It was a practice introduced by the German Social Democrats from the late nineteenth century on.[3] One might say that Marx's texts were treated in the same way that the bandit Procrustes reserved for his victims: if they were too long, they were amputated; if too short, stretched. In the best of circumstances, it is difficult to combine the requirements of popularization with the need to avoid theoretical impoverishment. But in the Soviet Union, first of Joseph Stalin (1878–1953), then of Nikita Khrushchev (1894–1971) and Leonid Brezhnev (1906–1982), things could hardly have been worse for the reception of Marx's work.

The dogmatic reduction of Marx's quintessentially critical theory resulted in the unlikeliest paradoxes. The thinker most resolutely opposed to "writing recipes . . . for the cook-shops of the future"[4] was converted into the progenitor of a new social system. The most painstaking thinker, never satisfied with the results he had produced, became the source of a dyed-in-the-wool doctrinairism. The steadfast champion of the materialist conception of history was wrenched more than any other author from his historical context. Even his insistence that "the emancipation of the working classes must be conquered by the working classes themselves"[5] was locked into an ideology that emphasized the primacy of political vanguards and parties as the forces propelling class consciousness and leading the revolution. The champion of the idea that a shorter working day was the prerequisite for the blossoming of human capacities found himself roped into support for the productivist creed of Stakhanovism. The convinced believer in the abolition of the state was built up into its firmest bulwark. Envisaging like few other thinkers the free development of individuality, he had argued that—whereas bourgeois right masked social disparities beneath a merely legal equality—"right would have to be unequal rather than equal."[6] Yet the same Marx was now falsely associated with a conception that erased the richness of the collective dimension in a featureless uniformity.

Recent research has refuted the various approaches that reduce Marx's conception of communist society to superior development of the productive forces. In particular, it has shown the importance he attached to the ecological question: on repeated occasions, he denounced the fact that expansion of the capitalist mode of production increased not only the theft of workers' labor but also the pillage of natural resources. Another question in which Marx took a close interest was migration. He showed that the forced movement of labor generated by capitalism was a major component of bourgeois exploitation and that the key to fighting this was class solidarity among workers, regardless of their origins or any distinction between local and imported labor.

Marx went deeply into many other issues which, though often underestimated, or even ignored, by scholars of his work, are acquiring crucial importance for the political agenda of our times. Among these are individual freedom in the economic and political sphere, gender emancipation, the critique of nationalism, the emancipatory potential of technology, and forms of collective ownership not controlled by the state.

Furthermore, Marx undertook thorough investigations of societies outside Europe and expressed himself unambiguously against the ravages of colonialism. It is a mistake to suggest otherwise. Marx criticized thinkers who, while highlighting the destructive consequences of colonialism, used categories peculiar to the European context in their analysis of peripheral areas of the globe. He warned a number of times against those who failed to observe the necessary distinctions between phenomena, and especially after his theoretical advances in the 1870s, he was highly wary of transferring interpretive categories across completely different historical or geographical fields. All this is now clear, despite the skepticism still fashionable in certain academic quarters.

Thus, thirty years after the fall of the Berlin Wall, it has become possible to read a Marx very unlike the dogmatic, economistic, and Eurocentric theorist who was paraded around for so long. Of course, one can find in Marx's massive literary bequest a number of statements suggesting that the development of the productive forces is leading to dissolution of the capitalist mode of production. But it would be wrong to attribute to him any idea that the advent of socialism is a historical inevitability. Indeed, for Marx the possibility of transforming society depended on the working class and its capacity, through struggle, to bring about social upheavals that led to the birth of an alternative economic and political system.

The new advances achieved in Marxian studies suggest that the exegesis of his work is likely to become more and more refined. In this perspective, the period covered in the present volume (1881–1883) and the themes that Marx dealt with during those years offer the contemporary reader plentiful scope for reflection on today's burning questions. For a long time, many Marxists foregrounded the writings of the young Marx (primarily the *Economic and Philosophic Manuscripts of 1844* and *The German Ideology*), while the *Manifesto of the Communist Party* remained his most widely read and quoted text. In those early writings, however, one finds many ideas that were superseded in his later work. It is above all in *Capital* and its preliminary drafts, as well as in the researches of his final years, that we find the most precious reflections on the critique of bourgeois society. These represent the last, though not the definitive, conclusions at which Marx arrived. If examined critically in the light of changes in the world since his death, they may still prove highly useful for the task of theorizing an alternative social-economic model to capitalism.

In 1881 and 1882, Marx made remarkable progress in relation to anthropology, precapitalist modes of production, non-Western societies, socialist revolution, and the materialist conception of history. He also closely observed the main events in international politics, as we can see from his letters expressing resolute support for the Irish liberation struggle and the populist movement in Russia, and firm opposition to British colonial oppression in India and Egypt and to French colonialism in Algeria. He was anything but Eurocentric, economistic, or fixated only on class conflict. Marx thought the study of new political conflicts, new themes, and geographical areas to be fundamental for his ongoing critique of the capitalist system. It enabled him to open up to national specificities and to consider the possibility of an approach to communism different from the one he had previously developed.

2. A FORGOTTEN CHAPTER: THE "LATE MARX"

Marx's ideas have changed the world. Yet despite the affirmation of Marx's theories, turned into dominant ideologies and state doctrines for a considerable part of humankind in the twentieth century, there is still no full edition of all his works and manuscripts. The main reason for this lies in the incompleteness of Marx's oeuvre. The works he published amount to less than the total number of projects left unfinished, not to speak of the mountainous *Nachlass* of notes connected with his unending researches.

Marx left many more manuscripts than those he sent to the printers.[7] Incompleteness was an inseparable part of his life: the sometimes grinding poverty in which he lived, as well as his constant ill health, added to his daily worries; his rigorous method and merciless self-criticism increased the difficulties of many of his undertakings; his passion for knowledge remained unaltered over time and always drove him on to fresh study. Nevertheless, his ceaseless labors would have the most extraordinary theoretical consequences for the future.[8]

In many biographies of Marx, the narrative of the main events in his life has been treated separately from his theoretical achievements.[9] Studies of an academic character have mostly ignored the existential vicissitudes, despite the fact that these considerably influenced the course of his labors. Quite a few authors have lingered over the differences between Marx's early and mature writings,[10] without showing a sufficiently thorough knowledge of the latter. Many other studies have based themselves on a misguided division between "Marx the philosopher" and "Marx the economist" or "Marx the politician."

Nearly all the intellectual biographies published to this day have given undue weight to an examination of Marx's youthful writings. For a long time, the difficulty of examining Marx's research in the final years of his life, especially the early 1880s, hampered our knowledge of the important gains he achieved. This is why all biographers devoted so few pages to his activity after the winding up of the International Working Men's Association, in 1872.[11] Not by chance, they nearly always used the generic title "the last decade" for this part of their work. Wrongly thinking that Marx had given up the idea of completing his work, they failed to look more deeply into what he actually did during that period. But if there was some justification for this in the past, it is hard to understand why the new materials available in MEGA[2] and the volume of research on the "late Marx" since the 1970s have not led to a more significant change in this tendency.[12]

The present book aims to fill a gap in the literature on Marx. However, the author is also aware that it is still a partial, incomplete contribution, not only because the volumes of MEGA² relating to the 1881–1883 period have not yet been published in their entirety,[13] but also because Marx's work spans the most diverse spheres of human knowledge, and his synthesis represents a peak difficult to climb. Besides, the need to contain this monograph to a reasonable number of pages made it impossible to analyze all of Marx's writings with the same degree of attention; it has often been necessary to summarize in a few words what should have taken at least a paragraph, or in one page what would have required a section to itself. In particular, the richness and complexity of *The Ethnological Notebooks* really demand exhaustive analysis, which will be attempted in a forthcoming work. It is in full awareness of these limitations that the reader is here offered the results of the research conducted up to this point.

In 1957 Maximilien Rubel (1905–1996), one of the most authoritative twentieth-century interpreters of Marx's work, wrote that a "monumental biography" had still to be written.[14] It is a judgment that remains valid today, at a distance of more than sixty years. The MEGA² series has given the lie to all the claims that Marx is a thinker about whom everything has already been written and said. But it would be wrong to argue—as do those who overexcitedly hail an "unknown Marx" after each new text appears for the first time—that recent research has turned upside down what was already known about him.

There is still so much to learn from Marx. Today it is possible to do this by studying not only what he wrote in his published works but also the questions and doubts contained in his unfinished manuscripts. This consideration is all the more valid for the material dating from the final years of his life.

The "late Marx" is also the most intimate Marx: he did not conceal his frailty in life yet continued to struggle, did not evade doubt but openly confronted it, chose to press on with his research rather than take refuge in self-certitude and lap up the uncritical adulation of the first "Marxists." This Marx is one of a very rare, radically subversive breed, quite unlike the twentieth-century image of a granite sphinx pointing to the future with dogmatic certainty. He beckons to a new generation of researchers and political activists, who are taking up and continuing the struggle to which he, like so many others before and since, devoted his whole existence.

Prelude

"STRUGGLE!"

IN AUGUST 1880 JOHN SWINTON (1829–1901), an influential American journalist with progressive views, was on a trip to Europe.[1] While there, he paid a visit to Ramsgate, a small coastal town of Kent, located a few kilometers from the southeastern extremity of England. This journey was made to conduct an interview for *The Sun*—the newspaper he edited, which at the time was one of the most widely read in the United States—with the man who had become one of the main representatives of the international workers' movement: Karl Marx.

Though German by birth, Marx had become stateless, after being banished by the French, Belgian, and Prussian governments when they stifled the revolutionary movements that emerged in their countries between 1848 and 1849. When Marx applied for naturalization in Britain in 1874, his request was denied because a Scotland Yard report labelled him a "notorious German agitator and advocate of communistic principles," who had "not been loyal to his own King and country."[2]

For more than a decade Marx had been a correspondent for the *New-York Tribune*; in 1867 he had published a major critique of the capitalist mode of production entitled *Capital*, and for eight years, beginning in 1864, he had been the guiding figure of the International Working Men's Association. In 1871 his name had featured in the pages of the most widely read European newspapers, when, having defended the Paris Commune in *The Civil War in France* (1871), the reactionary press had baptized him the "red terror doctor."[3]

In summer 1880, Marx was in Ramsgate with his family, under doctor's orders to "refrain from work of any kind"[4] and "to restore [his] nervous system by doing nothing."[5] His wife's health was worse than his. Jenny von Westphalen (1814–1881) was suffering from cancer and her condition had "suddenly been aggravated to a degree which menace[d] to tend to a fatal termination."[6] This was the situation in which Swinton, who had been chief editor at the *New York Times* throughout the 1860s, got to know Marx and drew a sympathetic, intense, and accurate portrait of him.

At a personal level, Swinton described Marx as a "massive-headed, generous-featured, courtly, kindly man in his 60s, with bushy masses of long reveling grey hair," who knew "not less finely than Victor Hugo . . . the art of being a grandfather."[7] His conversation, "so free, so sweeping, so creative, so incisive, so genuine," reminded Swinton of Socrates "with its sardonic touches, its gleams of humour, and its sportive merriment." He also noted "a man without desire for show or fame, caring nothing for the fanfaronade of life or the pretence of power."[8]

However, this was not the only Marx whom Swinton would describe to his readers. The interview that appeared on the front page of *The Sun*, on 6 September 1880, mainly presented the public face of Marx: "one of the most remarkable men of the day, who has played an inscrutable but puissant part in the revolutionary politics of the past forty years." Swinton wrote of him:

> [He is] without haste and without rest, a man of strong, broad, elevated mind, full of far-reaching projects, logical methods, and practical aims, he has stood and yet stands behind more of the earthquakes which have convulsed nations and destroyed thrones, and do now menace and appall crowned heads and established frauds, than any other man in Europe.[9]

The discussion with Marx convinced the New York journalist that he found himself in front of a man who was "deep in the times," whose hand "from the Neva to the Seine, from the Urals to the Pyrenees, [was] at work preparing the way for the . . . advent" of the new era. Marx impressed him because of his ability to "survey the European world, country after country, indicating the features and the developments and the personages on the surface and under the surface." Marx went on to speak

> of the political forces and popular movements of the various countries of Europe—the vast current of the spirit of Russia, the motions of the German

mind, the action of France, the immobility of England. He spoke hopefully of Russia, philosophically of Germany, cheerfully of France, and sombrely of England—referring contemptuously to the "atomistic reforms" over which the Liberals of the British Parliament spend their time.[10]

Swinton was also surprised by Marx's knowledge of the United States. He was an attentive observer and "his remarks upon some of the formative and substantive forces of American life were full of suggestiveness."

The day passed in a series of lively discussions. In the afternoon, Marx proposed "a walk along the shore to the beach" to meet his family, which Swinton described as "a delightful party—about ten in all." When evening fell, Marx's sons-in-law Charles Longuet (1839–1903) and Paul Lafargue (1842–1911) continued to keep the two men company; the talk was "of the world, and of man, and of time, and of ideas, as our glasses tinkled over the sea." It was at one of these moments that the American journalist, "over the thought of the babblement and rack of the age and the ages," immersing himself in the depth of "the talk of the day and the scenes of the evening," ventured to ask the great man in front of him a question "touching upon the final law of being." It was then, during a moment of silence, that he "interrogated the revolutionist and philosopher with a fateful question: "What is [the law of being]?" Swinton sensed that the mind of Marx had "inverted for a moment, while he looked upon the roaring sea in front and the restless multitude upon the beach." Finally, Marx replied in a deep and solemn tone: "Struggle!"[11]

1

NEW RESEARCH HORIZONS

1. THE ROOM ON MAITLAND PARK ROAD

A few months after the John Swinton interview, on a January night in 1881, a man with an almost white beard was seated in his room in North London reading through a pile of books and carefully noting down the most important passages. With great perseverance, he was continuing to carry out his life's purpose: to provide the workers' movement with the theoretical basis to destroy the capitalist mode of production.

His physique showed the signs of decades of hard daily work spent reading and writing. On his back and other parts of his body remained scars of the horrific boils that had appeared during the years when he was working on *Capital*. His spirit bore other wounds from a life of hardships and difficulties, mitigated from time to time by satisfaction at the blow he was inflicting on ruling-class bigwigs and political rivals in the same camp as his.

In winter, he was often tired and debilitated, as the ageing process began to limit his habitual energy, and his wife had reason to be increasingly anxious about the state of his health. But he was still Karl Marx. With the same passion as ever, he toiled away for the cause of working-class emancipation. He did it with the same method he had adopted since his early days at university: painstakingly rigorous and intransigently critical.

Seated on a wooden armchair, he had slogged all day and far into the night for years, at a modest desk no larger than three feet by two.[1] There was scarcely enough room on it for a green-shaded lamp, his sheets of writing paper, and a few books he was working on at the time. He needed nothing else.

His study was on the first floor, with a window overlooking the garden. The smell of tobacco vanished after the doctors forbade him to smoke, but the clay pipes from which he had inhaled for so many years were still there to remind him of the sleepless nights he spent taking apart the classics of political economy.

An impenetrable row of shelves concealed the walls, housing more books and newspapers than one would have thought possible. His library was not as imposing as that of bourgeois intellectuals of the same stature—and certainly greater wealth. In his years of greatest poverty, he had mostly used the resources of the British Museum reading room, but later he had managed to collect nearly two thousand volumes.[2] The largest section was of books on economics, but there were many classics of political theory, historical studies (especially French), and philosophical works mainly from the German tradition. The natural sciences were also well represented.

The range of languages matched this variety of disciplines. Books in German made up roughly a third of the total and those in English approximately a quarter, with French titles a little fewer in number. There were also works in other Romance languages such as Italian, but from 1869—when he began to learn Russian in order to study the changes taking place in the tsarist empire—books in the Cyrillic alphabet came to occupy a considerable section of their own.

But the shelves did not only feature academic texts. An anonymous *Chicago Tribune* correspondent, who visited the study in 1878, described its contents:

> A man can generally be judged by the books he reads, and you can form your own conclusions when I tell you a casual glance revealed Shakespeare, Dickens, Thackeray, Molière, Racine, Montaigne, Bacon, Goethe, Voltaire, Paine; English, American, French, Blue Books;[3] works political and philosophical in Russian, German, Spanish, Italian, etc.[4]

Paul Lafargue gave a similar account of Marx's literary interests and vast knowledge. Recalling his study—of which he said that "one must know that historic room before one can penetrate into the intimacy of Marx's spiritual life"—he wrote:

> He knew Heine and Goethe by heart and often quoted them in his conversations; he was an assiduous reader of poets in all European languages.

Every year he read Aeschylus in the Greek original. He considered him and Shakespeare as the greatest dramatic geniuses humanity ever gave birth to. . . . Dante and Robert Burns ranked among his favourite poets. he was a great reader of novels, his preference being for those of the eighteenth century, particularly Fielding's *Tom Jones*. The more modern novelists whom he found most interesting were Paul de Kock, Charles Lever, Alexander Dumas Senior and Walter Scott, whose *Old Mortality* he considered a masterpiece. He had a definite preference for stories of adventure and humour. He ranked Cervantes and Balzac above all other novelists. In *Don Quixote* he saw the epic of dying-out chivalry whose virtues were ridiculed and scoffed at in the emerging bourgeois world. He admired Balzac so much that he wished to write a review of his great work *La Comédie Humaine* as soon as he had finished his book on economics. . . . Marx could read all European languages. . . . He liked to repeat the saying: "A foreign language is a weapon in the struggle of life." . . . He took up the study of Russian . . . [and] in six months he knew it well enough to derive pleasure from reading Russian poets and prose writers, his preference going to Pushkin, Gogol and Shchedrin.[5]

Lafargue also dwelled upon Marx's relationship with his books. They were

tools for his mind, not articles of luxury. "They are my slaves and they must serve me as I will," he used to say. He . . . would turn down the corners of the pages, make pencil marks in the margin and underline whole lines. He never wrote on books, but sometimes he could not refrain from an exclamation or question mark when the author went too far. His system of underlining made it easy for him to find any passage he needed in any book.[6]

He paid them such heed that he defined himself as "a machine, condemned to devour them and, then, throw them, in a changed form, on the dunghill of history."[7]

Marx's library also contained his own works, which in the end were not as numerous as the ones he had planned to write but had to leave unfinished because of intense intellectual activity. There were copies of *The Holy Family* (1845) and *The Poverty of Philosophy* (1847), and certainly no shortage of the *Manifesto of the Communist Party* (1848)—written together with Engels (1820–1895) and timely published just before the 1848 revolutions, though widely circulated only from the 1870s on. Political texts such as such as *The Eighteenth Brumaire of Louis Bonaparte* (1852) and his polemical *The Story of the Life of Lord Palmerston* (1853–1854) lay alongside topical booklets such as *Revelations concerning the Communist Trial in Cologne* (1853) and *Secret Diplomatic History of the Eighteenth Century* (1856–1857), as well as the less noted *A Contribution to the Critique of Political Economy* (1859) and *Herr Vogt* (1860). Among the writings of which he was proudest were, of course, *Capital*, which at the time had already been translated into Russian and French, and the most important addresses and resolutions of the International Working Men's Association.

Packed away somewhere were also copies of papers and journals he had edited as a young man: the *German-French Yearbooks* [*Deutsch-Französiche Jahrbücher*]; the daily *New Rhenish Newspaper* [*Neue Rheinische Zeitung*], whose final issue in May 1849, before the victory of the counterrevolution, was published entirely in red ink; and copies of the monthly *New Rhenish Newspaper: Political-Economic Review* [*Neue Rheinische Zeitung. Politisch-ökonomische Revue*] from the following year. Other sections of the library contained dozens of notebooks of excerpts and incomplete manuscripts—although most of these were consigned to the loft, which accommodated all the projects he had started at various points in his life but never managed to finish. This mass of texts, some abandoned to "the gnawing criticism of the mice,"[8] consisted of a large number of scattered notebooks and folios.[9]

The papers included what would later become *The Economic and Philosophic Manuscripts of 1844* (1844) and *The German Ideology* (1845–1846), two of the most widely read and debated theoretical texts in the twentieth century. Marx—who never published "a single work without repeatedly revising it until he had found the most appropriate form" and who "would rather burn his manuscripts than leave them unfinished"[10]—would certainly have been surprised and felt negative about the publicity given to them.

The largest and most important manuscripts, however, were those related to the preliminary drafts of *Capital*, stretching, that is, from the *Grundrisse*—the "Foundations of the Critique of Political Economy" of 1857–1858—to the final notes he wrote in 1881. Most of the correspondence of Marx and Engels used to be called the "party archive," but in fact it was kept in Engels's house.

In the middle of Marx's crammed study was a leather sofa on which he lay down to rest from time to time. One of his regular rituals of relaxation was to pace around the room. Indeed, according to Lafargue, "one can say that he even worked walking in his room, only sitting down for short periods to write what he thought out while walking." Marx, he recalled, also "liked to walk up and down while talking, stopping from time to time when the explanation became more animated or the conversation serious." Another regular caller at the time said that he "had a habit, when at all interested in the discussion, of walking actively up and down the room, as if he were pacing the deck of a schooner for exercise."[11]

Another table stood in front of his desk. An occasional visitor would have felt bewildered by the chaos of papers on it, but anyone who knew Marx well was aware that the disorder was only apparent:

Everything was really in its intended place so that it was easy for him to lay his hand on the book or notebook he needed. Even during conversations he often paused to show in the book a quotation or figure he had just mentioned. He and his study were one: the books and papers in it were as much under his control as his own limbs.[12]

The last item of furnishing was a large chest of drawers. Here he placed photos of people he cherished such as the comrade Wilhelm Wolff (1809–1864), to whom he dedicated *Capital*. For a long time, the study also had a bust of Jove and two pieces of wall from the house of Gottfried Leibniz (1646–1716); both were presents from his doctor, and for many years dear friend, Ludwig Kugelmann (1828–1902), who gave them to Marx at Christmas 1867 and on his fifty-second birthday in 1870—when the house of the greatest German philosopher of the eighteenth century was demolished in Hanover.

Marx and his family lived in a terraced house at 41 Maitland Park Road, in North London. They had moved there in 1875, having rented larger and more expensive accommodation at No. 1 for the previous ten years.[13] At the time, the nuclear family consisted of Marx and his wife Jenny, his youngest daughter Eleanor (1855–1898), and Helene Demuth (1820–1890), the devoted governess who had lived with them for nearly forty years. There were also three dogs, of whom Marx was very fond. Toddy, Whisky, and a third whose name is not known were "animals of no particular breed, . . . [but] indeed formed important members of the household."[14] Marx had two other daughters, Jenny Longuet and Laura Lafargue (1845–1911), but they no longer lived with him after they got married.

In 1870, after Engels retired from business and left his Manchester home, he had taken accommodation at 122 Regent's Park Road, not much more than a kilometer from the home of the comrade with whom he had shared the political struggle and the sincerest of friendships since far back in 1844.[15]

Because of Marx's multiple health problems, "all night labour had for many years absolutely been interdicted by [his] medical advisers."[16] But he tirelessly continued to occupy his days with research, mainly in order to finish *Capital*, whose Volume II had been in preparation ever since Volume I was published in 1867.

Marx also critically followed all the main political and economic events of the time, attempting to predict the new scenarios that these might have produced for the emancipation of the working classes. In the end, his encyclopedic mind, guided by insatiable curiosity, drove him on to keep updating his knowledge and to stay abreast of the latest scientific developments. For this reason, in the final years of his life, Marx filled dozens of notebooks with comments and excerpts from numerous volumes on mathematics, physiology, geology, mineralogy, agronomy, chemistry, and physics; in addition to articles from newspapers and journals, he scoured parliamentary records, statistical material, and government reports and publications, as in the case of the "blue books." The time he devoted to these studies, in a number of languages, was rarely interrupted. Even Engels regretted this: he said that it was "only with great difficulty" that he managed "to persuade him to leave his room."[17] Apart from these exceptional cases, Marx left his work only for the usual breaks and appointments.

In the late afternoon, he would put on an overcoat and head for nearby Maitland Park, where he liked to stroll with his eldest grandson Johnny Longuet (1876–1938), or for the slightly more distant Hampstead Heath, where he spent many happy Sundays with his family. A friend of his youngest daughter, the actress Marian Comyn (1861–1938), succinctly described the scene they often witnessed:

> Many times, when Eleanor Marx and I were sitting on the rug in front of the drawing-room fire, talking in the twilight, we would hear the front door gently close, and immediately afterwards the doctor's figure, clad in a black cloak and soft felt hat (and looking, as his daughter remarked, for all the world like a conspirators' chorus), would pass along by the window, and not return until darkness closed in.[18]

Another time of relaxation was the meetings of the so-called Dogberry Club,[19] a name derived from a character in William Shakespeare's (1564–1616) *Much Ado about Nothing* (1598–1599). It involved readings from the Bard's works and dinners prepared for Engels, his closest acquaintances, and friends of Marx's daughters.[20] The sarcasm that Marx used to describe what he felt during these evenings was no less biting than that which he used to dismantle his theoretical adversaries: "It is a strange thing that one cannot well live altogether without company, and that when you get it, you try hard to rid yourself of it."[21]

The difficulties in the Marx household did not stop them from being open to visitors from various countries, who came to converse face-to-face with the highly regarded economist and famous revolutionary. The list in 1881 included the Crimean-born economist Nikolai Sieber (1844–1881), the Moscow university professor Nikolai Kablukov (1849–1919), the German journalist and future Reichstag deputy Louis Viereck (1851–1921), the long-standing Social Democrat Friedrich Fritzsche (1825–1905), and the Russian populist Leo Hartmann (1850–1908). Others who frequented Maitland Park Road were Carl Hirsch (1841–1900), a journalist linked to the Social Democratic Party of Germany [*Sozialdemokratische Partei Deutschlands*]; Henry Hyndman (1842–1921), who had founded the Democratic Federation in England earlier that year; and Karl Kautsky (1854–1938), a young socialist originally from Prague, who came to London to deepen his knowledge of politics through his relations with Marx and Engels, and became one of the influential theorists of the workers' movement.

No one in contact with Marx could resist the fascination of his personality or fail to be struck by his physical appearance. The Scottish politician Mountstuart Elphinstone (1829–1906), who met him at the beginning of 1879, found his gaze "rather hard but the whole expression rather pleasant than not, by no means that of a gentleman who is in the habit of eating babies in their cradles—which is I daresay the view which the Police takes of him."[22]

Eduard Bernstein (1850–1932), too, was struck by Marx's humanity and modesty: "I had expected to make the acquaintance of a somewhat suppressed, highly excitable old gentleman; and now I found myself in the presence of a very white-haired man whose dark eyes held a friendly smile, and whose speech was full of charity."[23]

Kautsky recalled that "Marx had the dignified look of a patriarch,"[24] that he beamed "a gentle smile that seemed almost paternal,"[25] and that, unlike the "always well dressed" Engels, he was "indifferent to external forms."[26]

Marian Comyn described his temperament well:

[His was] an extraordinarily forceful and dominating personality. His head was large, covered with longish grey hair that matched a shaggy beard and moustache; the black eyes, though small, were keen, piercing, sarcastic, with glints of humour in them. . . . As an audience he was delightful, never criticizing, always entering into the spirit of any fun that was going, laughing when anything struck him as particularly comic, until the tears ran down his cheeks—the oldest in years, but in spirit as young as any of us.[27]

If the Marx household was often bustling, its mailbox was always bursting with letters from activists and intellectuals that arrived each week from various countries. Their senders hoped to consult the leader of the International Working Men's Association about major political events of the day and asked for his suggestions about particular decisions or courses of action.

The background to Marx's days was the gray and rainy English climate. As he wrote to Nikolai Danielson (1844–1918) in February 1881, although his "health [had been] generally improving [since his] return from Ramsgate, the detestable weather, lasting for months," was the reason why he had "a perpetual cold and coughing [that were] interfering with sleep."[28] Ominously, Jenny was getting worse that winter, and with the return of spring Marx had to call in a new specialist, Bryan Donkin (1842–1927), in the hope of finding a cure for his wife.

He told his Russian friend Danielson of another depressing event. A French government amnesty in July 1880 allowed the return of hundreds of revolutionaries who had fled abroad to escape the post-Commune repression in 1871. Although the news itself could not but hearten Marx, the personal implications were inevitably painful. His eldest daughter Jenny's husband of ten years, the journalist and Communard Charles Longuet, had been offered a post as joint editor of *The Justice* [*La Justice*], the radical daily founded by Georges Clemenceau (1841–1929), and could therefore return with his children to the French capital. The parting caused much sadness to Marx and his wife, since their "three grandchildren . . . were inexhaustible sources of enjoyment of life."[29]

Over the following months, they were constantly aware of their absence, and Marx alternated between feelings of joy and melancholy. He always asked for news of the children in his letters to Jenny:

It's been boring ever since you left—without you and Johnny and Harra! and Mr. "Tea"![30] Sometimes I hurry across to the window when I hear children's voices which sound like those of our children, momentarily oblivious of the fact that the little chaps are on the other side of the Channel![31]

At the end of April, when Jenny gave birth to his fourth grandchild, Marx jokingly congratulated her and wrote that his "womankind" expected the "newcomer" to increase "the better half of the population." He added: "For my own part I prefer the 'manly' sex for children born at this turning point of history. They have before them the most revolutionary period men had ever to pass through."

These considerations, in which political hopes were mingled with preconceptions common to men of his generation, resulted in two major concerns. The first, strictly personal, came from regret that he could not help his daughter in Paris, who was now living a life of hardship that reminded him of the one he endured for a long time. In his letter to her, Marx passed on his wife's wishes for "all possible good things," but he did not see that "wishes" were "good for anything but glossing over one's powerlessness." His second, political regret was bound up with a realization that he would not live to experience the new and enthusiastic struggles of the international workers' movement: "The bad thing now is to be 'old' so as to be only able to foresee instead of seeing."[32]

Unfortunately, all the problems kept getting worse. In early June, Marx informed Swinton that his wife's illness was "assuming more and more a fatal character."[33] He himself continued to suffer new disorders and had to put up with Turkish baths because of a rheumatic leg.[34] He had also had a nasty "sempiternal" cold, although it now seemed to be "rapidly passing away." He greatly missed his eldest daughter and grandchildren: "There passes no day, when my thoughts are not with you and the lovely children." He sent Johnny a copy of Johann Wolfgang von Goethe's (1749–1832) *Renard the Fox* (1794) and enquired whether the "poor fellow" had "somebody to read it for him."[35] The first half of 1881 passed amid these difficulties.

2. NEW THEORETICAL EXPLORATIONS

In September 1879, Marx collected and read with great interest, in Russian, *Communal Landownership: The Causes, Course and Consequences of Its Decline* (1879) by Maksim Kovalevsky (1851–1916), whom he described as one of his "scientific friends."[36] The extracts he compiled were mainly from the parts of it dealing with landownership in countries under foreign rule. He summarized the various forms in which the Spanish in Latin America, the British in India, and the French in Algeria had regulated possession rights.[37]

In considering these three geographical areas, Marx's first reflections related to pre-Columbian civilizations. He observed that with the beginning of the Aztec and Inca empires "the rural population continued, as before, to own the land in common, but at the same time had to subtract part of its income in the form of payments in kind to its rulers." According to Kovalevsky this process laid "the bases for the development of the latifundia, at the expense of the property interests of those who owned the common land. The dissolution of the common land was only accelerated by the arrival of the Spanish."[38] The terrible consequences of their colonial empire were condemned both by Kovalevsky: the "original policy of extermination towards the Redskins"—and by Marx, who added, in his own hand, that "after the [Spanish] pillaged the gold they found there, the Indians [were] condemned to work in the mines."[39] At the end of this section of extracts, Marx observed that "the survival (in large measure) of the rural commune" was partly due to the fact that, "unlike in the British East Indies, there was no colonial legislation providing for regulations that would give clan members the possibility to sell their landholdings."[40]

More than half of Marx's extracts from Kovalevsky were on India under British rule. He paid special attention to parts of the book that reconstructed forms of common landownership in contemporary India as well as in the Hindu rajahs. Using Kovalevsky's text, he observed that the collective dimension remained alive even after the parcelization introduced by the British: "Between these atoms certain connections continue to exist, distantly reminiscent of the earlier communal village landowning groups."[41] Despite their shared hostility to British colonialism, Marx was critical of some aspects of Kovalevsky's historical account that wrongly projected the parameters of the European context onto India. In a series of brief but detailed comments, he reproached him for homogenizing two distinct phenomena. For although "the farming out of offices—by no means simply feudal, as Rome attests—and *commendatio*[42] [were] found in India," this did not mean that "feudalism in the West European sense of the term" developed there. In Marx's view, Kovalevsky left out the important fact that the "serfdom" essential to feudalism did not exist in India.[43] Moreover, since "according to Indian law the ruling power [was] not subject to division among the sons, thereby a great source of European feudalism [was] obstructed."[44] In conclusion, Marx was highly skeptical about the transfer of interpretive categories between completely different historical and geographical contexts.[45] The deeper insights that he gained from Kovalevsky's text were subsequently integrated through his study of other works on Indian history.

Finally, with regard to Algeria, Marx did not fail to highlight the importance of common landownership before the arrival of French settlers, or of the changes that these introduced. From Kovalevsky, he copied down: "Formation of private landownership (in eyes of French bourgeois) is a necessary condition for all progress in the political and social sphere." Further maintenance of communal property "as a form which supports communist tendencies in the minds is dangerous both for the colony and for the homeland."[46] He also extracted the following points from *Communal Landownership: The Causes, Course and Consequences of Its Decline*:

> The distribution of clan holdings is encouraged, even prescribed, first, as means of weakening subjugated tribes which are ever standing under impulsion to revolt; second, as the only way to a further transfer of land-ownership from the hands of the natives into those of the colonists. The same policy has been pursued by the French under all regimes. . . . The aim is ever the same: destruction of the indigenous collective property and its transformation into an object of free purchase and sale, and by this means the final passage made easier into the hands of the French colonists.[47]

As for the legislation on Algeria proposed by the Left Republican Jules War-nier (1826–1899) and passed in 1873, Marx endorsed Kovalevsky's claim that its only purpose was "expropriation of the soil of the native population by the European colonists and speculators."[48] The effrontery of the French went as far as "direct robbery," or conversion into "government property,"[49] of all uncultivated land remaining in common for native use. This process was designed to produce another important result: elimination of the danger of resistance by the local population. Again through Kovalevsky's words, Marx noted:

> The foundation of private property and the settlement of European colonists among the Arab clans [would] become the most powerful means to accelerate the process of dissolution of the clan unions. . . . The expropriation of the Arabs intended by the law had two purposes: (1) to provide the French as much land as possible; and (2) to tear away the Arabs from their natural bonds to the soil to break the last strength of the clan unions thus being dissolved, and thereby any danger of rebellion.[50]

Marx commented that this type of "individualization of landownership" had not only secured huge economic benefits for the invaders but also achieved a "political aim . . . : to destroy the foundation of this society."[51]

Marx's selection of points, as well as the few but forthright words condemning European colonial policies that he added to the extracts from Kovalevsky's text, demonstrate his refusal to believe that either Indian or Algerian society was destined to follow the same course of development as in Europe.[52] Whereas Kovalevsky thought that landownership would follow the European example as if by a law of nature, passing everywhere from common to private, Marx maintained that collective property could hold out in some cases and that it would certainly not disappear as a result of some historical inevitability.[53]

Having examined forms of landownership in India, through a study of Kovalevsky's work, Marx compiled a series of *Notes on Indian History (664–1858)*, in the period from autumn 1879 to summer 1880. These compendia, covering more than a thousand years of history, were taken from a number of books, in particular Robert Sewell's (1845–1925) *Analytic History of India* (1870) and Mountstuart Elphinstone's *History of India* (1841).

Marx divided his notes into four periods. The first set featured a rather basic chronology, from the Muslim conquest, beginning with the first Arab penetration in 664, to the beginning of the sixteenth century. A second set covered the Moghul Empire, founded in 1526 by Zahīr ud-Dīn Muhammad and lasting until 1761; it also contained a very brief survey of foreign invasions of India and a four-page schema of European merchant activity from 1497 to 1702. From Sewell's book, Marx copied down some specific points on Murshid Quli Khan (1660–1727), the first Nawab of Bengal and architect of a new tax system. Marx described it as "a system of unscrupulous extortion and oppression, which created a large surplus [out of] the taxes from Bengal that was duly sent to Delhi."[54] According to Quli Khan, it was this revenue that kept the entire Moghul Empire afloat.

The third and most substantial set of notes, covering the period from 1725 to 1822, referred to the presence of the British East India Company. Marx did not limit himself here to transcription of the main events, dates, and names, but followed in greater detail the course of historical events, particularly with regard to British rule in India. The fourth and final set of notes was devoted to the Sepoy revolt of 1857 and the collapse of the British East India Company the following year.

In the *Notes on Indian History (664–1858)*, Marx gave very little space to his personal reflections, but his marginal annotations provide important clues to his views. The invaders were often described with such terms as "British dogs,"[55] "usurpers,"[56] "English hypocrites," or "English intruders."[57] By contrast, the Indian resistance struggles were always accompanied with expressions of solidarity.[58] It was no accident that Marx always replaced Sewell's term "mutineers" with "insurgents."[59] His forthright condemnation of European colonialism was quite unmistakable.

Finally, Marx turned his attention to Australia, showing particular interest in the social organization of its Aboriginal communities. From "Some Account of Central Australia" (1879), by the ethnographer Richard Bennett (?), he acquired the necessary critical knowledge to use against those who argued that there were neither laws nor culture in Aboriginal society. He also read other articles in *The Victorian Review* on the state of the country's economy, including "The Commercial Future of Australia" (1880) and "The Future of North-East Australia" (1880).

Beginning in the autumn of 1879, Marx embarked on a profound study of the natural sciences. Despite his compromised health, an unquenched intellectual curiosity drove him on to update his knowledge in certain areas that had undergone major development in the second half of the 1800s. Rising to the challenge, Marx compiled voluminous extracts from recently published books such as *The Modern Theory of Chemistry and Its Meaning for Static Chemistry* (1872) by Lothar Meyer (1830–1895), the fourth edition of the *Short Manual of Chemistry after the New Conceptions of Science* (1873), and the two-volume *Treatise on Chemistry* (1877–1879), both co-authored by Henry Roscoe (1833–1915) and Carl Schorlemmer (1834–1892)—the latter a long-standing friend and associate of Engels in Manchester. Marx also read Schorlemmer's *Manual of the Chemistry of the Carbon Compounds, or Organic Chemistry* (1874) and copied some observations from Wilhelm Kühne's (1837–1900) *Manual of Physiological Chemistry* (1868). He used these texts to draft numerous charts and synoptic tables in both organic and inorganic chemistry,[60] paying particular attention to metals, carbon compounds, and molecular theory.

At the same time, Marx studied works in physics, physiology, and geology, compiling extracts from them in his usual manner. Among these texts were: *Physics, a Comprehensive Presentation in the Most Recent Light* (1858) by the mathematician Benjamin Witzschel (1822–1882), *Outlines of Human Physiology* (1863) by the physiologist Ludimar Hermann (1838–1914), *Foundations of Human Physiology* (1868) by the anthropologist and physiologist Johannes Ranke (1836–1916), and new synopses of the work of Jukes, which he had already studied in 1878.

In 1880, Marx also studied the *Manual of Political Economy* (1876) by Adolph Wagner (1835–1917), a professor of political economy at Berlin University and defender of state socialism. As was his wont, Marx compiled extracts from the main parts of the book, adding a weighty set of critical comments along the way. In the "Marginal Notes on Adolph Wagner's *Lehrbuch der politischen Ökonomie*" (1880), he observed that, even in the hypothetical society of what he sarcastically called the "academic socialists [*Kathedersozialisten*]," the fundamental contradictions of capitalism would remain almost unaltered. For "where the state is itself a capitalist producer, as in the exploitation of mines, forests, etc., its product is a 'commodity' and hence possesses the specific character of every other commodity."[61]

One of the other purposes in these notes was to demonstrate that Wagner had not understood the distinction between value and exchange value. He was therefore incapable of differentiating Marx's theory from that of David Ricardo (1772–1823), who had "concern[ed] himself with labour solely as a measure of the magnitude of value."[62] According to Wagner, use value and exchange value should be "derived . . . from the concept of value;"[63] whereas for Marx they should be analyzed on the basis of "a concrete object, the commodity."[64]

Wagner had asserted that Marx's theory of value was "the cornerstone of his socialist system."[65] Marx contested this and replied that, "instead of foisting such future proofs on [him]," Wagner "first ought to have proved" what he asserted only in principle: namely, that "a social process of production . . . had not existed in the very numerous communities which existed before the appearance of private capitalists (the Old Indian community, the South Slav family community, etc.)."[66] Marx pointed out that "in primitive communities in which means of livelihood are produced communally and distributed amongst the members of the community, the common product directly satisfies the vital needs of each community member, of each producer." In such cases, "the social character of the product, of the use-value, lies in its (common) communal character."[67]

Marx also objected to other of Wagner's theses: for example, that "profit on capital is also in fact . . . a 'constitutive' element of value, not, as in the socialist view, simply a deduction from, or 'robbery' of, the worker." In reply, Marx emphasized that he had "demonstrated in detail" that "the capitalist . . . not only 'deducts' or 'robs' but enforces the production of surplus value." It was a different mechanism, whereby the capitalist, in paying "the worker the real value of his labour power," benefited from the surplus value he produced. This was a "right" for the capitalist in "this mode of production,"[68] which did not infringe "the law corresponding to the exchange of commodities."[69] At any event, it did not mean—as Wagner postulated—that "profit on capital" was "the constitutive element of value."[70]

Marx further quoted Wagner's paradoxical statement that "Aristotle . . . was mistaken in not regarding the slave economy as transitory," whereas Marx was "mistaken in regarding [the capitalist] economy as transitory."[71] For the Bavarian economist, "the present organization of the economy and the legal basis for it"—"hence private ownership of . . . land and capital" etc.—are essentially "an immutable institution."[72] For Marx, on the contrary, they are a historical mode of production and can therefore be replaced with a radically different kind of economic and political organization: a classless society.

3. THE NOTEBOOKS ON ANTHROPOLOGY, ANCIENT SOCIETIES, AND MATHEMATICS

Nevertheless, Marx continued to work whenever circumstances allowed it. Even now—contrary to some biographers' claims that his intellectual curiosity and theoretical acumen faded in his final years—he not only pursued his research but extended it to new areas.[73]

In February, Marx wrote to Danielson: "An awful correspondence-indebtedness stares me in the face." This was largely due to his immersion in new studies and his determination "to struggle through an immense lot of blue books sent to [him] from different countries, above all from the United States."[74]

Between December 1880 and June 1881, Marx's research interests focused on another discipline: anthropology. He began with *Ancient Society* (1877), a work by the U.S. anthropologist Lewis Morgan (1818–1881), which the Russian ethnologist Maksim Kovalevsky had brought back from a trip to North America and sent to Marx two years after its publication.

What struck Marx most was the way in which Morgan treated production and technological factors as preconditions of social progress, and he felt moved to assemble a compilation of a hundred densely packed pages. These make up the bulk of what are known as the *The Ethnological Notebooks*[75] (1880–1881). They also contain excerpts from other works: *Java, or How to Manage a Colony* (1861) by James Money (1818–1890), a lawyer and Indonesia expert; *The Aryan Village in India and Ceylon* (1880) by John Phear (1825–1905), president of the supreme court of Ceylon; and *Lectures on the Early History of Institutions* (1875) by the historian Henry Maine (1822–1888), amounting to a total of another hundred sheets.[76] Marx's comparative assessments of these authors lead one to suppose that he compiled all this material in a fairly short period in an effort to get really on top of it.

In his previous research, Marx had already examined and extensively commented on past social-economic forms—in the first part of *The German Ideology*, in the long section of the *Grundrisse* entitled "Forms Which Precede Capitalist Production," and in *Capital, Volume I*. In 1879, his reading of Kovalevsky's *Communal Landownership: The Causes, Course and Consequences of Its Decline* directed him once more to the subject. But it was only with *The Ethnological Notebooks* that he engaged in more comprehensive and up-to-date study.

The aim of Marx's new research was to widen his knowledge of the historical periods, geographical areas, and thematic topics that he considered essential for his continuing critique of political economy. It also enabled him to acquire specific information about the social characteristics and institutions of the remote past, acquainting him with material that was not in his possession when he had written the manuscripts of the 1850s and 1860s. Finally, it acquainted him with the latest theories advanced by the most eminent contemporary scholars.

Marx devoted himself to these often time-consuming anthropological studies during the same period in which he aimed to complete *Capital, Volume II*. The precise theoretical-political purpose behind them was to reconstruct the most likely sequence in which the different modes of production had succeeded one another over time, with a particular focus on the birth of capitalism. He believed that this would give his theory of the possible communist transformation of society stronger historical foundations.[77]

In *The Ethnological Notebooks*, Marx therefore put together compilations and interesting notes on prehistory, on the development of family bonds, on the condition of women, on the origins of property relations, on community practices in precapitalist societies, on the formation and nature of state power, on the role of the individual, and on more modern aspects such as the racist connotations of certain anthropological approaches and the effects of colonialism.

On the particular theme of prehistory and the development of family ties, Marx drew a number of priceless indications from the work of Morgan. As Hyndman recalled: "When Lewis Morgan proved to Marx's satisfaction in his

Ancient Society that the gens[78] and not the family was the social unit of the old tribal system and ancient society generally, Marx at once abandoned his previous opinions."[79]

It was Morgan's research on the social structure of primitive peoples that allowed him to overcome the limits of traditional interpretations of kinship, including the one advanced by the German historian Barthold Niebuhr (1786–1831) in *The History of Rome* (1811–1812). In contrast to all previous hypotheses, Morgan showed that it had been a grave error to suggest that the gens "postdated the monogamous family" and was the result of "an aggregate of families."[80] His studies of prehistoric and ancient society led him to the conclusion that the patriarchal family should be seen not as the original basic unit of society but as a form of social organization more recent than was generally believed. It was an organization "too weak to face alone the hardships of life."[81] It was much more plausible to assume the existence of a form like that of the American native peoples, the sindiasmic family, which practiced a "communism in living."[82]

On the other hand, Marx constantly polemicized against Maine, who in his *Lectures on the Early History of Institutions* (1875) had visualized "the private family" as "the basis out of which the sept and clan developed." Marx's scorn for this attempt to reverse time's arrow by transposing the Victorian era into prehistory led him to assert that this "blockheaded Englishman started not from the gens but from the Patriarch, who later became the chief—what inanities!"[83] His mockery gradually reaches a crescendo: "Maine after all cannot get the English private family out of his head";[84] he "transports the Roman 'patriarchal' family into the very beginning of things."[85] Nor did Marx spare Phear, of whom he said: "The ass bases everything on private families!"[86]

Morgan gave Marx further food for thought with his remarks on the concept of the family, since in its "original meaning" the word *family*—which has the same root as *famulus*, or servan—"had no relation to the married pair or their children, but to the body of slaves and servants who laboured for its maintenance, and were under the power of the *pater familias*."[87] On this subject, Marx noted:

> The modern family contains the germ not only of slavery [*servitus*] but also serfdom, since it contains from the beginning a relation to services for agriculture. It contains in miniature all the antagonisms within itself, which are later broadly develop in society and its State. . . . The monogamous

family presupposed, in order to have an existence separate from others, a domestic class that was everywhere directly constituted by slaves.[88]

Developing his own thoughts elsewhere in the compendium, Marx wrote that "property in houses, lands and herds" was bound up with "the monogamous family."[89] In fact, as the *Manifesto of the Communist Party* suggested, this was the starting point of history as "the history of class struggle."[90]

In *The Origin of the Family, Private Property and the State* (1884)—a book that the author described as "the fulfilment of a behest" and no more than a "meagre substitute" for what his "dear friend" had not lived to write[91]—Engels completed Marx's analysis in *The Ethnological Notebooks*. Monogamy, he argued, represented

> the subjection of one sex by the other, as the proclamation of a conflict between the sexes hitherto unknown throughout preceding history. In an old unpublished manuscript, the work of Marx and myself in 1846, I find the following: "The first division of labour is that between man and woman for child breeding."[92] And today I can add: The first class antithesis which appears in history coincides with the development of the antagonism between man and woman in monogamian marriage, and the first class oppression with that of the female sex by the male. Monogamy . . . [is] the cellular form of civilized society, in which we can already study the nature of the antitheses and contradictions, which develop fully in the latter.[93]

Engels's thesis posited an overly schematic relationship between economic conflict and gender oppression that was absent from Marx's—fragmentary and highly intricate—notes.[94]

Marx too paid close attention to Morgan's considerations on parity between the sexes, which argued that pre-Greek ancient societies were more progressive in respect of the treatment and behavior of women. Marx copied the parts of Morgan's book that showed how, among the Greeks, "the change of descent from the female line to the male was damaging for the position and rights of the wife and woman." Indeed, Morgan had a very negative assessment of the Greek social model. "Greeks remained barbarians in their treatment of women at the height of their civilization; their education superficial, . . . their inferiority inculcated as a principle upon them, until it came to be accepted as a fact by the women themselves." Moreover, there was "a principle of studied selfishness among the males, tending to lessen the appreciation of women, scarcely found among savages." Thinking of the contrast with the myths of the classical world, Marx added an acute observation: "The condition of the goddesses on Olympus is a reminder of the position of women, once freer and more influential. Juno greedy for power, the goddess of wisdom springs from the head of Zeus."[95] For Marx, memory of the free divinities of the past provided an example for possible emancipation in the present.[96]

From the various authors he studied, Marx recorded many important observations on the role of women in ancient society. For example, referring to the work *Matriarchy* (1861) by the Swiss anthropologist Johann Bachofen (1815–1887), he noted: "The women were the great power among the gens and everywhere else. They did not hesitate, when occasion required, 'to knock off the horns,' as it was technically called, from the head of a chief, and send him back to the ranks of warriors. The original nomination of the chiefs also always rested with them."[97]

Marx's reading of Morgan also gave him an angle on another important question: the origin of property relations. For the celebrated anthropologist established a causal relation between the various types of kinship structure and social-economic forms. In his view, the factors in Western history that accounted for the affirmation of the descriptive system—which described blood relatives and specified everyone's kinship (e.g., "brother's son for nephew, father's brother for uncle, father's brother's son for cousin")—and the decline of the classificatory system—which grouped blood relatives into categories without specifying proximity or distance in relation to Ego ("e.g., my own brother and my father's brother's sons are in equal degree my brothers")—had to do with the development of property and the state.[98]

Morgan's book was divided into four parts: (1) growth of intelligence through inventions and discoveries, (2) growth of the idea of government, (3) growth of the Idea of the family, and (4) growth of the idea of property. Marx changed the order to (1) inventions, (2) family, (3) property, and (4) government, in order to bring out more clearly the nexus between the last two.

Morgan's book argued that, although "the rights of wealth, of rank and of official position" had prevailed for thousands of years over "justice and intelligence," there was ample evidence that "the privileged classes" were a "burdensome"[99] influence on society. Marx copied out almost in full one of the final pages of *Ancient Society* on the distortions that property could generate; it operated with concepts that made a deep impression on him:

Since the advent of civilization, the outgrowth of property has been so immense, its forms so diversified, its uses so expanding and its management so intelligent in the interests of its owners, that it has become, on the part of the people, an unmanageable power. The human mind stands bewildered in the presence of its own creation. The time will come, nevertheless, when human intelligence will rise to the mastery over property, and define the relations of the state to the property it protects, as well as the obligations and the limits of the rights of its owners. The interests of society are paramount to individual interests, and the two must be brought into just and harmonious relations.[100]

Morgan refused to believe that the "final destiny of mankind" was the mere pursuit of riches. He issued a stark warning:

The dissolution of society bids fair to become the termination of a career of which property is the end and aim; because such a career contains the elements of self-destruction. Democracy in government, brotherhood in society, equality in rights and privileges, and universal education, foreshadow the next higher plane of society to which experience, intelligence and knowledge are steadily tending. It (a higher plan of society)[101] will be a revival, in a higher form (of society), of the liberty, equality and fraternity of the ancient gentes.[102]

Bourgeois "civilization," then, was itself a transitory stage. It had arisen at the end of two long epochs, the "savage state" and the "barbaric state" (the terms current at the time), which followed the abolition of communal forms of social organization. These forms imploded following the accumulation of property and wealth and the emergence of social classes and the state. But sooner or later prehistory and history were destined to join up once again.[103]

Morgan considered ancient societies to have been very democratic and solidaristic. As for the present, he limited himself to a declaration of optimism about the progress of humanity, without invoking the necessity of political struggle.[104] Marx, however, did not envisage a socialist revival of "the myth of the noble savage." He never hoped for a return to the past, but—as he made clear when copying Morgan's book—looked to the advent of a "higher form of society"[105] based on a new mode of production and consumption. This would come about not through mechanical evolution, but only through conscious working-class struggle.

All of Marx's anthropological reading had a bearing on the origins and functions of the state. The excerpts from Morgan summarized its role in the transition from barbarism to civilization, while his notes on Maine concentrated on analysis of the relations between the individual and the state.[106] Consistent with his most significant theoretical texts on the subject, from the *Critique of Hegel's Philosophy of Law* (1843)[107] to *The Civil War in France* (1871),[108] *The Ethnological Notebooks* also present the state as a power subjugating society, a force preventing the full emancipation of the individual.

In the notes he wrote in 1881, Marx stressed the parasitic and transitory character of the state:

> Maine ignores the much deeper point: that the seeming supreme independent existence of the state is only seeming and that it is in all its forms an excrescence of society; just as its appearance itself arises only at a certain stage of social development, it disappears again as soon as society has reached a stage not yet attained.

Marx followed this up with a critique of the human condition under the given historical circumstances. The formation of civilized society, with its transition from a regime of common to individual property, generated a "still one-sided . . . individuality."[109] If the "true nature . . . [of the state] appears only when we analyse its content," that is, its "interests," then this shows that these interests "are common to certain social groups" and therefore "class interests." For Marx, "the state is built on and presupposes classes." Hence the individuality that exists in this type of society is "a class individuality," which in the last analysis is "based on economic presuppositions."[110]

In *The Ethnological Notebooks*, Marx also made a number of observations on the racist connotations of many of the anthropological reports he was studying.[111] His rejection of such ideology was categorical, and he commented caustically on the authors who expressed it in this way. Thus, when Maine used discriminatory epithets, he firmly interjected: "Again this nonsense!" Moreover, expressions such as "the devil take this 'Aryan' jargon!"[112] keep recurring.

Referring to Money's *Java, or How to Manage a Colony* and Phear's *The Aryan Village in India and Ceylon*, Marx studied the negative effects of the European presence in Asia. He was not at all interested in Money's views on colonial policy, but he found his book useful for the detail it gave about commerce.[113] He adopted a similar approach to Phear's book, focusing mainly on what he reported about the state in Bengal and ignoring his weak theoretical constructions.

The authors whom Marx read and summarized in *The Ethnological Notebooks* had all been influenced—with various nuances—by the evolutionary conceptions of the age, and some had also become firm proponents of the superiority of bourgeois civilization. But an examination of *The Ethnological Notebooks* clearly shows that their ideological assertions had no influence on Marx.

Theories of progress, hegemonic in the nineteenth century and widely shared by anthropologists and ethnologists, postulated that events would follow a pregiven course because of factors external to human action; a rigid sequence of stages had the capitalist world as its sole and uniform destination.

Within the space of a few years, a naïve belief in the automatic advance of history also took root in the Second International. The only difference from the bourgeois version was the prediction that a final stage would follow the inevitable "collapse" of the capitalist system: namely, the advent of socialism (itself subsequently defined as "Marxist"!).[114]

Not only was this analysis cognitively unsound; it produced a kind of fatalistic passivity, which became a stabilizing factor for the existing order and weakened the social and political action of the proletariat. Opposing this approach that so many regarded as "scientific," and which was common to the bourgeois and socialist visions of progress, Marx rejected the siren calls of a one-way historicism and preserved his own complex, flexible, and variegated conception.

Whereas, in comparison with the Darwinist oracles, Marx's voice might seem uncertain and hesitant,[115] he actually escaped the trap of economic determinism into which many of his followers and ostensible continuators tended to fall—a position, light years from the theories they claimed to have inspired them, which would lead many into one of the worst characterizations of "Marxism."

In his manuscripts, notebooks, and letters to comrades and activists, as well as in the few public interventions he could still make against a backdrop of family dramas and declining physical capacities, Marx persevered with his efforts to reconstruct the complex history of the passage from antiquity to capitalism. From the anthropological studies that he read and summarized, he drew confirmation that human progress had proceeded more quickly in epochs when the sources of subsistence were expanding, from the birth of agriculture on. He treasured the historical information and data, but did not share the rigid schemas suggesting an inescapable sequence of stages in human history.

Marx spurned any rigid linking of social changes to economic transformations alone. Instead, he highlighted the specificity of historical conditions, the multiple possibilities that the passing of time offered, and the centrality of human intervention in the shaping of reality and the achievement of change.[116] These were the salient features of Marx's theoretical elaboration in the final years of his life.

In 1881, alongside his ethnological research, Marx resumed his study of organic chemistry and, continuing with interests from 1879, produced tables on paraffin, benzine, and various aromatic compounds.[117] Above all, however, he returned in the first half of the year to the study of mathematics—a challenge he had already taken up on several previous occasions.

In early 1858, he wrote to Engels that he had made so many mistakes of calculation in writing the *Grundrisse* that "in despair [he had] applied [himself] to a rapid revision of algebra." "I have never felt at home with arithmetic," he confessed, "but by making a detour with algebra I shall quickly get back into the way of things."[118] Initially, therefore, Marx's interest in the science of numbers was tied to his studies of political economy and an urgent need to solve certain theoretical problems that they posed. But once he got down to it, there was a profound change in his attitude. Apart from being useful for *Capital*, mathematics became a source of cultural interest in itself, acquiring a really special place in his intellectual activities.

As early as 1860, when his wife was ill with smallpox and his daughters were away for fear of catching it themselves, Marx—who had taken on the role of "nurse"—wrote to Engels: "Writing articles [for the *New-York Tribune*] is almost out of the question. The only occupation that helps me maintain the necessary quietness of mind is mathematics."[119] He kept up this habit until the end of his days. He stressed the pleasure this gave him in many letters to Engels. In spring 1865, he wrote that in breaks from *Capital*—to complete which he was "working like a horse," as the carbuncles, though still with him, did not "disturb the brain-pan"—he was "doing some differential calculus." "Any other kind of reading always drives me back to my writing-desk."[120] Marx kept this up during the 1870s,[121] and from the end of the decade he went about it more methodically, writing hundreds of pages that came to be known as the *Mathematical Manuscripts*.[122]

In 1881, Marx focused his attention on the mathematical theories of Isaac Newton (1643–1727) and Gottfried Wilhelm Leibniz (1646–1716), who independently of each other[123]—the first in England, the second in Germany—had invented differential calculus and integral calculus, the two components of infinitesimal calculus. Following these studies, Marx wrote two short manuscripts, "On the Concept of the Derived Function" and "On the Differential," that methodically presented his interpretation of differential calculus and illustrated the method he had discovered. Both texts were dedicated to Engels, and as soon as he had finished Marx sent them off for him to give his judgment.

Marx's studies on the history of differential calculus, beginning with its origins, were accompanied with various notes and preliminary drafts[124] and served a precise objective: to criticize the foundations of infinitesimal calculus, refuting the existence of a prime mathematics with dx and dy differentials.[125] In the course of this research, he particularly noted the "mystical" foundation of the differential calculus developed by Newton and Leibniz, neither of whom gave any formal explanation of how this had happened. Marx criticized them for introducing it without defining it.[126]

This negative aspect had already been seized upon by other mathematicians, such as Jean D'Alembert (1717–1783) and Joseph-Louis Lagrange (1736–1813), whose theses Marx studied with great interest. Both these men, however—the first using the rationalist method and the notion of limit, the second using the purely algebraic method and the concept of derived function—had failed to solve the problem that Marx identified.

Still dissatisfied at the end of these studies, Marx decided to seek a rigorous formal definition of differential calculus, conceptually based rather than "mystical." But he was not familiar with the latest research on the subject, since his knowledge of the specialist literature stopped with the discoveries at the beginning of the nineteenth century. He did not manage to read the works by two contemporary mathematicians: Augustin Cauchy (1789–1857) and Karl Weierstrass (1815–1897),[127] which would probably have enabled him to advance toward the objective he had set for himself.[128]

Engels, for his part, finally "plucked up the courage" in August 1881 "to make a thorough study" of Marx's *Mathematical Manuscripts*. He wrote to him offering his congratulations. "Here at last we are able to see clearly what has long been maintained by many mathematicians who were unable to produce rational grounds for it, namely that the differential quotient is the prototype, while the differentials dx and dy are derived." Engels was so involved in the matter that it not only "kept going round in his head all day" but he "actually had a dream in which [he] gave a fellow [his] studs to differentiate them and he made off with the lot."[129]

Discussions of the question among Marx, Engels, and their mutual friend Samuel Moore (1838–1911) continued until the end of the following year. In November 1882, Marx was still convinced that he could "dismiss the whole of this historical development of analysis by saying that, in practice, no essential change has been brought about in the geometrical application of differential calculus, i.e. in geometrical symbolization."[130] Contrary to expectations, however, Marx would have no further opportunity to continue his research at the British Museum library and "to return to a detailed discussion of the various methods."

In this very last period of his life, Marx's interest in differential calculus was no longer directly related to his work on *Capital*. He focused more on pure mathematics rather than its application to economics, whereas in the 1870s he had wanted "to determine mathematically the principal laws governing crises."[131] Despite what some experts have argued,[132] Marx's limited energies make it unlikely that he ever intended to write a mathematical text of his own.

The *Mathematical Manuscripts* from this final period do show, however, what was most distinctive about Marx's preoccupation with mathematics. First and foremost, it was a useful intellectual stimulus in his search for a method of social analysis. In the end, mathematics became almost a physical space for him: sometimes a ludic space, but above all one where he could take refuge at moments of great personal difficulty.

4. CITIZEN OF THE WORLD

Totally absorbed though he was in intensive theoretical studies, Marx never stopped taking an interest in the economic and international political events of his time. In addition to reading the main "bourgeois" newspapers, he received and regularly looked through the German and French working-class press. Curious as ever, he always began the day by perusing the news reports in order to remain on top of what was happening in the world. Correspondence with leading political and intellectual figures from various countries was often another valuable source of information, giving him fresh stimuli and deeper knowledge of a wide range of subjects.

Early in 1881 Ferdinand Domela Nieuwenhuis (1846–1919), a leading figure in the Social Democratic League [*Sociaal-Democratische Bond*]—the main socialist political force in the Netherlands at the time—gave Marx the opportunity to explain once more his views on the transition to communism. In the run-up to a socialist congress later that year,[133] which was intended to unify the largest parties of the European proletariat in a new International, Nieuwenhuis turned to Marx with a question that he considered of decisive importance: what legislative measures of a political and economic nature would a revolutionary government have to take after it came to power in order to guarantee the success of socialism?

As in the past, Marx said he was opposed to answering such questions with a general formula; in fact, he considered them "pointless," since "what is to be done, and done immediately at any given, particular moment in the future, depends wholly and entirely on the actual historical circumstances in which action is to be taken." Posed in the abstract, it was "a fallacious problem to which the only answer can be a critique of the question as such."[134] He was not interested in making predictions about what the free society of the future would look like, but focused on the conditions that would make it achievable. Marx therefore replied in peremptory fashion to Nieuwenhuis that it was impossible to "solve an equation that does not comprise within its terms the elements of its solution." He was sure, moreover, that

> a socialist government will not come to the helm in a country unless things have reached a stage at which it can, before all else, take such measures as will so intimidate the mass of the bourgeoisie as to achieve the first desideratum—time for effective action.[135]

For Marx, it was clear that the establishment of a socialist system of production and consumption would be a long and complex process, certainly not achievable simply through the capture of the palace of power. Indeed, there would be nothing "specifically socialist about the predicaments of a government that has suddenly come into being as a result of a popular victory." The Paris Commune—the only actual experience of a revolutionary government—could by no means be considered the reference model. For it had been a very special case, "merely an uprising of one city in exceptional circumstances," most of whose political leadership "was in no sense socialist, nor could it have been."[136]

In comparing the position of the working class of his time with that of the French bourgeoisie before the fall of the ancien régime, Marx maintained that the proletarian front was not more backward:

> The general demands of the French bourgeoisie before 1789 were *mutatis mutandis* just as well-defined as are today, with a fair degree of uniformity, the primary, immediate demands of the proletariat in all countries where there is capitalist production. But could any 18th century Frenchman

a priori have the least idea of the manner in which the demands of the French bourgeoisie would be implemented?[137]

More generally, Marx never abandoned his conviction:

> A doctrinaire and of necessity fantastic anticipation of a future revolution's programme of action only serves to distract from the present struggle. The dream of the imminent end of the world inspired the struggle of the early Christians against the Roman Empire and gave them confidence in victory. Scientific insight into the inevitable disintegration, now steadily taking place before our eyes, of the prevailing social order; the masses themselves, their fury mounting under the lash of the old governmental bogies; the gigantic and positive advances simultaneously taking place in the development of the means of production—all this is sufficient guarantee that the moment a truly proletarian revolution breaks out, the conditions for its immediate initial (if certainly not idyllic) *modus operandi* will also be there.[138]

Ending the letter with some remarks on the forthcoming socialist congress mentioned by Nieuwenhuis, Marx did not conceal his skepticism about the possibility of immediately creating a new transnational organization along the lines of the one he had coordinated for almost a decade:

> My own conviction is that the critical conjuncture for a New International Working Men's Association has not yet arrived; hence I consider all labour congresses and/or socialist congresses, in so far as they do not relate to the immediate, actual conditions obtaining in this or that specific nation, to be not only useless but harmful. They will invariably fizzle out in a host of rehashed generalized banalities.[139]

Some of Marx's correspondents also raised with him a proposal made by the U.S. economist Henry George (1839–1897) in his *Progress and Poverty* (1879), a work sold in millions of copies in a number of languages. George's argument, much talked about in the press of the day, was that a single tax on land value should replace all other existing taxes:

> Government already takes some rent in taxation. With a few changes in our tax laws, we could take almost all. . . . Therefore, I propose that we

appropriate land rent for public use, through taxation. . . . In its form, ownership of land would remain just as it is now. No owner need be dispossessed. No restriction need be placed upon the amount of land any one could hold. If rent were taken by the state in taxes, then land would really be common property—no matter in whose name or in what parcels it was held. Every member of the community would participate in the advantages of its ownership. . . . In fact, when rent exceeds current government revenues, it will be necessary to actually increase the land tax to absorb excess rent. Taxation of rent would increase as we abolish other taxes. So, we may put our proposition into practical form by proposing: To abolish all taxes—except on land values.[140]

When the German revolutionary émigré Friedrich Sorge (1828–1906), as well as John Swinton and the American socialist Willard Brown (?), asked for his opinion about this proposal to solve the paradox of the coexistence of progress and poverty, Marx felt obliged to reply. His "very brief assessment of the book" was, as often happened, contemptuous. Marx recognized that George was a "talented writer" and that most of the praise heaped on the book in the United States was due to the fact that it represented "a first, if unsuccessful, attempt at emancipation from orthodox political economy." But apart from these two small concessions, Marx hit out against the views of the economist on the other side of the ocean, who, as a theoretician, seemed to him "totally backward." He had "understood nothing of the nature of surplus value" and lost himself in "speculations about those portions of surplus value that have become independent—about the relations between profit, rent, interest, etc."

Marx not only contested George's "basic tenet"[141] but also denied its originality. In their younger days, Marx and Engels themselves had argued in the *Manifesto of the Communist Party* for the "abolition of property in land and application of all rents of land to public purposes,"[142] as one of the ten measures to be taken in the most advanced countries after the conquest of power by the working class.

Marx reminded Swinton that "the older disciples of Ricardo—the radical ones—fancied already that by the public appropriation of the rent of land everything would be righted."[143] Marx had criticized this notion in 1847, in *The Poverty of Philosophy*, when he made it clear that if "such economists as Mill, Cherbuliez, Hilditch and others demand[ed] that rent should be handed over to the state to serve in place of taxes," it was "a frank expression of the hatred the industrial capitalist bears towards the landed proprietor, who seems to him a useless thing, an excrescence upon the general body of bourgeois production."[144] It was certainly not enough to remove the inequalities in contemporary society.

In his reply to Sorge, Marx mentioned other authors who had proposed similar ideas in the past. Jean Hyppolite Colins (1783–1859), for example, had tried to make "a socialist panacea of this desideratum of the English radical bourgeois economists, declaring this procedure to be a solution of the antagonisms inherent in today's mode of production." And the economist Adolph Samter (1824–1883), "a shallow-pated Prussian banker and lottery collector" and follower of Johann Rodbertus (1805–1875), had "distended this 'socialism' to fill a hefty tome," under the title *Social Doctrine: On the Satisfaction of Needs in Human Society* (1875).

For Marx, George's book fitted into this tradition of thought, although it was "all the more inexcusable" than other examples. A citizen of the United States, "where the land was [once] relatively accessible to the great mass of the people and to a certain degree still [was]," should have explained how it was possible that "the capitalist economy and the corresponding enslavement of the working class ha[d] developed more rapidly and brazenly than in any other country."[145] However, he declared:

> All these "socialists" . . . have this in common—they allow wage labour and hence also capitalist production to subsist, while endeavouring to delude themselves and the world into believing that the transformation of rent into taxation paid to the State must bring about the automatic disappearance of all the abuses of capitalist production.[146]

Whatever their intentions, then, the theories of George and like-minded writers were "merely an attempt, tricked out with socialism, to save the capitalist *régime* and, indeed, to re-establish it on an even broader basis than at present."[147] In conclusion, Marx attacked George's "revolting presumptuousness and arrogance," which he saw as "the unmistakable hallmark of all such panacea-mongers."[148]

In the course of 1881, Marx continued to observe world events and to comment on them with comrades and family members. In particular, he wrote a long letter to Danielson in February that contained some priceless observations on the situation in several countries.

The study of economic crashes—always a priority for Marx—and the Great Depression that, in 1873, struck a number of countries, particularly England, stimulated the researcher's interest and intensified the militant's hopes. On the financial events in the United Kingdom, he wrote: "If the great industrial and commercial crisis England has passed through went over without the culminating financial crash at London, this exceptional phenomenon was only due to—French money."[149]

These considerations were accompanied with a description of the general economic context. The recession had manifested itself in a marked drop in productivity and a dramatic stagnation of exports. Britain had ceased to be the workshop of the world, and the "Victorian prosperity" of the previous decades had remained no more than a memory. In particular, Marx noted:

> The English railway system rolls on the same inclined plane as the European Public Debt system. The ruling magnates amongst the different railway-nets directors contract not only—progressively—new loans in order to enlarge their networks, i.e. the "territory," where they rule as absolute monarchs, but they enlarge their respective networks in order to have new pretexts for engaging in new loans which enable them to pay the interest due to the holders of obligations, preferential shares, etc., and also from time to time to throw a sop to the much ill-used common shareholders in the shape of somewhat increased dividends. This pleasant method must one day or another terminate in an ugly catastrophe.[150]

Marx showed no less interest in events on the other side of the Atlantic. One of these was the San Francisco Riot of July 1877, with its ethnic violence directed against the Chinese community. In November 1880, Marx repeatedly requested Sorge to send him "meaty stuff" from the United States on "economic conditions in California." He had agreed to press on with his analysis of the region, which he considered highly important "because in no other place ha[d] revolution by capitalist centralization been effected with such effrontery at such great speed."[151] Shortly afterwards, having received the materials for his research, Marx made some extracts from George's article "The Kearney Agitation in California" (1880), which had appeared in *The Popular Science Monthly*. Stimulated by this piece, in the context of growing poverty resulting from the Great Depression onwards, Marx too focused on the racist demagogy of Dennis Kearney (1847–1907) against the Chinese workers and the countermobilization organized by the Workingmen's Party of the United States. Using the slogan "The Chinamen Must Go!,"[152] Kearney had speculated that the workers' rage at the continuing crisis could be turned against migrants and used to stir up clashes among the poor. Marx copied George's observation that "communism or socialism (understanding by these terms the desire for fundamental social changes)" had failed to win the support of most workers, because "the presence of the Chinese ha[d] largely engrossed the attention of the labouring classes, offering what has seemed to them a sufficient explanation of the fall of wages and difficulty of finding employment."[153] Marx was well aware that conflicts among workers, particularly after waves of migration, were a powerful weapon that the bourgeoisie could use to distract them from the real problems of capitalist society. But although he was increasingly alert to the difficulties and contradictions of the class struggle, he retained great expectations of the revolutionary potential of the workers' movement.[154]

Marx also closely followed the financial collapse of Jay Gould (1836–1892), a major U.S. railroad builder, who, by means of huge speculative operations, had become one of the richest and most unscrupulous men of his time—with a not undeserved reputation as "king of the robber barons."[155] He owned the Erie Railroad Company, which operated the historic line between New York and the Northeast, and in 1879 he had taken control of three major networks, including the Union Pacific Railroad, in many Pacific coast states, and the Missouri Pacific Railroad, which ran services east of the Mississippi River. All this added up to 16,000 kilometers of track—a ninth of the country's total. In 1881, he further expanded his empire by taking over Western Union as well.

Interested as he was in developments in American society, Marx could not have failed to follow Gould's ascent or to comment on the way in which he defended himself from public attacks:

In the United States the railway kings have become the butt of attacks, not only, as before this, on the part of the farmers and other industrial "entrepreneurs" of the West, but also on the part of the grand representative of commerce—the New York Chamber of Commerce. The octopodus railway king and financial swindler Gould has, on his side, told the New York commercial magnates: "You now attack the railways, because you think them most vulnerable considering their present unpopularity; but take heed: after the railways every sort of corporation . . . will have its turn; then, later on, all forms of associated capital; finally, all forms of capital;

you are thus paving the way to—Communism, whose tendencies are already more and more spreading among the people."[156]

"Mr Gould has a good nose," Marx joked,[157] hoping that this tendency would indeed assert itself in the United States.

In the same letter, he also touched on events in India and went so far as to predict that "serious complications, if not a general outbreak, [was] in store for the British government."[158] The degree of exploitation had become more and more intolerable:

> What the English take from them annually in the form of rent, dividends for railways useless to the Hindoos, pensions for military and civil servicemen, for Afghanistan and other wars, etc. etc.—what they take from them without any equivalent and quite apart from what they appropriate to themselves annually within India, speaking only of the value of the commodities the Indians have gratuitously and annually to send over to England, it amounts to more than the total sum of income of the 60 millions of agricultural and industrial labourers of India! This is a bleeding process, with a vengeance! The famine years are pressing each other and in dimensions till now not yet suspected in Europe! There is an actual conspiracy going on wherein Hindus and Mussulmans cooperate; the British government is aware that something is "brewing," but this shallow people (I mean the governmental men), stultified by their own parliamentary ways of talking and thinking, do not even desire to see clear, to realize the whole extent of the imminent danger! To delude others and by deluding them to delude yourself—this is: parliamentary wisdom in a nutshell! Just as well![159]

Ever since the 1860s, Marx had also paid close attention to the Irish cause. Some of his reflections are to be found in a letter of 11 April to his daughter Jenny Longuet, who had for many years been a supporter of the Fenian movement. Marx was totally opposed to the occupation of Ireland and the terrible injustices that the British perpetrated there. Thus, when William Gladstone (1809–1898)—that "arch-hypocrite and casuist of the old-fashioned school"[160]—heard in 1868 that he had been appointed prime minister, he declared that his political "mission" was to "pacify Ireland."[161]

The first measures that Gladstone took to address the decisive question of landownership totally failed to live up to the expectations he had aroused. The

Landlord and Tenant (Ireland) Act, passed in 1870 as an amendment to existing legislation, merely made the situation worse. For by the end of the decade, Ireland was the scene of numerous protests against the landowners' terrible exactions, and a revolt against British rule was indeed "brewing."

When the Liberals submitted a second piece of legislation in April 1881—the Land Law (Ireland) Act—Marx again rounded on a government that, contrary to the claims of its supporters, had not really sought to curb the English landowners' arbitrary power over their tenants. In reality, he wrote to Jenny, "Gladstone, by his disgraceful preliminary measures (incl. abolishing the freedom of speech of members of the Lower House), has brought about the conditions under which mass evictions are now taking place in Ireland."[162] In Marx's view, the proposed reforms were "pure humbug, seeing that the Lords, who can get anything they want from Gladstone, and no longer have to tremble before the Land League,[163] will doubtless throw it out or else so castrate it that the Irish themselves will end up voting against it."[164] Marx was wrong in so far as the British parliament approved the measures, but he was right in predicting that they would not solve the problems of Ireland. As a result of the new legislation, only a few hundred farmers were able to purchase land, and the agitation picked up again a few years later.

In another letter to Jenny sent a few weeks later, Marx returned to the charge. He saw that it had been a "very fine trick" on Gladstone's part, "at a moment when landed property in Ireland (as in England) [was being] depreciated by the import of corn and cattle from the United States," to offer big landlords the possibility "to sell that property at a price it does no longer possess."[165] He asked Jenny to get her husband, Charles Longuet, to read the speech given in Cork by Charles Parnell (1846–1891), the main figure in the Irish Parliamentary Party: "He will find in it the substance of what ought to be said about Gladstone's new Land Act."[166] In the end, for Marx:

> the real intricacies of the Irish land problem—which indeed are not especially Irish—are so great that the only true way to solve it would be to give the Irish Home-rule and thus force them to solve it themselves. But John Bull is too stupid to understand this.[167]

In general, it certainly cannot be said that Marx was enthusiastic about living under the English monarchy. The death of Benjamin Disraeli (1804–1881), twice prime minister and for many years leader of the Conservative Party, occurred on 19 April and elicited a campaign of "exaltation." This seemed to Marx "the last London craze," which "gave John Bull the satisfaction of admiring his own magnanimity." In fact, Disraeli's second government (1874–1880) had seen one negative episode after another: in foreign policy, the Second Afghan War and the bloody conflict in South Africa known as the Anglo-Zulu War; and in the economy, the downturn in agricultural and industrial production. These were the reasons for his crushing defeat in the general elections of 1880.

Reflecting on Disraeli's posthumous return to popularity, Marx commented: "Is it not 'grand' to act the sycophant with regard to a dead man whom just before his kicking the bucket you had saluted with rotten apples and foul eggs?" Perhaps, he noted sarcastically, this was meant to teach "the lower classes" that, "however their natural 'superiors' might fall out amongst each other during the struggle for 'place and pelf,' death brings out the truth that the leaders of the 'ruling classes' are always 'great and good men.'"[168]

He also hated the English climate. On 6 June, he complained bitterly to his daughter of the "infernal rainy and cold weather today and yesterday," which had coincided with Irish protest actions in the English capital. It was "one of the bad tricks the celestial father has always in store for his London plebeian cattle and sheep. Yesterday he spoiled by the rain the Hyde Park demonstration of Parnell's."[169]

Of course, Marx by no means neglected the two main countries on the Continent: Germany and France. As in the past, he took an active interest in them whenever possible, meeting left-wing political leaders, authors of books of socialist theory, and others who wrote in papers and reviews in support of the proletarian movement.

In the course of 1880, Marx was particularly assiduous with regard to the French workers' movement, contributing to its advance in ways that seemed opportune and practicable. In October of the previous year, the Federation of the Socialist Workers of France [*Fédération du parti des travailleurs socialistes de France*], born out of a fusion of various socialist currents, met in congress in Marseilles. Its proceedings were marked by a conflict between the "Possibilists," headed by the former anarchist Paul Brousse (1844–1912), and another current closer to Marx's ideas, led by Jules Guesde (1845–1922). When the latter won a majority, Marx commented to Sorge: "The anti-communist gang, composed of very heterogeneous elements, was finally defeated at the Marseilles Congress."[170]

Guesde, who, with elections in the offing, had to draw up a political program, turned to Marx for assistance, and Paul Lafargue arranged for them to meet in London in May 1880. This was the origin of the *Electoral Programme of the Socialist Workers* (1880), which appeared in various French dailies in the spring and was adopted at Le Havre in November at the founding congress of the French Workers' Party [*Parti ouvrier français*]. Marx's contribution in setting forth the primary demands of the working class was decisive.[171] Starting from the point that workers could never be free in a system of production based on wage labor, Marx declared that their emancipation would be achieved only after "the political and economic expropriation of the capitalist class and the return of all the means of production to collective ownership."[172] The working class, he continued, should fight any kind of discrimination and operate in such a way as to end women's subaltern position in relation to men: "The emancipation of the productive class is that of all human beings without distinction of sex or race."[173] The economic part of the *Electoral Programme of the Socialist Workers* clearly spelled out two key points: "Legal prohibition of bosses employing foreign workers at a wage less than that of French workers," and "equal pay for equal work, for workers of both sexes."[174]

The workers should support a form of government that could guarantee their broadest participation. They should fight for "suppression of the public debt,"[175] for "the transformation of all direct taxes into a progressive tax on incomes," and for an end to state support for religious orders. The working class should also demand the right to publicly funded education for all and fight for "annulment of all the contracts that have alienated public property (banks, railways, mines, etc.)." At the same time, it should mobilize for "the operation of all state-owned workshops to be entrusted to the workers who work there." The political organization of the proletariat, including the constitution of "a distinct political party"[176] competing with democratic parties and fighting against bourgeois ones, was essential for the achievement of these aims.

In a letter to Sorge, Marx explained that "with the exception of some stupidities such as a minimum wage fixed by law"—which risked turning into the maximum any capitalist would accept[177]—the economic section of the document consisted "solely of demands that have, in fact, arisen spontaneously out of the workers' movement itself." For Marx, "to bring the French workers down to earth out of their verbal cloud-cuckoo land was a tremendous step forward, and therefore aroused much resentment among all those French intellectual frauds who make a living as 'cloud-gatherers.'" He also stressed that, for the first time, the program had been discussed by the workers themselves—"proof that this [was] the first real workers' movement in France."[178] Marx clearly distinguished this phase from the one that had gone before, when "sects there received their slogans from their founders, while the bulk of the proletariat followed the radical or pseudo-radical bourgeois and fought for them when the day came, only to be slaughtered, deported, etc., on the morrow by the very laddies they had placed at the helm."[179]

In March 1880, Marx had offered his support for another political initiative of the Federation of the Socialist Workers of France. He drafted the *Workers' Questionnaire* (1880), a long, 101-point questionnaire that was published in the April issue of the *Socialist Review* [*La Revue socialiste*], before being distributed in 25,000 copies "all over France." In one of the usual accounts he sent across the Atlantic to Sorge, he reported that this journal too—though edited by Benoît Malon (1841–1893), a man formerly close to Bakunin's positions—now "felt bound . . . to espouse modern scientific socialism."[180]

In his brief introduction to the questionnaire, Marx wrote that workers "alone can describe with full knowledge the misfortunes from which they suffer, and that only they, and not saviours sent by Providence, can energetically apply the healing remedies for the social ills to which they are a prey." Their answers would be used to expose "the facts and crimes of capitalist exploitation"—a "statement of grievances" that were "the first act which socialist democracy must perform . . . to prepare the way for social regeneration."[181] Elsewhere, Marx had described the political significance of initiatives like the International Working Men's Association,[182] and the investigations contained in the English Factory Inspectors' Reports, the so-called blue books, were fundamental, also at a purely theoretical level, for the composition of *Capital, Volume I*.

Along with the gathering of as much information as possible about the working conditions of the French proletariat, Marx's aim was to help workers become more critically aware of the capitalist *modus operandi*. The *Workers' Questionnaire* was divided into four parts. In the first, workers were asked to describe the factory where they were employed, and in particular to supply as much detail as possible about "the division of labour" and "the muscular and nervous strain required and its general effect on the[ir] health." There were also questions on matters such as workplace incidents and "effluvia . . . harmful for the health and [productive of] specific diseases."[183]

The second part asked for details about the workers' jobs: how many days and hours they worked, whether they also had to work nights, how much they were fined for lateness, whether the laws prohibiting child labor were respected, what kind of schooling, if any, existed for children and young people in their trade, and whether it took place in special premises.[184]

The third part mainly concentrated on wages. Workers were asked to specify whether they were paid time or piece rates, the amount of "wages paid to women and children" in the same shop, the length of the "credit given to the employer . . . before receiving payment for work . . . already carried out," and whether they were paid "after a week [or] a month." What were the effects of "delayed payment of wages,"[185] and were these sufficient for basic expenses?

The fourth and final part of the *Workers' Questionnaire* concerned class struggles. Marx wanted to know, from the actual participants, the reasons why they took strike action, whether any "resistance associations existed" for mutual aid, and how these were managed. Were there cooperative guilds in the workers' trade, and if so, how were they controlled? Were there "any workshops in [the] trade in which payment [was] made to the workers partly in the form of wages and partly in the form of so-called profit-sharing?"[186] For Marx, such "profit-sharing" was the new mystification that the bourgeoisie was trying to peddle to the working class.[187]

In the more than thirty years he spent in London, as well as on the few journeys he was able to make, Marx got to know hundreds of militants and intellectuals committed to the cause of the working classes. He took special pleasure in receiving visits from young people, since, as he liked to put it: "I must train people to continue communist propaganda after me."[188]

It was also in 1881 that Marx first met Kautsky, but his impressions of him were far from positive. Although "a decent fellow in his own way," he was essentially "a mediocrity, narrow in outlook, overwise (only 26 years old), a know-all, hard-working after a fashion, much concerned with statistics out of which, however, he makes little sense, by nature a member of the philistine tribe." Therefore, Marx jokingly confided to his daughter Jenny that he had decided to "unload him onto *amigo* Engels as much as [he could]," adding that Engels had become "much more tolerant" toward him on receiving "proof of his considerable drinking ability."[189]

That summer, Marx closely followed events leading up to the French elections. Léon Gambetta (1838 1882) was likely to become prime minister and his Republican Union to win a majority of seats in parliament. Two weeks before the ballot, he shared his predictions with Engels:

It may be that the extreme left will slightly increase its numbers, but the chief upshot of this will probably be victory for Gambetta. Things being

what they are in France, the shortness of the election period will decide
the issue in favour of humbugs with numerous strongholds in their possession, prospective bestowers of places in the machinery of government,
and the men who control the "exchequer," etc. The "Grévystes"[190] could
have licked Gambetta if, after the latter's recent failures, they had had the
energy to throw his appendages, Cazot, Constans and Farre, out of the
cabinet. Since they didn't, the place-hunters, speculators on the Bourse,
etc., etc., are saying to themselves, "Gambetta is the man!" . . . The general onslaughts daily made upon him in the radical and reactionary press
contribute to enhance him despite all his tomfooleries. On top of which
the peasants regard Gambetta as the *nec plus ultra* in possible republican-
ism.[191]

Later that month, Marx wrote to Engels about "the state of the workers' party
[the Federation of the Socialist Workers of France] in Paris." Prosper-Olivier
Lissagaray (1838–1901), a revolutionary and author of *The History of the Paris
Commune of 1871* (1876), whom Marx considered "wholly impartial in this
respect," had told him that "although only existing as a seedling, it alone counts
for anything vis-à-vis the bourgeois parties of all nuances." Its organization,
"though still tenuous and more or less fictitious," was "nevertheless sufficiently
disciplined for it to be able to put up candidates in every arrondissement—to
make its presence felt at meetings and annoy the official society people." Marx
had verified everything on the spot, by reading "Paris papers of every com-
plexion" and noting that "there's not one that doesn't grind its teeth at that
general nuisance—the collectivist workers' party."[192]

The whole world was contained in his room as he sat there at his desk.
Through his study of social changes in the United States, his hopes for an end
to colonial oppression in India, his support for the Fenian cause, analysis of the
economic crisis in Britain, and interest in the elections in France, Marx constantly observed the signs of social conflict developing at every latitude around
the world. He tried to keep up with them, wherever they emerged. Not without
reason he could say of himself: "I am a citizen of the world and act wherever I
am."[193] The last years of his life did not belie this mode of existence.

2

CONTROVERSY OVER THE
DEVELOPMENT OF CAPITALISM
IN RUSSIA

1. THE QUESTION OF THE AGRARIAN COMMUNE

In his political writings, Marx had always identified Russia as one of the main obstacles to working-class emancipation on the European stage. In the *New-York Tribune* articles and the *Secret Diplomatic History of the Eighteenth Century* (1856–1857), as well as in his voluminous correspondence, he had emphasized that Russia's social backwardness, sluggish economic development, despotic political regime, and conservative foreign policy helped to make the vast tsarist empire the advance post of counterrevolution.

Marx continued to hold this judgment over time. But in his final years, he began to look rather differently at Russia, having recognized some possible conditions for a major social transformation in certain changes that were under way there. Indeed, Russia seemed more likely to produce a revolution than Britain, where capitalism had created the proportionately largest number of factory workers in the world, but where the workers' movement, enjoying better living conditions partly based on colonial exploitation, had grown weaker and undergone the negative conditioning of trade union reformism.

In 1882, in their "Preface to the Second Russian Edition of the *Manifesto of the Communist Party*," Marx and Engels recalled that "during the Revolution of 1848–49, not only the European princes, but the European bourgeois as well, found their only salvation from the proletariat, which was just beginning to awaken, in Russian intervention. The Tsar was proclaimed the chief of European reaction." They added, however, albeit with an element of political propaganda:

"Today he is a prisoner of war of the revolution in Gatchina[1] and Russia forms the vanguard of revolutionary action in Europe."[2]

Marx followed—and greeted very favorably—the peasant movements in Russia that preceded the abolition of serfdom in 1861.[3] From 1870, having learned to read Russian, he then kept up-to-date with events by consulting statistics and more thorough texts on social-economic changes, and by corresponding with prominent Russian scholars.[4] Looking back in 1877 at his own trajectory, Marx wrote: "in order to reach an informed judgment on Russia's economic development, I learned Russian and then for many years studied official and other publications relating to the question."[5] Marx went so deep in his studies of Russia that they became a theme of banter with Engels.[6]

In the seventies, there was a key encounter with the work of the Russian socialist philosopher and writer Nikolai Chernyshevsky (1828–1889). Marx procured many of his writings,[7] and the views of the main figure in Russian populism [Narodnichestvo],[8] which at this time was a left-wing, anticapitalist movement. Chernyshevsky became an always useful reference for his analysis of the social changes taking place in Russia. Marx thought that his economic works were "excellent,"[9] and in early 1873 he already declared himself "familiar with a major part of his writings";[10] he even spoke of "publishing something" about Chernyshevsky's "life and personality, so as to create some interest in him in the West."[11]

Reading Chernyshevsky was one of main incentives for Marx to learn Russian. In studying the work of the author whom he had described as "the great Russian scholar and critic,"[12] Marx discovered original views about whether, in some parts of the world, economic development could bypass the capitalist mode of production and the terrible social consequences it had had for the working class in Western Europe. In particular, in his "Critique of the Philosophical Prejudices against Communal Ownership of the Land" (1859), Chernyshevsky had asked "whether a given social phenomenon has to pass through all the logical moments in the real life of every society."[13] His answer had been negative. In what would become one of the manifestoes of the populist movement, in which events following the arrival of the British in New Zealand were taken as a reference, he had summarized his view in five points:

1. When a social phenomenon has reached a high level of development in one nation, its progression to that stage in another, more backward nation may occur rather more quickly than it did in the advanced nation.

(The British needed more than 1,500 years of civilized life to reach the free market system. The New Zealanders definitely did not take that long.)

2. This acceleration takes place thanks to the contact that the backward nation has with the advanced nation. . . .

3. This acceleration consists in the fact that in a backward nation, thanks to the influence of the advanced nation, the development of a certain social phenomenon leaps directly from the lower to the higher level, avoiding intermediate stages along the way. . . .

4. In this accelerated process of development, the intermediate stages, skipped over by the once backward nation now profiting from the experience and science of the advanced nation, attain only a theoretical existence, as logical moments, without actually becoming a reality. (New Zealanders will know from books about the existence of the protectionist system, but it will have no application in their real lives.)

5. Even if these intermediate stages attain actual existence, they will be of truly insignificant dimensions and have even less relevance for practical life.[14]

On the basis of these observations, Chernyshevsky put forward "two conclusions"[15] that helped to define the political demands of the Russian populists and to provide them with a scientific foundation:

1. The higher stage of development coincides in form with its source.

2. Under the influence of the high development which a certain phenomenon of social life has attained among the most advanced peoples, this phenomenon can develop very swiftly among other peoples, and rise from a lower level straight to a higher one, passing over the intermediate logical moments.[16]

We should note that Chernyshevsky's theories differed markedly from those of many Slavophile thinkers of his time. To be sure, he shared their denunciation of the effects of capitalism and their opposition to the proletarianization of labor in the Russian countryside.[17] But he was decidedly averse to the positions of the aristocratic intelligentsia, which hoped to preserve the structures of the past, and he never described the *obshchina*—the peasant village community—as an idyllic form typical only of the Slavic peoples.[18] Indeed, he saw no reason to "be proud of the survival of such vestiges of primitive antiquity." For Chernyshevsky, their persistence in certain countries "testified only to the slowness and weakness of historical evolution." In agrarian relations, for example, "the preservation of communal ownership, which had disappeared in this sense among other peoples," was by no means a sign of superiority but demonstrated that the Russians had "lived less."[19]

Chernyshevsky was strongly convinced that Russia's development could not proceed regardless of the gains achieved in Western Europe. The positive features of the rural commune needed to be preserved, but they could ensure the well-being of the peasant masses only if they were inserted into a different productive context.[20] The *obshchina* could contribute to an incipient stage of social emancipation, but only if it became the embryo of a new and radically different organization of society. Communal ownership of the land had to be backed up with a collective form of farming and distribution. Moreover, without the scientific discoveries and technological acquisitions associated with the rise of capitalism, the *obshchina* would never become an experiment in truly modern agricultural cooperativism.[21] In Russia, progress stemming from in-dustrialization—this was the key point—must not bring about the conditions of poverty and exploitation typical of capitalism. Chernyshevsky found the theoretical basis for this transition from an archaic to a postcapitalist orga-nization of production in German philosophy. In his view, it was thanks to Hegel and Schelling that it was possible to say that "in all spheres of life . . . , the higher level of development, in terms of form, is analogous to the principle that is its source."[22]

The "primitive stage" was characterized by "communal ownership of the land." In a "second stage," following the intensification of productive develop-ment, the land became the private property of those who invested capital in its cultivation. In a third and final stage, "communal ownership is necessary not only for the well-being of the agricultural class but also for the progress of agriculture itself." It is again affirmed as "a higher form of man's relations with the land."[23]

Though based more on dialectics than on concrete historical-analytic re-search, Chernyshevsky's conception had the merit of countering those who saw historical development in terms of unshakeable linear progress toward a predefined end. Politically, this meant that it would be possible to avoid passing through the second stage, and that the "communal ownership of the land" still alive in rural communes would not necessarily have to be destroyed through the spread of private property.[24] Indeed, the strengthening of communal ownership would enable the birth of a system of agrarian collectivism capable of ensuring social justice to the peasantry and satisfying the needs of the whole population.

Starting from these foundations, the populists made it the dual aim of their program to impede the advance of capitalism in Russia and to utilize the emancipatory potential of the existing rural communes. Chernyshevsky presented this prospect in a striking image. "History," he wrote, "like a grandmother, is terribly fond of its smallest grandchildren. To latecomers it gives not the bones but the marrow, whereas in trying to break the bones Western Europe has hurt its fingers ever so badly."[25]

In arguing along these lines, Chernyshevsky had drawn inspiration from the theories of Alexander Herzen (1812–1870). For example, in "An Open Letter to Jules Michelet" (1851), Herzen had asserted that "the history of the West provides us with certain lessons, but no more: we do not consider ourselves the legal executors of your past."[26]

The study of the work of Chernyshevsky was very useful for Marx. In 1881, as his growing interest in archaic forms of community led him to study contemporary anthropologists, and as his reflections constantly reached beyond Europe, a chance happening encouraged him to deepen his study of Russia.

In mid-February 1881, he received a brief but intense and engaging letter from Vera Zasulich (1848–1919), a populist militant, who had made an attempt on the life of the St. Petersburg police chief.[27] Written in French, it had been sent on 16 February from Geneva, where she had taken refuge from the tsarist police.

A great admirer of Marx, who she thought must be aware of the great popularity of *Capital* in Russia, Zasulich wanted to know whether he also knew of the influence it had had on Russian comrades discussing "the agrarian question and the rural commune [*obshchina*]." She stressed that he, "better than anyone," could understand the urgency of the problem—a "life and death question" for Russian revolutionaries—and added that "even the personal fate of our revolutionary socialists depended"[28] on his answer. Zasulich then summarized the two different viewpoints that had emerged in the discussions:

Either the rural commune, freed of exorbitant tax demands, payment to the
nobility and arbitrary administration, is capable of developing in a socialist
direction, that is, gradually organizing its production and distribution on

a collectivist basis. In that case, the revolutionary socialist must devote all his strength to the liberation and development of the commune.

If, however, the commune is destined to perish, all that remains for the socialist, as such, is more or less ill-founded calculations as to how many decades it will take for the Russian peasant's land to pass into the hands of the bourgeoisie, and how many centuries it will take for capitalism in Russia to reach something like the level of development already attained in Western Europe. Their task will then be to conduct propaganda solely among the urban workers, while these workers will be continually drowned in the peasant mass which, following the dissolution of the commune, will be thrown onto the streets of the large towns in search of a wage.[29]

Zasulich further pointed out that some of those involved in the debate argued that "the rural commune is an archaic form condemned to perish by history, scientific socialism and, in short, everything above debate." Those who held this view called themselves Marx's "disciples *par excellence*": "Marxists." Their strongest argument was often: "Marx said so."

For this reason, she addressed a heartfelt plea to Marx: "You would be doing us a great favour if you were to set forth your ideas on the possible fate of our rural commune, and on the theory that it is historically necessary for every country in the world to pass through all the phases of capitalist production." The question was so vital, and Zasulich so eager to know the thinking of the most prestigious living socialist, that she ended by requesting an answer "at least in the form of a letter,"[30] which, if time did not allow a more detailed exposition, could be translated and published in Russia.

The question posed by Zasulich arrived at the right moment, just when Marx was absorbed in the study of precapitalist communities. Her message thus induced him to analyze an actual historical case of great contemporary relevance, closely related to his theoretical interests at that time.[31] The full complexity of his response can be appreciated only in the context of his reflections on capitalism and the transition to socialism.

2. IS CAPITALISM A NECESSARY PREREQUISITE FOR A COMMUNIST SOCIETY?

The conviction that expansion of the capitalist mode of production is a necessary prerequisite for the birth of communist society runs through the whole of

Marx's work. In the *Manifesto of the Communist Party*, he and Friedrich Engels declared that attempts at a working-class revolution during the age of the overthrow of feudal society had been doomed to failure, owing to "the then undeveloped state of the proletariat, as well as to the absence of the economic conditions for its emancipation, conditions that had yet to be produced, and could be produced by the impending bourgeois epoch alone."[32]

Exploiting new geographical discoveries and the birth of the world market, the bourgeoisie had "given a cosmopolitan character to production and consumption in every country."[33] More important still, it had created "the weapons that bring death to itself" and the human beings who would wield those weapons: "the modern working class—the proletarians,"[34] who were increasing at the same rhythm at which capitalism was expanding. For Marx and Engels, "the advance of industry, whose involuntary promoter is the bourgeoisie, replaces the isolation of the labourers, due to competition, by their revolutionary combination, due to association."[35]

Marx expressed a similar judgment, in a more political optic, in the brilliant "Speech at the Anniversary of the *People's Paper*" (1856). Recalling that historically unprecedented industrial and scientific forces had been born together with capitalism, he told the militants attending the event that "steam, electricity and the self-acting mule were revolutionists of a rather more dangerous character than even citizens Barbes, Raspail and Blanqui."[36]

In the *Grundrisse*, Marx repeated several times the idea that capitalism "creates bourgeois society and the universal appropriation of nature and of the social nexus itself by the members of society." In this text, he clearly affirmed that:

> Capital drive[s] beyond national boundaries and prejudices and, equally, beyond nature worship, as well as beyond the traditional satisfaction of existing needs and the reproduction of old ways of life confined within long-established and complacently accepted limits. Capital is destructive towards, and constantly revolutionizes, all this, tearing down all barriers which impede the development of the productive forces, the extension of the range of needs, the differentiation of production, and the exploitation and exchange of all natural and spiritual powers.[37]

One of Marx's most analytic accounts of the positive effects of capitalist production is to be found toward the end of *Capital, Volume I*, in the section entitled "Historical Tendency of Capitalist Accumulation." In the passage in question, he summarizes the six conditions generated by capitalism—particularly by its centralization[38]—that constitute the basic prerequisites for the birth of communist society. These are: (1) the cooperative labor process; (2) the scientific-technological contribution to production; (3) the appropriation of the forces of nature by production; (4) the creation of machinery that workers can only operate in common; (5) the economizing of all means of production; and (6) the tendency to the creation of the world market. For Marx:

> Hand in hand . . . with this expropriation of many capitalists by a few, other developments take place on an ever-increasing scale, such as the growth of the cooperative form of the labour process, the conscious technical application of science, the methodical cultivation of the soil, the transformation of the instruments of labour into instruments of labour only usable in common, the economizing of all means of production by their use as the means of production of combined, socialized labor, the entanglement of all peoples in the net of the world market, and, with this, the international character of the capitalistic regime.[39]

Marx well knew that the concentration of production in the hands of a small number of bosses increased "the mass of misery, oppression, slavery, degradation and exploitation" for the working class,[40] but he was also aware that "the cooperation of wage-labourers is entirely brought about by the capital that employs them."[41] He was convinced that the extraordinary growth of the productive forces under capitalism, greater and faster than in all previously existing modes of production, had created the conditions to overcome the social-economic relations that capitalism had itself brought about—and therefore to achieve the transition to socialist society.

In *Capital, Volume I*, Marx wrote that "the capitalist mode of production presents itself to us historically as a necessary condition for the transformation of the labour process into a social process."[42] In his view, "the socially productive power of labour develops as a free gift to capital, whenever the workmen are placed under given conditions, and it is capital that places them under such conditions."[43] Marx understood that the most favorable circumstances for communism could be realized only through the expansion of capital:

> Fanatically bent on making value expand itself, [the capitalist] ruthlessly forces the human race to produce for production's sake; he thus forces the

development of the productive powers of society, and creates those material conditions, which alone can form the real basis of a higher form of society, a society in which the full and free development of every individual forms the ruling principle.[44]

Further reflections on the decisive role of the capitalist mode of production in preparing the way for communism occur throughout Marx's critique of political economy. As he wrote in the *Grundrisse*, although one of the tendencies of capital is "to create disposable time," it subsequently "converts it into surplus labour."[45] It valorizes labor to the maximum, while "the quantity of labour necessary for the production of a certain object is in fact reduced to the minimum." For Marx this was an absolutely essential point; it would redound "to the advantage of emancipated labour" and was "the condition for its emancipation."[46] Hence capital was "instrumental, despite itself, in creating the means of social disposable time, of reducing labour time for the whole of society to a declining minimum, and of thus setting free the time of all for their own development."[47]

Not only did Marx believe that capitalism, in respect of its capacity to expand the productive forces to the maximum, was the best system that had ever existed. He also recognized that, despite the ruthless exploitation of human beings, it had a number of potentially progressive elements, which allowed, much more than in earlier societies, the valorization of individual potentials. Although he was profoundly averse to the productivist principle of capitalism, to the imperative of the production of surplus labor, Marx considered the increase in productive capacities in relation to the growth of individual faculties. Indeed, in the *Grundrisse* he argued:

> In the act of reproduction itself are changed not only the objective conditions—e.g. village becomes city, the wilderness becomes cultivated clearings, etc.—but also the producers, who transform themselves in that they evolve new qualities from within themselves, develop through production new powers and new ideas, new modes of intercourse, new needs, and new speech.[48]

This more intense and complex advance of the productive forces generated "the richest development of individuals"[49] and the "universality" of relations among human beings.[50]

In *Capital, Volume I*, too, Marx outlined "how the exchange of commodities breaks through all local and personal bounds inseparable from direct barter, and develops a whole network of social relations spontaneous in their growth and entirely beyond the control of the actors."[51] This "imperiously calls for" production to take place "under a form appropriate to the full development of the human race."[52]

Finally, Marx thought certain tendencies in capitalism were favorable to the emancipation of women and the modernization of relations in the domestic sphere. In the important "Instructions for the Delegates of the Provisional General Council: The Different Questions" (1866), drafted for the first congress of the International Working Men's Association, he wrote that, although "under capital it was distorted into an abomination . . . , the tendency of modern industry to make children and juvenile persons of both sexes cooperate in the great work of social production [was] a progressive, sound and legitimate tendency."[53]

Similar views are expressed in *Capital*:

> However terrible and disgusting the dissolution, under the capitalist system, of the old family ties may appear, nevertheless, modern industry, by assigning as it does an important part in the process of production, outside the domestic sphere, to women, to young persons, and to children of both sexes, creates a new economic foundation for a higher form of the family and of the relations between the sexes.[54]

Marx added that, while "capitalist production completely tears asunder the old bond of union which held together agriculture and manufacture in their infancy," this "collects the population in great centres, . . . causing an ever increasing preponderance of town population [and] concentrating the historical motive power of society."[55]

In sum, on the basis of the dialectical method he used in *Capital* and in its preparatory manuscripts, Marx maintained that "the elements for the formation of a new society" mature along with "the material conditions and the combination on a social scale of the processes of production."[56] These "material premises" are decisive for the achievement of a "higher synthesis in the future,"[57] and, although revolution will never arise solely through economic dynamics but will always require a political factor too, the advent of communism "demands for society a certain material groundwork or set of conditions of existence which in their turn are the spontaneous product of a long and painful process of development."[58]

Similar ideas that confirm the continuity of Marx's thought are contained in short but significant writings of a political character that he wrote after *Capital*. In "Notes on Bakunin's Book *Statehood and Anarchy*" (1874), which documents his radical differences with the Russian revolutionary over the prerequisites for an alternative to capitalist society, Marx said of the social subject that will lead the struggle:

> A radical social revolution is bound up with definite historical conditions of economic development; these are its premises. It is only possible, there-fore, where alongside capitalist production the industrial proletariat ac-counts for at least a significant portion of the mass of the people.[59]

In the *Critique of the Gotha Programme* (1875), he further argued the need "to prove concretely how in present capitalist society the material, etc., con-ditions have at last been created which enable and compel the workers to lift this historical curse."[60] Finally, also in one of his last short published pieces, the "Preamble to the Programme of the French Workers Party," he stressed that one essential requirement for the producers to appropriate the means of production is "the collective form, whose material and intellectual elements are shaped by the very development of capitalist society."[61]

In his work, Marx carefully avoided formulations that might suggest a uni-versal model of socialist society, which he considered unhelpful and counter-productive. This is why, in the "Afterword to the Second German Edition" (1873) of *Capital, Volume I*, he intimated that "writing recipes for the cook-shops of the future" was by no means one of his interests,[62] and why in 1879–1880, in response to criticisms made by the German economist Adolph Wagner (1835–1917), he wrote categorically: "I have never established a 'socialist system.'"[63]

Just as Marx never showed a wish to envisage what socialism should be like, he did not assert in his reflections on capitalism that human society was everywhere destined to follow the same path or to pass through the same stages. Nevertheless, he found himself obliged to confront the thesis, falsely attributed to him, that the bourgeois mode of production was everywhere a historical in-evitability. The controversy on the prospect of capitalist development in Russia provides clear evidence of this.

Presumably in November 1877, Marx had drafted a long letter to the editorial board of *Patriotic Notes* [*Otechestvennye Zapiski*], in which he set out to reply to an article on the future of the rural commune (*obshchina*) in Russia—"Karl

Marx before the Tribunal of Mr. Zhukovsky"—by the literary critic and sociologist Nikolai Mikhailovsky.[64] Marx reworked the letter a couple of times, but in the end it remained in draft form, with signs of deletions, and was never actually sent. However, it contained some interesting anticipations of the arguments that Marx would later use in his reply to Zasulich.

In a series of essays, Mikhailovsky had raised a question very similar, nuances apart, to the one that Zasulich would pose four years later. For Zasulich, the crux of the matter was the impact that possible changes in the rural commune would have on the propaganda activity of the socialist movement. Mikhailovsky, on the other hand, was concerned to discuss at a more theoretical level the various positions regarding the future of the *obshchina*—ranging from the thesis of liberal economists that Russia should simply do away with the *obshchina* and embrace a capitalist regime, to the argument that the commune might develop further and avoid the negative effects of the capitalist mode of production on the rural population.[65]

Whereas Zasulich approached Marx to discover his views and to receive indications for practical work, Mikhailovsky, an eminent representative of the more moderate, liberal wing of Russian populism, clearly leaned toward the second thesis and thought that Marx had a preference for the first. While Zasulich wrote that "Marxists" were arguing that the development of capitalism was indispensable, Mikhailovsky went further and claimed that the author of this thesis was Marx himself in *Capital*. He wrote:

> All this "maiming of women and children" we have still before us, and from the point of view of Marx's historical theory, we should not protest against them because it would mean acting to our own detriment. . . . A Russian disciple of Marx . . . must reduce himself to the role of an onlooker. . . . If he really shares Marx's historical-philosophical views, he should be pleased to see the producers being divorced from the means of production, he should treat this divorce as the first phase of the inevitable and, in the final result, beneficial process. He must, in a word, accept the overthrow of the principles inherent in his ideal. This collision between moral feeling and historical inevitability should be resolved, of course, in favour of the latter.[66]

But Mikhailovsky was unable to support this with precise quotations and instead cited Marx's polemical reference to Herzen in an appendix to the first German edition of *Capital*:

If, in Continental Europe, the influence of capitalist production—which saps the human race through overwork, division of labour, subjugation to the machine, crippling of immature female bodies, bad living conditions, etc.—continues to develop hand in hand with competition over the size of the national soldiery, government debt, taxes, dashing warfare, etc., then the rejuvenation of Europe by the knout and compulsory infusions of Kalmuck blood, which the half-Russian and totally Muscovite Herzen seriously prophesies (Herzen the belletrist, let it be noted, who made his discoveries about "Russian" communism not in Russia but in the works of the Prussian state secretary Haxthausen) may eventually become inevitable.[67]

The omission of this note from subsequent editions of *Capital* does not provide evidence that Marx changed his judgment of Herzen[68]—on the contrary. In "A Letter to the Editorial Board of *Otechestvennye Zapiski*" (1877), he maintained in the same terms as in 1867 "that he [Herzen] discovered 'Russian' communism not in Russia but in the book by Haxthausen . . . and that in his hands the Russian community serve[d] only as an argument to prove that the old, rotten Europe must be regenerated by the victory of Pan-Slavism."[69] Marx's ideas on socialism were always antithetical to Herzen's. In "Revolution in Russia" (1857), Herzen had argued that although the circle of people ready to move "in the name of the people and for their benefit . . . might not be very large," it was certainly not "inferior in consciousness and development to any circle in the West. If it [was] unaccustomed to the consideration of social movement, it [was] freer of everything traditional, and [was] newer, simpler, and more youthful than Western society."[70] Marx did not share the assumption that the Russian people was naturally predisposed to communism. His openness to the possibility of a revolution in Russia cannot be traced back to Herzen's positions, with regard either to the forms necessary for the capture of political power or to the prerequisites for the birth of a postcapitalist society.

In the letter to *Otechestvennye Zapiski*, Marx stated rather drily that his polemic with Herzen could not be turned into a falsification of his own judgments, or, as Mikhailovsky had claimed, into a dismissal of "the efforts by the Russian people to find for their motherland a road of development different from the one along which Western Europe has proceeded and still proceeds."[71]

In 1875, in a pamphlet "On Social Relations in Russia" that he wrote in reply to the "Open Letter to Mr Friedrich Engels" by the Blanquist-inclined

Pyotr Tkachev (1844–1886), Engels too intervened on the possibility of a social revolution in Russia.[72]

> The revolution that modern socialism strives to achieve is, briefly, the victory of the proletariat over the bourgeoisie and the establishment of a new organization of society by the destruction of all class distinctions. This requires not only a proletariat to carry out this revolution, but also a bourgeoisie in whose hands the social productive forces have developed so far that they permit the final destruction of class distinctions. Among savages and semi-savages there likewise often exist no class distinctions, and every people has passed through such a state. It could not occur to us to re-establish this state, for the simple reason that class distinctions necessarily emerge from it as the social productive forces develop.

To remove any possible doubts, he added:

> Only at a certain level of development of these social productive forces, even a very high level for our modern conditions, does it become possible to raise production to such an extent that the abolition of class distinctions can constitute real progress, can be lasting without bringing about stagnation or even decline in the mode of social production. But the productive forces have reached this level of development only in the hands of the bourgeoisie. The bourgeoisie, therefore, in this respect also is just as necessary a precondition for the socialist revolution as is the proletariat itself. Hence a man who says that this revolution can be more easily carried out in a country where, although there is no proletariat, there is no bourgeoisie either, only proves that he has still to learn the ABC of socialism.[73]

Marx shared Engels's views,[74] and both men were always in radical disagreement with Herzen and all those who, like Bakunin and Tkachev, had inherited his ideas. They had committed the mistake of depicting the Russian peasants as "the true vehicles of socialism, as born communists, in contrast to the workers of the ageing, decayed European West, who would first have to go through the ordeal of acquiring socialism artificially."[75]

Concerning the debate with Mikhailovsky, Marx intended with his letter to the editorial board of *Otechestvennye Zapiski* to "speak straight out" and to express the conclusions he had reached after many years of study. He began with the following sentence, which he later crossed out in the manuscript: "if Russia continues along the path it has followed since 1861, it will lose the finest chance ever offered by history to a people and undergo all the fateful vicissitudes of the capitalist regime."[76]

Marx's first key clarification concerned the areas to which he had referred in his analysis. He recalled that, in the section of *Capital* entitled "The So-Called Primitive Accumulation,"[77] he had sought to describe how "dissolution of the economic structure of feudal society" set free the elements of "the economic structure of capitalist society" in "Western Europe." The process did not occur throughout the world, therefore, but only in the Old Continent.

Marx referred to a passage in the French edition of *Capital, Volume I* (1872–1875), where he asserted that the basis for the separation of the producers from their means of production was the "expropriation of the agricultural producers," adding that "only in England [had this been] accomplished in a radical manner," but that "all the other countries of Western Europe [were] following the same course."[78]

This is the spatial horizon within which we should understand the famous statement in the preface of *Capital, Volume I*: "The country that is more developed industrially only shows, to the less developed, the image of its own future." Writing for a German readership, Marx observed that, "just like the rest of Continental Western Europe, we suffer not only from the development of capitalist production, but also from the incompleteness of that development." In his view, alongside "the modern evils," the Germans were "oppressed by a whole series of inherited evils, arising from the passive survival of archaic and outmoded modes of production, with their accompanying train of anachronistic social and political relations."[79] It was for the German who might "in optimistic fashion comfort himself with the thought that in Germany things are not nearly so bad," that Marx asserted *"De te fabula narratur!"*[80]

Marx also displayed a flexible approach to other European countries, since he did not think of Europe as a homogeneous whole. In a speech he gave in 1867 to the German Workers' Educational Society in London, later published in *The Harbinger* [*Der Vorbote*] in Geneva, he argued that German proletarians could successfully carry out a revolution because, "unlike the workers in other countries, they need not go through the lengthy period of bourgeois development."[81]

As far as Russia is concerned, in "A Letter to the Editorial Board of *Otechest-vennye Zapiski*," Marx shared Mikhailovsky's view that it might "develop its own historical foundations and thus, without experiencing all the tortures of the [capitalist] regime, nevertheless appropriate all its fruits." He accused Mikhailovsky of "transforming [his] historical sketch of the genesis of capitalism in Western Europe into a historico-philosophical theory of the general course fatally imposed on all peoples, whatever the historical circumstances in which they find themselves."[82]

Continuing his argument, Marx pointed out that in his analysis in *Capital* the historical tendency of capitalist production lay in the fact that it "created the elements of a new economic order, giving the greatest impetus both to the productive forces of social labour and to the all-round development of each individual producer"; in effect, it "already rested upon a collective mode of production" and could "not but be transformed into social property."[83]

Mikhailovsky, then, could apply this historical sketch to Russia in only one way: if Russia was tending to become a "capitalist nation, on the model of the countries of Western Europe"—and in Marx's view it had been moving in that direction in the previous few years—she would not succeed "without having first transformed a large proportion of its peasants into proletarians; and after that, once it has been placed in the bosom of the capitalist system, it will be subjected to its pitiless laws, like other profane peoples."[84]

Marx was most annoyed because he thought his critic had set out "to transform [his] historical sketch of the genesis of capitalism in Western Europe into a historico-philosophical theory of the general course fatally imposed on all peoples, whatever the historical circumstances in which they [found] themselves placed."[85] He added with a touch of sarcasm: "But I beg his pardon. That is to do me both too much honour and too much discredit."

Using the example of the expropriation of peasants in ancient Rome, and their separation from the means of production, he noted how they became "not wage-labourers but an idle mob." What then developed was not capitalism but a slave mode of production. From this Marx concluded that "events of striking similarity, taking place in different historical contexts, [lead] to totally disparate results." To understand real historical transformations, it was necessary to study individual phenomena separately; only then could they be compared with one another. It would never be possible to interpret them "with the master-key of a general historico-philosophical theory, whose supreme virtue consists in being supra-historical."[86]

Thus Mikhailovsky, who did not know Marx's real theoretical position well, criticized it in a way that seemed to anticipate one of the cardinal points of twentieth-century Marxism, which was already spreading insidiously among Marx's followers in Russia and elsewhere. Marx's critique of this conception was all the more important because it related not only to the present but also to the future.[87] He never published it, however,[88] and the idea that Marx considered capitalism to be an obligatory stage for Russia, too, rapidly took hold and had serious consequences for what became Marxism in Russia.[89]

3. THE OTHER POSSIBLE ROAD

For nearly three weeks, Marx remained immersed in his papers, well aware that he had to provide an answer to a highly significant theoretical question and to express his position on a crucial political matter.[90] The fruits of his labor were four drafts—three of them very long and sometimes containing contradictory arguments—and the eventual reply he sent to Zasulich. All were written in French and began in the same way.

To summarize his analysis of the passage from "feudal production to capitalist production,"[91] Marx chose a quotation from the French edition of *Capital* that he had inserted in November 1877 into a (never sent) letter to the editorial board of *Patriotic Notes*. In the next line, Marx repeated that he had "expressly restricted ... the historical inevitability" of the passage from feudalism to capitalist to "the countries of Western Europe."[92] Taking this as a kind of premise, he then developed some rich and detailed thoughts on the *obshchina*, as the germ of a future socialist society, and examined the concrete possibilities that this might come to pass in reality.

In the first, and longest, of the four drafts, Marx analyzed what he saw as the "only serious argument" why the "dissolution of the Russian peasant commune" should be inevitable. Analyzing history, Marx saw a constant change: "By going back a long way, communal property of a more or less archaic type may be found throughout Western Europe; everywhere it has disappeared with increasing social progress." Therefore, he asked why Russia should "be able to escape the same fate."[93] In his reply, Marx repeated that he would "not take this argument into account except in so far as it is based on European experiences."[94] As to Russia:

> If capitalist production is to establish its sway in Russia, the great majority of the peasants, i.e. of the Russian people, must be converted into wage-earners and consequently expropriated by the advance abolition of their communist property. But in any event, the Western precedent would not prove anything at all![95]

Marx did not exclude the possibility that the rural commune would break up and end its long existence. But if that happened, it would not be because of some historical predestination.[96] Referring to his self-styled followers who argued that the advent of capitalism was inevitable, he commented to Zasulich with his typical sarcasm: "The Russian 'Marxists' of whom you speak are quite unknown to me. To the best of my knowledge, the Russians with whom I am in personal contact hold diametrically opposed views."[97]

These constant references to Western experiences were accompanied with a political observation of great value. Whereas in the early 1850s, in his *New-York Tribune* article "The Future Results of British Rule in India" (1853), he had maintained that "England has to fulfill a double mission in India: one destructive, the other regenerating the annihilation of old Asiatic society, and the laying the material foundations of Western society in Asia,"[98] there was an evident change of perspective in his reflections on Russia.

Already in 1853, he had been under no illusion about the basic characteristics of capitalism. He well knew that the bourgeoisie had never "effected a progress without dragging individuals and people through blood and dirt, through misery and degradation."[99] But he had also been convinced that, through world trade, development of the productive forces, and the transformation of production into something scientifically capable of dominating the forces of nature, "bourgeois industry and commerce [had] created the material conditions of a new world."[100]

Limited and sometimes superficial readings have seen this as evidence of Marx's Eurocentrism or orientalism,[101] but in reality, it reflected no more than a partial, ingenuous vision of colonialism held by a man writing a journalistic piece at barely thirty-five years of age. Nowhere in Marx's works is there the suggestion of an essentialist distinction between the societies of the East and the West.

In 1881, after three decades of profound theoretical research and careful observation of changes in international politics, not to speak of his massive synopses in *The Ethnological Notebooks*, he had quite a different view of the transition from past communal forms to capitalism.[102] Thus, referring to the "East Indies," he noted: "Everyone except Sir Henry Maine and others of his ilk realizes that the suppression of communal landownership out there was nothing but an act of English vandalism, pushing the native people not forwards but backwards."[103] All the British "managed to do was to ruin native agriculture and double the number and severity of the famines."[104]

Thus, the Russian *obshchina* was not predestined to suffer the same fate as similar Western European forms in earlier centuries, where "the transition from a society founded on communal property to a society founded on private property"[105] was more or less uniform. To the question whether this was inevitable in Russia, Marx drily replied: "Absolutely not."

Beyond his resolute refusal to apply the same historical model schematically in different contexts, Marx also suggested why the distinctive characteristics of the *obshchina* made a close study of it desirable. In Western Europe, "the expropriation of the agricultural producers . . . served to transform the private and parcelled property of the labourers into the private and concentrated property of the capitalists." But it had to be emphasized that in Russia "it would be a question of substituting capitalist property for communist property."[106] Moreover, "in Western Europe the death of communal property and the birth of capitalist production [were] separated from one another by an immense interval embracing a whole series of economic revolutions and evolutions."[107]

With his usual flexibility and lack of schematism, Marx considered the possibility that the rural commune might change. In his view, the *obshchina* was open to two kinds of evolution: "Either the element of private property . . . will gain the upper hand over the collective element, or the latter will gain the upper hand over the former. . . . All this depends on the historical surroundings in which it finds itself";[108] those existing at the time did not exclude a socialist development.

The first point that Marx underlined was the coexistence of the rural commune with more advanced economic forms. Marx observed that Russia was

> contemporary with a higher culture; it is linked to a world market dominated by capitalist production. By appropriating the positive results of this mode of production, it is thus in a position to develop and transform the still archaic form of its rural commune, instead of destroying it.[109]

For Marx the peasantry "can thus incorporate the positive acquisitions devised by the capitalist system without passing through its Caudine Forks."[110] Addressing those who denied the possibility of leaps and saw capitalism as an indispensable stage for Russia too, Marx asked ironically whether Russia had had "to pass through a long incubation period in the engineering industry . . . in order to utilize machines, steam engines, railways, etc." Similarly, had it not been possible "to introduce in the twinkling of an eye, the entire mechanism of exchange (banks, credit institutions, etc.), which it took the West centuries to devise?"[111]

Russia could not slavishly repeat all the historical stages travelled by England and other West European countries. Logically, therefore, even the socialist transformation of the *obshchina* could happen without its being necessary to pass through capitalism.

In the end, Marx thought it essential to assess the historical moment at which this hypothesis was being considered. The "best proof" that a socialist development of the rural commune was "in keeping with the historical tendency of the age" was the "fatal crisis [here Marx's political hopes led him to write one "fatal" too many] which capitalist production has undergone in the European and American countries where it has reached its highest peak." Drawing on ideas suggested by his reading of the anthropologist Lewis Morgan, he expected that the economic crisis then under way might create favorable conditions for the "destruction" of capitalism and "the return of modern society to a higher form of the most archaic type-collective production and appropriation."[112]

This makes it clear that Marx was not thinking of the "primitive type of cooperative or collective production [resulting] from the weakness of the isolated individual," but of the fruits of the "socialization of the means of production."[113] The *obshchina*, he noted, was "the most modern form of the archaic type" of communist property, which had itself "passed through a whole series of evolutions."[114]

It was these studies and analyses, not abstract schemas, which influenced Marx's choice. The Russian rural communes were not based on "blood relations between their members," but were potentially the "first social grouping of free men not held together by blood ties."[115]

Marx criticized the "isolation" of the archaic agricultural communes, for, being closed in on themselves, having no contact with the outside world, they were politically speaking the economic form most in keeping with the reactionary tsarist regime: "The lack of connection between the life of one commune and that of the others, this localized microcosm, . . . always gives rise to central despotism over and above the communes."[116]

Marx had certainly not changed his complex critical judgment on the rural communes in Russia, and the importance of individual development and social production remained intact in his analysis. He did not suddenly become convinced that the archaic rural communes were a more advanced locus of emancipation for the individual than the social relations existing under capitalism. Both remained remote from how he conceived of communist society.

The drafts of Marx's letter to Zasulich show no glimpse of the dramatic break with his former positions that some scholars have detected.[117] Marx did not suggest, as a matter of theoretical principle, that Russia, or other countries where capitalism was still underdeveloped, should become the special locus for revolution to break out; nor did he think that countries with a more backward capitalism were closer to the goal of communism than others with a more advanced productive development. In his view, sporadic rebellions or resistance struggles must not be confused with the establishment of a new social-economic order on a communist basis. The possibility he considered at a highly particular moment in Russia's history, when favorable opportunities arose for a progressive transformation of agrarian communes, could not be elevated into a more general model. French-ruled Algeria or British India, for example, did not display the special conditions that Chernyshevsky had identified, and the Russia of the early 1880s could not be compared with what might happen there in the future. The new element in Marx's thinking was an ever greater theoretical openness, which enabled him to consider other possible roads to socialism that he had never before taken seriously or had regarded as unattainable.[118]

In the second half of the nineteenth century, following the reforms under Tsar Alexander II (1818–1881), the conditions of the *obshchina* had already changed and presented a number of contradictory aspects:

> Freed from the strong but tight bonds of natural kinship, communal ownership of the land and the social relations stemming from it guarantee it a solid foundation, at the same time as the house and the courtyard, the exclusive domain of the individual family, parcel farming and the private appropriation of its fruits give a scope to individuality incompatible with the organism of more primitive communities.[119]

This "dualism" might turn into "the germ of decomposition" and showed that "the commune carrie[d] the elements of corruption in its own bosom."[120] But also threatening its survival were "destructive influences" from outside, such as state legislation in support of "some branches of the Western capitalist system," which, "without developing the productive forces of agriculture in any way . . . cooperated in the enrichment of a new capitalist vermin, sucking the already impoverished blood of the "rural commune."[121]

Marx therefore concluded that the alternative envisaged by the Russian populists was achievable:

> Theoretically speaking, then, the Russian "rural commune" can preserve itself by developing its basis, the common ownership of land, and by eliminating the principle of private property which it also implies; it can become a direct point of departure for the economic system towards which modern society tends; it can turn over a new leaf without beginning by committing suicide; it can gain possession of the fruits with which capitalist production has enriched mankind, without passing through the capitalist regime.[122]

If it was to come to pass, however, this hypothesis had to "descend from pure theory to the Russian reality."[123] To this end, Marx tried to identify the "capacity for further development"[124] of the *obshchina*. At that precise moment,

> [it] occupies a unique position, without precedent in history. Alone in Europe, it is still the predominant organic form of rural life throughout an immense empire. The common ownership of land provides it with the natural basis for collective appropriation, and its historical setting, its contemporaneity with capitalist production, lends it—fully developed—the material conditions for cooperative labour organized on a vast scale. It can thus incorporate the positive acquisitions devised by the capitalist system; . . . it can gradually replace parcel farming with combined agriculture assisted by machines; . . . it may become the direct starting point for the economic system towards which modern society tends and turn over a new leaf without beginning by committing suicide.[125]

What Marx writes here is therefore very similar to what Chernyshevsky had written in the past.[126] This alternative was possible, and it was certainly better suited to Russia's social-economic context than "capitalized farming on the English model."[127] But it could survive only if "collective labour supplanted parcel labour—the source of private appropriation." For that to happen, two things were required: "the economic need for such a change and the material conditions to bring it about."[128] The fact that the Russian agricultural commune was contemporaneous with capitalism in Europe offered it "all the conditions necessary for collective labour,"[129] while the peasant's familiarity with the *artel*[130] would facilitate the actual transition to "cooperative labour."[131]

As regards the separation of the communes from one another, which favored the despotic character of the political regime in Russia, this could "easily be eliminated."[132] "It would simply be necessary to replace the *volost*[133]—the government body—with an assembly of peasants elected by the communes themselves, serving as the economic and administrative organ for their interests."[134]

Political will and a favorable set of historical circumstances were therefore the basic prerequisites for the survival and radical transformation of the *obshchina*. In other words, despite all the upheavals that capitalism threatened to bring about, the socialist transformation of an archaic form of community like the *obshchina* was still possible:

> It is no longer a matter of solving a problem; it is simply a matter of beating an enemy. To save the Russian commune, a Russian revolution is needed. . . . If revolution comes at the opportune moment, if it concentrates all its forces so as to allow the rural commune full scope, the latter will soon develop as an element of regeneration in Russian society and an element of superiority over the countries enslaved by the capitalist system.[135]

Marx returned to similar themes in 1882. In January, in the "Preface to the Second Russian Edition of the *Manifesto of the Communist Party*," which he co-authored with Engels, the fate of the Russian rural commune is linked to that of proletarian struggles in Western Europe:

> In Russia we find, face to face with the rapidly developing capitalist swindle and bourgeois landed property, which is just beginning to develop, more than half the land owned in common by the peasants. Now the question is: can the Russian *obshchina*, a form of primeval common ownership of land, even if greatly undermined, pass directly to the higher form of communist common ownership? Or must it, conversely, first pass through the same process of dissolution as constitutes the historical development of the West? The only answer possible today is this: If the Russian Revolution becomes the signal for a proletarian revolution in the West, so that the two complement each other, the present Russian common ownership of land may serve as the starting point for communist development.[136]

The basic thesis that Marx had frequently expressed in the past remained the same, but now his ideas were related more closely to the historical context and the various political scenarios they opened up.[137] Marx and Engels's brief preface was published in *People's Will* [*Narodnaya Volya*], together with a triumphant note stating that the editors were "particularly glad to underline [its] concluding words," which they saw as "confirmation of one of the fundamental theoretical positions of People's Will."[138]

As to the reply to Zasulich, so long under composition, he eventually sent it off on 8 March 1881. Although he had written several long and closely argued drafts, spending much precious time and energy on them, he decided to send her quite a short final version. He excused himself for not having provided a version "intended for publication" that she had requested[139] adding that he had already undertaken to intervene on the matter—without actually doing so—with the St. Petersburg Committee of the populist organization People's Will.[140]

Still, his "few lines" were meant to "dispel any doubts" that Zasulich might have "as to the misunderstanding in regard to my so-called theory."[141] Marx referred her to the quotation on the "expropriation of the agricultural producer" from the French edition of *Capital, Volume I*—the same as the one he had inserted in the draft letter to *Patriotic Notes (Otechestvennye Zapiski)*—and stressed that his analysis was "expressly limited to the countries of Western Europe," which saw "the transformation of one form of private property into another form of private property."[142] In the Russian case, by contrast, "communal property would have to be transformed into private property."[143] Hence his conclusion:

> The analysis provided in *Capital* does not adduce reasons either for or against the viability of the rural commune, but the special study I have made of it, and the material for which I drew from original sources, has convinced me that this commune is the fulcrum of social regeneration in Russia, but in order that it may function as such, it would first be necessary to eliminate the deleterious influences which are assailing it from all sides, and then ensure for it the normal conditions of spontaneous development.[144]

Marx's dialectical position therefore did not lead him to claim that a new economic system, based on the association of the producers, could come about through a fixed sequence of predefined stages. At the same time, he denied that the development of the capitalist mode of production was a historical inevitability in any part of the world.[145] In the final text that he sent to Zasulich, Marx's considerations were decidedly more concise, and his tone more cautious, than in the preliminary drafts. This probably indicates that he thought his treatment of such a complex question was still too superficial, and that some theoretical uncertainties continued to hound him. He began by saying that "a nervous complaint which has assailed me periodically over the last ten years has prevented me from replying any sooner to your letter . . . [and] providing you with a concise exposé . . . of the question."[146] In reality, the multiple drafts indicate how much time he had devoted to the matter, without resolving it in a way that satisfied him.[147]

Those who did not agree with his final reflections tried to downplay them as the unimportant musings of an old man, whose theoretical capacities were nearing exhaustion;[148] while those who agreed with them saw them as Marx's intellectual testament, perhaps even more valuable than the texts he finished and published in his lifetime. But the fact is that the reply to Zasulich is in keeping with Marx's habitual style of work. In the process of elaborating his theories, he usually spent a long time in extensive research, formulating hypotheses that were invariably followed by self-criticism and fresh doubts about their validity. He then arrived at new hypotheses, which also required further study and raised fresh doubts. The writings from the last part of his life do not depart from this schema. They should therefore not be lightly dismissed as being of lesser value, nor regarded as the terminus of Marx's thinking on these matters. What they do help us to understand is a key conclusion that Marx reached: hypotheses about the possible course of history should not base themselves on abstract laws but always be commensurate with the diversity of existing contexts.

Marx's densely argued considerations on the future of the *obshchina* are poles apart from the equation of socialism with the productive forces—a conception involving nationalist overtones and sympathy with colonialism, which asserted itself within the Second International and social-democratic parties. They also differ profoundly from the supposedly "scientific method" of social analysis preponderant in the twentieth century in the international communist movement.

Engels too was guilty of a passive acceptance of the course of history. In a number of writings and letters from the last part of his life, he adopted a position similar to the one expressed in a letter of 1893 to Danielson: "The process of replacing some 500,000 landowners and some eighty million peasants by a new class of bourgeois landed proprietors cannot be carried out but under fearful sufferings and convulsions." He added that "history is about the most cruel of all goddesses, and she leads her triumphal car over heaps of corpses, not only in war, but also in 'peaceful' economic development. And we men and women are unfortunately so stupid that we never can pluck up the courage needed for real progress unless urged to it by sufferings that seem almost out of proportion."[149] Marx's doubting was replaced by a conviction that, even in a country like Russia, capitalism was an inescapable stage for economic development.[150]

4. ASSESSMENT OF THE POPULIST MOVEMENT

In this period, Marx also took the opportunity to express his views on various revolutionary tendencies in Russia. With regard to the populist movement, he appreciated the down-to-earth character of their political activity and the fact that, in the dissemination of their ideas, they did not resort to senseless ultra-revolutionary flourishes or counterproductive generalizations.

Three positions took shape, in accordance with how revolutionaries viewed the relationship between the political and the economic sphere. Those who held that any transformation in the latter could be imposed through the former tended to share the neo-Blanquist positions of Tkachev (1844–1886) or the anarchist approach of Bakunin (1814–1876).

The first Russian revolutionary movement to emerge in the 1870s was Land and Freedom [*Zemlya i Volya*]. It believed that socialism could be achieved even where bourgeois society had not previously undergone significant development.[151] This organization then split in 1879 into two currents: a minority around Black Repartition [*Chernyi Peredel*] ruled out any idea that revolution in the political sphere alone could bring about a fundamental change in economic relations. Its name derived from the proposal to distribute the land among the peasantry—where the adjective *chernyi* had connotations of popular or plebeian. Among its main leaders were Vera Zasulich and Georgii Plekhanov (1856–1918), one of the first Russian "Marxists," who moved toward a gradualist vision and eventually accepted that, with no immediate prospect of revolution, the only way forward was to concentrate all energies on the task of organization, while awaiting the further development of capitalism.[152]

The majority successor to Land and Freedom, which called itself People's Will, had a more clearly articulated position.[153] In an article entitled "Political Revolution and the Economic Problem" (1881), signed A. Doroshenko—a pseudonym for Nikolai Kibalchich (1853–1881)—it was argued that "free political institutions [cannot] be maintained without some historical preparation in the economic sphere."[154] Equally flexible was their position on the revolutionary subject: "It appears that the first signal for a revolution will come from the town and not from the village. But once success has been achieved in the town, this will raise the banner of revolt for millions of starving peasants."[155] In short, the revolutionaries who belonged to the People's Will thought that significant social upheavals were possible in Russia at that time, but that it was necessary to seize the opportunities that presented themselves. The second issue of the journal *People's Will* made the programmatic point that, if revolutionaries knew how to "take advantage of this moment, they would be able to hand over power to the people and prevent the Tsar from giving it to the bourgeoisie. But there was no time to be lost. . . . Now or never; that is our dilemma."[156] Thus, one reason for Marx's close attention to developments in Russia was related to the question—fundamental for revolutionaries who came after him—of the weight of subjective and objective factors in the historical process.

In a letter that Marx sent to Friedrich Sorge toward the end of 1880, his judgment on the socialist organizations in Russia showed that he was not influenced by personal attachments to their members, still less by declarations of loyalty to his own theories. He described the active forces as follows: "On the one hand, we have the critics (mostly young university professors, some of them personal friends of mine, some also *littérateurs*), on the other, the terrorist Central Committee," that is, the People's Will organization. Marx told Sorge that the latter's pragmatic character, which he viewed favorably, enraged the former group of people: that is, the Black Repartition militants. On these—for the most part—voluntary exiles, he commented:

> Unlike the terrorists, who risk life and limb, [they] constitute the so-called Propaganda Party. (In order to disseminate propaganda in Russia—they remove to Geneva. What a *quid pro quo*.) These gentry are all of them opposed to politico-revolutionary action. Russia is to leap head-over-heels into the anarchist-communist-atheist millennium! Meanwhile they pave the way for that leap by tedious doctrinarianism.[157]

In a letter of April 1881 to his daughter Jenny, he again lambasted the attitude of the Russian intellectuals who had taken refuge in Switzerland: they were "mere doctrinaires, confused anarchist socialists, and their influence upon the Russian 'theatre of war' is zero."[158] As to the trials of the St. Petersburg assassins, he approved of their political position and methods of propaganda:

> They are sterling chaps through and through, without melodramatic pose, simple, matter-of-fact, heroic. Shouting and doing are irreconcilable opposites. The Petersburg Executive Committee,[159] which took such vigorous

action, issues manifestoes of exquisite "moderation." It is remote indeed from the bungling way in which Most and other puerile ranters advocate tyrannicide as a "theory" and panacea. . . . They, on the other hand, are at pains to teach Europe that their *modus operandi* is a specifically Russian and historically inevitable mode of action, which no more lends itself to moralizing—for or against—than does the earthquake in Chios.[160]

Thus, Marx's views on the possibility of socialism in Russia were not based only on the economic situation there. In 1881, his contact with Russian populists—as with the Paris Communards a decade earlier—helped him to develop a new conviction: he was now more flexible in considering the irruption of revolutionary events and the subjective forces that shaped them, as well as the succession of modes of production in the course of history. It brought him closer to a true internationalism on a global, not only European, scale.[161]

The more pronounced multilinear conception that Marx developed in his final years led him to look even more attentively at the historical specificities and unevenness of political and economic development in different countries and social contexts. This approach certainly increased the difficulties he faced in the already bumpy course of completing the second and third volumes of *Capital*.

But Marx did not change the vision of communist society that he outlined in the *Grundrisse* without ever falling into abstract utopianism.[162] Guided by doubt and hostility toward past schematism and new dogmatisms arising in his name, he thought it possible that the revolution would break out in conditions and forms that he had never considered before. The future was in the hands of the working class and depended on the capacity of its organizations and struggles to bring about profound social upheavals.

3

THE TRAVAILS OF "OLD NICK"

1. THE EARLY DISSEMINATION OF *CAPITAL* IN EUROPE

In 1881, Marx was not yet the towering theoretical reference for the international workers' movement that he would become in the twentieth century. Over the course of the 1840s, the number of political leaders and intellectuals influenced by his work had been quite limited; what the international police and political adversaries called "the Marx party"[1] was, in fact, composed of only a handful of militants. Things did not change for the better in the next decade, when, following the defeat of the 1848 revolutions, only a small number of refugees, mostly in Great Britain, could be considered "Marxian."[2]

The development of the International Working Men's Association and the Europe-wide resonance of the Paris Commune altered the picture, giving Marx a certain notoriety and ensuring a reasonable dissemination of his works. *Capital* had begun to circulate in Germany, where a new edition appeared in 1873; Russia, where it had been translated in 1872; and France, where it appeared in installments between 1872 and 1875. Even there, however, Marx's ideas had to compete—often from a minority position—with those of other socialists of his time.

In Germany, the Gotha fusion congress of the Social Democratic Workers' Party [*Sozialdemokratische Arbeiterpartei Deutschlands*], linked to Marx, and the General Association of German Workers [*Allgemeiner Deutscher Arbeiter-Verein*], founded by Ferdinand Lassalle (1825–1864), adopted a program in 1875 that bore the marks more of Lassalle. In France, as in Belgium, the theories of Pierre-Joseph Proudhon (1809–1865) were more influential in the working class, and the groups inspired by Marx were not much more significant, in numbers or political initiative, than those that modelled themselves on Auguste Blanqui (1805–1881). In Russia, a distinctive complication was that Marx's critique of the capitalist mode of production was read and interpreted in a backward social, economic, and political setting quite remote from the West European model of capitalist development. In Britain, on the other hand, Marx remained virtually unknown,[3] and his writings had difficulty finding an audience in Italy, Spain, and Switzerland, where the influence of Mikhail Bakunin was greater in the 1870s. On the other side of the Atlantic, few indeed had ever heard of him.

Another reason for this was the incompleteness of his works, beginning with *Capital* itself. Indicatively, when Karl Kautsky asked him, in 1881, whether the time had not come to publish his collected writings, he caustically replied that "first of all, they would need to be written."[4]

Thus, although Marx did not live to see the worldwide take-up of his ideas, the final years of his life did bring an ever-growing interest in his theories—particularly his *magnum opus*—in many parts of Europe. This aroused contrasting reactions. Sometimes—Engels wrote to Bernstein in late 1881—"jealousy of Marx" even reared its head. The internal life of the Socialist Workers' Party Federation of France, for example, involved conflict between two main currents: the "possibilists" headed by ex-anarchist Paul Brousse (1844–1912) and a group closer to Marx's ideas led by Jules Guesde (1845–1922). In the period before the inevitable split—which resulted in two new parties: the reformist Federation of the Socialist Workers of France and the first French "Marxist" party, the French Workers' Party [*Parti ouvrier français*]—the rival groups engaged in intense ideological battles. Marx was eventually drawn into these, and in June 1880, together with Guesde and Paul Lafargue, he wrote the "Electoral Programme of the French Workers' Party," the political platform of the French Left.

In this climate Brousse and Benoît Malon (1841–1893), a Communard and socialist writer, used every means to discredit Marx's theories. Commenting on their harsh polemics, Engels blamed Malon in particular, who, he said, was "at pains to find or impute other progenitors (Lassalle, Schäffle and actually De Paepe!) on whom to father Marx's discoveries." He further railed against the editors of the weekly *The Proletarian* [*Le Prolétaire*], who had accused Guesde and Lafargue of being Marx's "mouthpieces" and "wanting to sell the French workers to Bismarck."[5] Friedrich Engels interpreted Malon's and Brousse's hostility as a sign of chauvinism:

> To the majority of French socialists it is an anathema that the nation which confers upon the world the boon of French ideas . . . —and Paris, the centre of the Enlightenment—must now all of a sudden import its socialist ideas ready-made from a German, Marx. But there's no denying the fact and, what is more, Marx's genius, his almost excessive scientific scrupulousness and his incredible erudition place him so far above all the rest of us that anyone who ventures to criticize his discoveries is more likely to burn his fingers than anything else. That is something which must be left to a more advanced epoch.[6]

Unable to understand "how anyone can be envious of genius," Engels went on:

> But what mainly annoys the small-minded carpers who count for nothing, yet like to think themselves all-important, is the fact that Marx, thanks to his theoretical and practical achievements, has attained a position in which he enjoys the complete trust of the best people in all the labour movements in the various countries. At critical junctures it is to him they turn for advice, when they generally find that his advice is the best. He occupies that position in Germany, in France, and in Russia, not to speak of the smaller countries. Hence it is not Marx who imposes his opinion, let alone his will, on these people; rather it is these people who come to him of their own accord. And it is precisely on this that Marx's peculiar influence rests, an influence of the utmost importance to the movement.[7]

Contrary to what Brousse and his followers maintained, Marx had no special animosity toward them. Engels made it clear that "Marx's attitude . . . towards the French [was] the same as towards the other national movements" with which they were "constantly in touch . . . in so far as it was worthwhile and opportunities present[ed] themselves." In conclusion, Engels stressed that "any attempt to influence people against their will [would] only do us harm [and] destroy the old trust that dates from the International."[8]

Independently of Guesde and Lafargue, a number of other French militants had got in touch with Marx. In early 1881, he informed his son-in-law Charles Longuet that he had been contacted by Édouard Fortin (1854–1947), a socialist militant and publicist:

> [He] has written me several letters addressing me as: "My dear Master." His demand is very "modest." While he studies *Capital* he proposes to make monthly summaries which he will be so kind as to send over to me monthly, whereupon I shall correct them monthly, elucidating the points he might have misunderstood. In this quiet way, when he has done with the last monthly résumé, and I have sent it back corrected, he will have a manuscript ready for publication and—as he says—inundate France with torrents of light.[9]

Preoccupied as he was with rather more important matters, Marx had to inform Fortin that he would be unable to grant his request.[10] But something good came of it all, when Fortin later translated *The Eighteenth Brumaire of Louis Bonaparte* into French and had it published in 1891.

A popular compendium from *Capital*—the third after those by Johann Most (1846–1906) in 1873[11] and by Carlo Cafiero (1846–1892) in 1879[12]—appeared in Dutch in 1881.[13] Its originator, Ferdinand Domela Nieuwenhuis, appended to it: "The author dedicates this work to Karl Marx, the acute thinker and noble fighter for workers' rights, as a token of his most devoted esteem."[14] He expressed an appreciative recognition of Marx's work that was beginning to spread in a number of European countries.

In February 1881, with an eye on a future second edition, Marx told Nieuwenhuis that he thought he had done a good job and intended to make some suggestions of his own: "The amendments I consider necessary relate to details; the main thing, the spirit of the thing, is there already."[15] In the same letter, he referred to a biography of himself by the Dutch liberal journalist Arnoldus Kerdijk (1846–1905), which had appeared in 1879 in a series called *Important People of Our Time* [*Mannen van beteekenis*]. Its publisher, Nicolas Balsem (1835–1884), had previously been in touch with Marx for material about his life, making it clear that, although he did not share his views, he recognized their importance. Marx "habitually turned down such requests," and he was angry later to read the text and find himself accused of "deliberate misquotation." He communicated to Nieuwenhuis:

A Dutch journal proposed to open its columns to me [to reply], but on principle I do not reply to pin-pricks of this kind. I have never, even in London, taken the slightest notice of such literary yapping. Any other course would mean wasting the better part of my time on making rectifications all over the place, from California to Moscow. In my younger days I sometimes did some hard hitting, but wisdom comes with age, at least in so far as one avoids useless dissipation of force.[16]

Marx had come to this conclusion some years before. In an interview published on 5 January 1879 in the *Chicago Tribune*, he quipped: "If I denied everything that has been said and written of me, I would require a score of secretaries."[17] Engels fully concurred with this attitude. In a letter to Kautsky, written shortly before Marx's one to Nieuwenhuis, he said of the numerous inaccuracies and misunderstandings that the German economist Albert Schäffle (1831–1903) and other "armchair socialists [*Kathedersozialisten*]"[18] displayed in relation to Marx's work:

To refute, for example, all the monstrous twaddle which Schäffle alone has assembled in his many fat tomes is, in my opinion, a sheer waste of time. It would fill a fair-sized book were one merely to attempt to put right all the misquotations from *Capital* inserted by these gentlemen between inverted commas.[19]

And he concluded in peremptory fashion: "They should first learn to read and copy before demanding to have their questions answered."[20]

Apart from misinterpretations and inexactitudes, as well as associated attempts at political ostracization, Marx's work also suffered from veritable acts of sabotage. In a letter he wrote to Danielson in February, having read his article "Sketches of Our Post-Reform Social Economy" (1880), which he found "in the best sense original," Marx pointed out:

If you break through the webs of routine thought, you are always sure to be "boycotted" in the first instance; it is the only arm of defence, which in their first perplexity the routiniers know how to wield. I have been "boycotted" in Germany for many many years, and am still so in England, with that little variation that from time to time something so absurd and asinine is launched against me that I would blush to take any public notice of it.[21]

In Germany, however, sales of his *magnum opus* had been creeping up, and in October 1881, with the second edition going out of print, the publisher Otto Meissner (1819–1902) asked Marx to make some amendments or additions in preparation for a third edition. Two months later, Marx confessed to his friend Friedrich Sorge that this was "at a moment anything but opportune";[22] he had written shortly before to his daughter Jenny that he "wanted to apply all [his] time—as soon as [he] felt himself able again—exclusively to the finishing of the second volume."[23] He said the same to Danielson—"I want to finish off Volume Two . . . as soon as possible"—adding:

> I will arrange with my editor that I shall make for the third edition only the fewest possible alterations and additions, but, on the other hand, that he must this time only draw off 1,000 copies, instead of 3,000, as was his wont. When these . . . are sold, I may change the book in the way I should have done at present under different circumstances.[24]

Marx's ideas were beginning to spread, though more slowly than elsewhere, in the country where he had lived since 1849. In June 1881, Hyndman published a book, *England for All* (1881), that set forth the guiding principles for what he intended to make of the Democratic Federation. Two of its eight chapters—entitled "Labour" and "Capital"—were put together from translations, or in some cases paraphrases, of *Capital*. Yet its author—who since late 1880 had been a regular visitor at Maitland Park Road[25] and was working on a summary of Marx's theories—did not mention *Capital* or even Marx's name in *England for All*. He merely stated: "For the ideas and much of the matter contained in Chapters II and III, I am indebted to the work of a great thinker and original writer, which will, I trust, shortly be made accessible to the majority of my countrymen."[26]

Marx learned of Hyndman's pamphlet only after it had been published. He was vexed and astonished, since, apart from anything else, the extracts from *Capital* were "separated by no marks of quotation from a remainder, much of which is not exact or even implies misunderstandings."[27] He therefore wrote to him at the beginning of July:

> I confess to some astonishment at the discovery that, during your stay at London, you should have so closely kept the secret of your plan, then matured and executed, to publish, with certain modifications, the rejected

article of *The Nineteenth Century* as chapters II and III of *England for All*, that is to say, of your comments on the Federation's Foundation Program.[28]

Marx returned to the matter in December in a letter to Friedrich Sorge:

> Vis-à-vis myself, the fellow wrote stupid letters of excuse, for instance, that "the English don't like to be taught by foreigners," that "my name was so much detested, etc." With all that his little book—so far as it pilfers the *Capital*—makes good propaganda, although the man is a "weak" vessel, and very far from having even the patience—the first condition of learning anything—to study a matter thoroughly.[29]

After the breaking-off of their relations, Marx branded Hyndman as one of those "amiable middle-class writers [who] have an itching to make money or name or political capital immediately out of any new thoughts they may have got at by some favourable windfall."[30] The harshness of Marx's words was certainly not due to disappointment that he had not been credited by name. For he remained of the opinion

> that to have named the *Capital* and its author would have been a big blunder. Party programs ought to keep free of any apparent dependence upon individual authors or books. But allow me to add that they are also no proper place for new scientific developments, such as those borrowed by you from *Capital*, and that the latter are altogether out of place in a commentary on a Program with whose professed aims they are not at all connected. Their introduction might have been appropriate for the exposition of a Program for the foundation of a distinct and independent working-class party.[31]

Along with Hyndman's lack of manners, the chief motive for Marx's anger was his concern that *Capital* should not be used for a political project so clearly at odds with the ideas contained in it.[32] The differences between the two men were indeed profound. Hyndman was not at all inclined to the idea that power should be conquered through revolutionary action; his position, which came to characterize British reformism, was that changes could be achieved only by peaceful, gradual means. In February 1880, he had told Marx: "The object which every Englishman should have is to bring about the coming mobilization, political and social, without troublous, dangerous conflict."[33]

Conversely, Marx—who was opposed to any preconceived schematism—replied to Hyndman in late 1880 that his "party consider[ed] an English revolution not necessary, but—according to historic precedents—possible." The expansion of the proletariat had made an "evolution" of the social question "inevitable":

> If [this evolution] turns into a revolution, it would not only be the fault of the ruling classes, but also of the working class. Every pacific concession of the former has been wrung from them by "pressure from without." Their action kept pace with that pressure and if the latter has more and more weakened, it is only because the English working class know not how to wield their power and use their liberties, both of which they possess legally.[34]

He followed this judgment with a comparison with events in Germany, where

> the working class were fully aware from the beginning of their movement that you cannot get rid of a military despotism but by a Revolution. At the same time they understood that such a Revolution, even if at first successful, would finally turn against them without previous organization, acquirement of knowledge, propaganda. . . . Hence they moved within strictly legal bounds. The illegality was all on the side of government, which declared them outside the law. Their crimes were not deeds, but opinions unpleasant to their rulers.[35]

Such considerations are further proof that for Marx revolution was not simply a rapid overthrow of the system, but a long and complex process.[36]

Although Marx's ideas led to sharp polemics and disputes, they were beginning to have an impact even in England. Thus, at the end of 1881, Marx observed in a letter to Sorge that "the English have latterly begun to take rather more notice of *Capital*." In October, *The Contemporary Review* had published an article, "The Socialism of Karl Marx and the Young Hegelians,"[37] which Marx judged "very inadequate [and] full of mistakes," but also indicative of a new interest. He added sardonically that it was "fair," because its author, John Rae (1845–1915), "does not suppose that for the forty years I have been spreading my pernicious theories I was instigated by 'bad' motives. I must praise his 'magnanimity.'" Nevertheless, Marx tersely summed up his view of all such publications: "The fairness of making yourself at least sufficiently acquainted with the subject of your criticism seems a thing quite unknown to the penmen of British philistinism."[38]

Another English journal, *Modern Thought*, gave Marx a more respectful treatment and was prepared to recognize the scientific character of his work. An article by the journalist and lawyer Ernest Belfort Bax (1854–1926) defined *Capital* as a book that "embodies the working out of a doctrine in economy, comparable in its revolutionary character and wide-reaching importance to the Copernican system in astronomy, or the law of gravitation in mechanics generally."

Hoping for an English translation soon, Bax not only maintained that *Capital* was "one of the most important books of the century," but also admired Marx's style and compared it to Arthur Schopenhauer's (1788–1860) in its "fascination and verve," its "humour," and its "readily comprehensible presentation of the most abstract principles."[39]

Marx was pleased with this "first English publication of that kind which is pervaded by a real enthusiasm for the new ideas themselves and boldly stands up against British philistinism." He noted that "much [was] wrong and confused . . . in the exposition of my economic principles and in his translations (i.e. quotations from *Capital*)." However, he praised the author for his efforts and was heartened that "the appearance of this article, announced in large letters by placards on the walls of the West End of London, ha[d] produced a great sensation."[40]

The wider circulation of Marx's ideas, already noticeable in the 1870s, therefore continued at the beginning of the new decade. Now, however, they not only penetrated a small circle of followers and political activists but began to achieve a wider audience. The interest in Marx was not limited to his political writings—the *Manifesto of the Communist Party*, for example, and the resolutions of the International Working Men's Association—but extended to his main theoretical contribution: the critique of political economy. The theories contained in *Capital* were starting to be discussed and appreciated in various European countries, and just a few years later—to quote an expression that would become famous—Engels did not hesitate to describe his friend's work as "the Bible of the working class."[41] Who knows whether Marx, no friend of sacred texts, would have appreciated the choice.

2. WHY COULD MARX NOT COMPLETE *CAPITAL*?

Between 1877 and early 1881, Marx wrote two new versions of various parts of Volume II of *Capital*. In March 1877, he started by compiling quite an extensive index of the materials he had already collected,[42] then concentrated almost exclusively on Part I, "The Metamorphoses of Capital and Their Circuit,"[43] with a more advanced account of the circulation process of capital. Subsequently, despite his poor health and the fact that the necessity of further research made his work very irregular, Marx continued to busy himself with a number of matters, including the final chapter, "Accumulation and Reproduction on an Expanded Scale." Also dating from this period is the so-called Manuscript VIII of *Capital, Volume II*,[44] in which Marx, after a recapitulation of previous texts, composed new drafts that he thought useful for the continuation of the work. He also realized that he had committed, and for a long time repeated, an error of interpretation, when he had considered monetary representations to be merely a cover for the real content of economic relations.[45]

In summer 1877, when "insomnia and a correspondingly chaotic condition of the cranial nerves assumed serious dimensions,"[46] Marx was forced yet again to set aside a period for rest in Karlsbad and the Black Forest. He had learned over the years that "one has to treat one's physique with as much diplomacy as everything else."[47]

Once he was back in England, although his health had not improved much, Marx re-immersed himself in his manuscripts. He complained to Sorge of the "damned insomnia" that had afflicted him during the year and made him "tremendously remiss about writing," since he had had "to devote all [his] more tolerable moments to work."[48] In November 1877, Marx wrote to the young Frankfurt banker Sigmund Schott (1852–1910) that he was "applying himself to various parts of the book in turn." He "began by writing *Capital* in a sequence (starting with the third, historical section[49]) quite the reverse of that in which it was presented to the public, saving only that the first volume—the last [he] tackled—was got ready for the press straight away, whereas the two others remained in the rough form which all research originally assumes."[50]

In this period, too, Marx did not neglect further study but concentrated on banking and trade, compiling extracts from the *History of Banking* (1874) by the Italian economist Pietro Rota (1846–1875), from the *History of Byzantine Commerce* (1808) and *History of the Commerce of the Greeks* (1839) by the first rector of Bonn University Karl Hüllmann (1765–1846), and from the *Natural History of the Raw Materials of Commerce* (1872) by the legal scholar and statistician John Yeats (1822–1902).[51] At the end of March 1878, Marx wrote to Schott that he had found "very useful"[52] a book by A. Saling (?), the editor of a stock exchange yearbook. He also read and compiled extracts from the works of the Russian economist Illarion Ignatevich Kaufman (1848–1916), particularly *Theory and*

Practice of the Banking System (1873–1877); while criticizing its "high-falutin style" and "enthusiastic apology" for capitalism, he concluded that the author, "unbeknown" to himself, "ends up demonstrating . . . the correlation between the necessary product of the present system of production . . . and what your philistine condemns as 'abuse,' 'malpractice,' etc."[53] Marx's development of his knowledge in these areas continued in the autumn, when he perused, among many other works, *Paper Money, the Root of Evil* (1872) by the economist Charles A. Mann (?), and *Principles of the Science of Banking* (1873) by Pietro Rota.

Along with this research and his reading of the most up-to-date publications, Marx deepened his knowledge of economic developments in Russia and the United States. In April, thanks to his friend Danielson who had been advised by German Lopatin (1845–1918), he received "a whole lot of the latest 'Russian' publications from Petersburg."[54] Among the authors was the celebrated jurist and philosopher Boris Nikolaevich Chicherin (1828–1904), of whose mediocrity Marx wrote: "He is evidently unacquainted with the very elements of Political Economy and fancies that, by being edited under his name, the trivialities of the Bastiat school become transformed into original and self-evident truths."[55] Marx subsequently commissioned Danielson to write a survey of Russian financial policy over the previous fifteen years as well as a summary report on the productivity of agricultural labor.

In April 1876, Marx had written to Sorge that, in order to make further headway with *Capital, Volume II*, he would need "to see for [himself] . . . what ha[d] appeared that might . . . be of use as regards American agriculture and relations of landownership, ditto . . . credit (panic, money, etc., and anything connected therewith)."[56] This was also why now, more than two years later, he asked the London bookseller George Rivers (?) to send him catalogues of his "American and secondhand books."[57] Soon after he had received and begun to use them, Marx remarked to Danielson that the "most interesting field for the economist [was] now certainly to be found in the United States; . . . transformations which . . . require[d] in England centuries were here realized in a few years." He therefore advised his friend to pay particular attention to developments in "the newer states" across the Atlantic, such as Ohio and California, rather than the "older ones."[58]

Marx himself had begun to use the approach he recommended to Danielson in his own work. In May 1878, Marx studied the *Ohio Bureau of Labor Statistics—First Annual Report* (1877), and in the following months, thanks to the material that Sorge sent him from the United States, he turned his attention to Pennsylvania and Massachusetts. It may be that he planned to follow the dynamics of the capitalist mode of production more extensively and on a more global scale in the volumes of *Capital* that remained to be written. If England was his field of observation for Volume I, the United States could have represented a new field of observation that would have allowed him to expand his work. It may be assumed, moreover, that he was keen to verify more closely the forms in which the capitalist mode of production developed in different contexts and periods.[59]

At any event, between the spring and summer of 1878, geology, mineralogy, and agrarian chemistry were more central to his studies than political economy. From late March to early June, he compiled extracts from a number of texts, including *The Natural History of the Raw Materials of Commerce* (1872) by John Yeats, *The Book of Nature* (1848) by the chemist Friedrich Schoedler (1813–1884), and *Elements of Agricultural Chemistry and Geology* (1856) by the chemist and mineralogist James Johnston (1796–1855).[60] Between June and early September, he was grappling with Joseph Jukes's (1811–1869) *Student's Manual of Geology* (1857),[61] from which he compiled the largest number of extracts. These excerpts concentrate on questions of scientific methodology, the stages of the development of geology as a discipline, and its usefulness for industrial and agricultural production.

These new insights awakened in Marx a need to develop his ideas regarding profit, with which he had last intensively occupied himself in the mid-1860s, in Part VI of *Capital, Volume III*, entitled "The Transformation of Surplus-Profit into Ground Rent." None of the summaries of natural-scientific texts had the aim of throwing greater light on the material he was studying. But other compilations, more geared to theoretical aspects, were meant to be used in the completion of Volume III. Engels later recalled that Marx "combed . . . prehistory, agronomy, Russian and American landownership, geology, etc., in particular to work out, to an extent . . . never previously attempted, the section on ground rent in *Capital, Volume III*."[62]

Meanwhile, in the summer of 1878, Marx's state of health made another pause necessary. His daughter Eleanor told the German journalist and activist Carl Hirsch that Marx had been "working too hard latterly and [would] be absolutely forced to do nothing for some time."[63]

When he resumed work later that month, Marx read *The Reform of the Monetary System* (1869) by the German economist Adolph Samter (1824–1883). Among the ostensible quotations in it from *Capital* was the phrase "gold and silver are by their nature money," although Marx's actual words had been "are not by nature money." He commented testily to Engels that "the art of reading would appear to be increasingly on the wane among the 'educated' estates in Germany."[64]

On the other hand, those who met Marx were indeed greatly struck by his erudition and boundless culture. An anonymous correspondent who interviewed him for the *Chicago Tribune* in December 1878 was greatly struck by his "intimacy with American questions . . . during the past twenty years."[65] The two discussed multiple themes, and Marx, showing great political flexibility, maintained that "many points" in the program of the German Party had "no significance outside of Germany." The workers' movement in "Spain, Russia, England and the United States," he explained, had "platforms suited to their particular difficulties. The only similarity in them [was] the end to be attained," which Marx defined less as "workers' power" (which the interviewer had suggested) than as "the emancipation of labour."[66] When asked "what Socialism [had] done so far," he focused on two main aspects. First:

> Socialists have shown the general universal struggle between capital and labour—the cosmopolitan character, in one word—and consequently tried to bring about an understanding between the workmen in the different countries, which became more necessary as the capitalists became more cosmopolitan in hiring labour, pitting foreign against native labour not only in America, but in England, France and Germany. International relations sprang up at once between the workingmen in the different countries, showing that Socialism was not merely a local, but an international problem, to be solved by the international action of workmen.[67]

Marx again stressed that "the working classes moved spontaneously," without bourgeois philanthropists or revolutionary sects to decide for them what to do. "Socialists invent no movement, but merely tell the workmen what its character and its ends will be."[68]

The American journalist then asked him to confirm the words attributed to him by the religious evangelist Josephus Cook (1838–1901), the author of various popular books on science and socialism. According to Cook, Marx had said that in 1871, at the time of the Paris Commune, the revolutionaries totaled a maximum of 3 million, but that within twenty years they would grow to 50–100 million; they would "rise against odious capital" and "the past [would] disappear like a hideous nightmare," in a "popular conflagration kindled at a hundred points at once."[69] Marx replied that he "never wrote a word" of the text that had appeared in the French conservative daily *Le Figaro*; he never penned "such melodramatic nonsense," but if he had to deny "everything said and written [about him], he would require a score of secretaries." What interested Marx was the critique of capitalism: "This system," he said, was "merely an historical phase, which will pass away and give place to a higher social condition."[70] In contrast to those who associated his ideas with an immediate and ineluctable collapse of capitalism, the journalist detected a "firm conviction in the realization of his theories, if not in this century, at least in the next."[71]

Marx put forward similar ideas to the Scottish politician Elphinstone, who met him early in 1879. When the latter envisaged a scenario in which "your Revolution has taken place and . . . you have your Republican form of Government," and provocatively suggested that it would "still be a long long way to the realization of the special ideas of yourself and your friends," Marx calmly replied: "Doubtless, but all great movements are slow. It would merely be a step to better things as your Revolution of 1688 was—a mere stage on the road."[72]

As to the continuation of *Capital*, Marx told Danielson—the Russian translator of Volume I—in November 1878 that the "second volume" would not go to print "before the end of 1879."[73] In April 1879, he said he had been informed that, following the adoption of the Anti-Socialist Laws in Germany, it would not be possible to publish further volumes "so long as the present regime was maintained in its present severity."[74] Marx, aware that he was still far from completing the work he had first begun in 1867, took the bad news quite well.

First, he wanted to wait until the industrial crisis in England reached a climax. Even if, as he expected, "it [would] pass over, like its predecessors, and initiate a new "industrial cycle" with all its diversified phases of prosperity," the further course of the crisis and its detailed observation were "most important" for "the student of capitalistic production."

Second, Marx wrote that "the bulk of materials [he had] received from Russia . . . and the United States [had given him] a "pretext" for continuing his studies, instead of winding them up finally for the public."[75] The United States, though still behind in "the extent of acquired wealth," had already "overtaken England in the rapidity of economic progress."[76] Marx was also particularly interested in the development of joint stock companies and the impact of railway construction on the economy. As he saw it, the railways "allowed, and even forced, states where capitalism was confined to a few summits of society, to suddenly create and enlarge their capitalistic superstructure in dimensions altogether disproportionate to the bulk of the social body carrying on the great work of production in the traditional modes." They had therefore "accelerated social and political disintegration" in countries where capitalism was less developed, just as they had "hastened the final development of capitalism" in the countries where it was more advanced.[77] Furthermore, the advent of this major new infrastructure had not only provided "means of communication adequate to the modern means of production but also, insofar as they were the basis of immense joint-stock companies, formed . . . a new starting point for . . . banking companies." Rail transport had given "an impetus never before suspected to the concentration of capital," but also to the "cosmopolitan activity of loanable capital," thus embracing the whole world in what Marx called "a network of financial swindling and mutual indebtedness, the capitalistic form of 'international' brotherhood."[78]

It took time to understand these phenomena—which was why, in June 1880, Marx reiterated to Nieuwenhuis, the main representative of the Social Democratic League of the Netherlands, that "under present circumstances the second part of *Capital* [could] not appear in Germany" and he was "quite glad of this." For "certain economic phenomena [were just then] entering upon a new phase of development and hence call[ed] for fresh appraisal."[79]

The third and last reason why it was taking longer to conclude Volume II was the instructions of Marx's doctor that he should "shorten considerably [his] working day."[80] Marx had already confessed to Danielson, in April 1879, that when he cancelled his "annual trip to Karlsbad"[81] because of the political climate in Germany and Austria after the enactment of antisocialist laws, his health had never really been good.[82] Marx spent two weeks in August between St. Aubin and St. Helier, two small towns on the "delightful island"[83] of Jersey, a few miles off the Normandy coast. The place had been chosen by Eleanor, his customary travelling companion, who was happy to try somewhere new. Father and daughter set off in the second part of August to join the rest of the family in Ramsgate, where Jenny Longuet had given birth to another boy. They remained there until the middle of September.

Marx tested whether his capacity for work had improved, by looking through some "mathematical notebooks" he had brought with him, but, as he confessed to Engels, "his head [was] not quite right yet" and he "very soon had to abandon the premature job."[84] Shortly afterwards, he wrote to Sorge that his health had worsened and that his "nervous condition" had "latterly made all brain work virtually 'unfeasible.'"[85] Nevertheless, as he wrote to Engels, the fortnight in Ramsgate—where "the air suit[ed] [him] extraordinarily well"—put him back on his feet and made him feel "much better."[86] Marx also kept Danielson informed, reporting that, after a period when he had had to "suspend all work . . . and been unable to do justice to the mental food" from St. Petersburg, he was feeling better and planned to "set to work with a will."[87] But he was well aware of the arduous labors ahead of him. Not only did he need to go back over some parts of the manuscript and improve their content; a more pressing task was to face some complex theoretical problems that remained unresolved.[88]

Engels also told Johann Philipp Becker (1809–1886) of the improvement in Marx's health: "Marx is fitter than last year, although he still isn't really up to the mark. Mrs Marx has long been subject to bouts of indigestion and is seldom entirely well. Volume Two is making slow progress, nor is it likely to progress any faster until a summer better than the last one enables Marx to recover properly for once."[89] Such a summer would never arrive, however.

Similar worries and difficulties accompanied the revision work on *Capital, Volume I*. In 1872, the publication of the French edition of *Capital* got under way. Entrusted to Joseph Roy, who had previously translated some of Ludwig Feuerbach's (1804–1872) texts, it was scheduled to appear in batches with the French publisher Maurice Lachâtre (1814–1900), between 1872 and 1875. Marx agreed that it would be good to bring out a "cheap popular edition."[90] "I applaud your idea of publishing the translation . . . in periodic instalments," he wrote. "In this form the work will be more accessible to the working class and for me that consideration outweighs any other." Aware, however, that there was a "reverse side" of the coin, he anticipated that the "method of analysis" he had used would "make for somewhat arduous reading in the early chapters," and that readers might "become discouraged when they were 'unable to carry straight on.'" He did not feel he could do anything about this "disadvantage, . . . other than constantly caution and forewarn those readers concerned with the truth. There is no royal road to learning and the only people with any chance of scaling its sunlit peaks are those who have no fear of weariness when ascending the precipitous paths that lead up to them."[91]

In the end, Marx had to spend much more time on the translation than he had planned for the proof correction. As he wrote to Danielson, Roy had "often translated too literally" and forced him to "rewrite whole passages in French, to make them more palatable to the French public."[92]

Earlier that month, his daughter Jenny had told Kugelmann that her father was "obliged to make numberless corrections," rewriting "not only whole sentences but entire pages"[93]—and a month later she added that the translation was so "imperfect" that he had been "obliged to rewrite the greater part of the first chapter."[94] Subsequently, Engels wrote in similar vein to Kugelmann that the French translation had proved a "real slog" for Marx and that he had "more or less had to rewrite the whole thing from the beginning."[95] At the end of his labors, Marx himself remarked that they had "consumed so much of [his] time that [he would] not again collaborate in any way on a translation."[96]

In revising the French version,[97] moreover, Marx decided to introduce some additions and modifications. These mostly concerned the section on the process of capital accumulation, but also some specific points such as the distinction between "concentration" and "centralization" of capital. In the postscript to the French edition, he did not hesitate to attach to it "a scientific value independent of the original."[98] It was no accident that in 1877, when an English edition already seemed a possibility, Marx wrote to Sorge that a translator "must without fail . . . compare the 2nd German edition with the French edition, in which [he had] included a good deal of new matter and greatly improved [his] presentation of much else."[99] In a letter of November 1878, in which he weighed the positive and negative aspects of the French edition, he wrote to Danielson that it contained "many important changes and additions," but that he had "also sometimes been obliged—principally in the first chapter—to simplify [*aplatir*] the matter."[100] For this reason, he felt it necessary to clarify later in the month that the chapters "Commodities and Money" and "The Transformation of Money into Capital" should be "translated exclusively from the German text."[101]

The drafts of *Capital, Volume II* were left in anything but a definitive state. The manuscripts of *Capital, Volume III*, have a highly fragmentary character, and Marx never managed to update them in a way that reflected the progress of his research.[102] It should also be borne in mind that he was unable to complete a revision of *Capital, Volume I*, that included the changes and additions he intended to improve his *magnum opus*.[103] In fact, neither the French edition of 1872–1875 nor the German edition of 1881 can be considered the definitive version that he would have liked it to be.

The critical spirit with which Marx composed his *Capital* reveals just how distant he was from the dogmatic author that many of his adversaries and self-styled disciples presented to the world.

3. THE CAROUSEL OF LIFE

In the first two weeks of June 1881, Jenny Marx's health took a further turn for the worse. Her "constant and increasing loss of flesh and strength" was alarming and resistant to any treatment. Dr. Bryan Donkin persuaded her to get away from the London climate, hoping that this would stabilize her enough for a planned trip to visit her daughter Jenny and her beloved grandchildren in Paris. Marx and his wife therefore decided to spend some time in Eastbourne, on the Channel coast.

At this time, Marx was not in good health either, and it was hoped that a spell by the sea would not only allow him to be by his wife's side, as he wished, but bring some benefit to him too. Engels wrote to Jenny Longuet in the second half of the month that "the change [would] be equally favourable to Moor:[104] he wants a bit of bracing up too, his cough is not so bad at nights and he sleeps better, that is one thing."[105] Marx himself spoke of his plight to Sorge, confiding on 20 June that he had been "suffering continuously for 6 months and more from a cough, cold, sore throat and rheumatism, which only seldom permit[ted him] to go out and [kept him] out of society."[106]

Marx and his wife left for Eastbourne toward the end of the month and remained there for approximately three weeks. The costs of the trip, and of the necessary consultations with doctors, were borne by Engels. In July, he calmed his friend: "You can now have £100 to £120, and it's simply a question of whether you want it all at one go and how much is to be sent there and how much is for here."[107]

Laura and Eleanor took it in turns to spend some time with their parents and to offer them comfort.[108] But Jenny Marx's health did not improve. As she wrote to Laura: "In spite of the propitious circumstances, I do not feel better and have . . . actually sunk to a Bath-chair, a thing that I, the pedestrian par excellence, should have regarded as beneath my dignity a few months ago."[109]

Upon her return to London, the doctor found Jenny somewhat better and accepted her wish to see her daughter and grandchildren in Paris for the first time in five months or more. Marx sent "£5" to his daughter Jenny, as she would "have to pay cash for the hire of bed-linen, etc." that he insisted was indispensable if she was to receive them both in her home. "The remainder," he added, would be "paid when we arrive."[110]

On 26 July, Marx and his wife, accompanied by Helene Demuth, landed in France and travelled on to Argenteuil, the suburb of Paris where Jenny Longuet lived with her husband. Marx immediately wanted to meet the family doctor, Gustave Dourlen (?), who said he was available to take care of Jenny Marx. He wrote to Engels that, for the first day of their visit, "the little ones ha[d] rightly laid claim to 'Old Nick.'"[111] This name, with its diabolic associations, was used in the family as an alternative to "Moor," and especially in the last few years of his life, Marx often signed letters to his daughters, Engels, and Paul Lafargue in this way, amused more than pleased by the reference to his illustrious namesake.[112]

The news of Marx's return to France, though for strictly personal motives, was bound to arouse suspicions. Longuet had speculated that as soon as they heard of it, "the anarchists [would] impute to [Marx] the malicious intention of swinging the vote" in forthcoming elections, but then he heard from his friend Georges Clemenceau (1841–1929) that Marx "had absolutely nothing to fear from the police."[113] Eleanor Marx had also informed Carl Hirsch (1841–1900), the Paris correspondent of the German social democratic press, of her parents' arrival, so that Marx joked that his presence was already "an open secret."

Engels, spending a fortnight in Bridlington, Yorkshire, was entertained and reassured by what his friend had told him and wrote back with his usual thoughtfulness: "I have got some cheques with me, so if you need anything, don't hesitate to let me know roughly how much you want. Your wife must not and shall not want for anything; if there's something she would like to have or something you know would give her pleasure, then have it she must." He also filled Marx in about one of his great pleasures in life: "Here one can pretty well do without German beer, for the bitter ale in the little café on the pier is excellent, and has a head on it like German beer."[114]

On the other side of the Channel, Marx was not having such a good time. He thanked Engels for his help: "Drawing so heavily on your exchequer is a great embarrassment to me, but the anarchy which has wrought havoc with the housekeeping over the past two years and given rise to all sorts of arrears has been oppressing me for some considerable time."[115] He then reported how his wife was doing: "Every day we experience the same ups and downs here as we did in Eastbourne, only with the difference—as for instance yesterday—that there are sudden and frightful bouts of pain," when Dr. Dourlen was ready to administer opiates. Marx did not conceal his fears: "The temporary 'improvements' do not, of course, inhibit the natural course of the disease, but they delude my wife and fortify Jenny [Longuet]—despite my objurgations—in the belief that our stay in Argenteuil should last as long as possible."[116]

This constant oscillation between hopes and fears had not been at all good for his own health, even interfering with his moments of rest: "Last night, in fact, was the first occasion on which I had anything like a decent sleep. My thoughts are so dull and dead, as if a mill-wheel was turning in my head." He had therefore not yet "been into Paris or written a single line" to comrades in the capital to invite them round to his daughter's house.[117] Their first day trip to the center of Paris came only on 7 August and gave Jenny Marx great pleasure. To Marx—who had not been there since 1849—it "gave the impression of a perpetual fair."

Back in Argenteuil, fearing that his wife's state might suddenly deteriorate, Marx wrote to Engels that he had tried to persuade her to return to London. Her maternal feelings had prevailed, however, and she said she wanted to stay as long as possible with her daughter Jenny. She had "already played a trick . . . by sending out a mass of washing"[118] that would be returned only early the following week.[119] Marx ended with a few lines about himself: "Oddly enough, though I get damned little rest at night and my days are racked with worry, everyone tells me how well I look—as is, indeed, the case."[120]

In the end, it was another painful event that forced him to leave France in great haste. On 16 August, Marx received news that his third daughter, Eleanor, was gravely ill. He immediately set off for London, where he was joined a few days later by his wife and Helene Demuth. It soon became clear that Tussy—his pet name for Eleanor—was in a state of extreme depression.[121] Anxious that she was "looking pale and thin" and had not eaten "literally for weeks," Marx turned to his other daughter, Jenny, and reported that her sister was tormented by "continuous sleeplessness, trembling of the hands, neuralgic convulsions of the face, etc." and that she would be in "the greatest danger in the case of further delay."[122] Fortunately, to sustain him in the crisis, Marx had the memory of the fine weeks he had just spent, despite everything, in Argenteuil: "The pleasure to be with you and the dear children has given me a more substantial satisfaction than I could have found anywhere else."[123]

Barely two days later, news arrived from Argenteuil that "Longuet and little Harry" were "very ill." Marx commented to Engels: "Nothing but misfortune in the family at the moment."[124] There seemed no end in sight to the trials and tribulations.

4. THE DEATH OF HIS WIFE

The task of caring for Eleanor, which absorbed much of his energies in the second half of the summer, together with the course of Jenny Marx's illness— which "day by day [was] drawing closer to its consummation"[125]—prevented the Marx family from keeping up any social relations. At the beginning of the month, he wrote to Minna Kautsky (1837–1912)—a former actress and now author of socially committed novels—and apologized for not being able to invite her to London, because his "wife's shocking and [he feared] fatal illness" had "put a stop to [their] intercourse with the outside world."[126] To Kautsky, Minna's son, he had written the same day that he was a "sick nurse."[127]

During this period Marx resumed his study of mathematics. Paul Lafargue later recalled his father-in-law's highly distinctive approach to the subject:

> Besides the poets and novelists, Marx had another remarkable way of relaxing intellectually—mathematics, for which he had a special liking. Algebra even brought him moral consolation and he took refuge in the most distressing moments of his eventful life. During his wife's last illness, he was unable to devote himself to his usual scientific work and the only way in which he could shake off the oppression caused by her sufferings was to plunge into mathematics. During that time of moral suffering he wrote a work on infinitesimal calculus. . . . He saw in higher mathematics the most logical and at the same time the simplest form of dialectical movement. He held the view that science is not really developed until it has learned to make use of mathematics.[128]

In mid-October, Marx's health, which was feeling the weight of family events, faltered once more, as bronchitis developed into a severe case of pleurisy. This time, Eleanor spent all her time at her father's bedside, trying to help him ward off the danger of pneumonia. She stopped her sister from travelling over to join them from Argenteuil.[129]

A worried Engels wrote to Bernstein on 25 October: "He has been in bed for the past 12 days with bronchitis and all kinds of complications, but since Sunday—due precautions having been taken—there has no longer been any danger. I've been anxious enough, I can tell you."[130] A few days later, he also informed the long-standing comrade Becker: "At his time of life and considering the general state of his health, [the bronchitis and pleurisy] were certainly no laughing matter. Fortunately, the worst is over and, so far as Marx is concerned, all danger has been completely eliminated for the time being, though he has to spend the greater part of the day in bed and is greatly weakened."[131]

At the end of November, Engels sent a further medical bulletin to Bernstein: "Marx is still very run down, isn't allowed to leave his room or engage in any serious occupation, but he is visibly gaining weight." Meanwhile, "if any one outside event has contributed to putting Marx more or less to rights again, then it is the elections."[132] On 27 October 1881, the German Social Democrats had obtained more than 300,000 votes in the ballot for the new parliament—a unique score in Europe.[133]

Jenny Marx, too, was very pleased with the result, but it would be one of the last joys in her life. The following weeks brought terrible conditions for her. Her daughter Eleanor recalled Dr. Donkin saying that "to give her a little change" she and other helpers should "lift her—in her sheets—from her bed to the chair-bed" and back again.[134] Jenny was heavily sedated with morphine because of the intense pain. Eleanor later recalled:

> Our mother lay in the large front room, Moor in the little room behind. . . . Never shall I forget the morning when he felt strong enough to go into my mother's room. When they were together they were young again—she a loving girl and he a loving youth, on the threshold of life, not an old man devastated by illness and an old dying woman parting from each other for life.[135]

On 2 December 1881, Jenny Marx, the woman who, by Marx's side, had shared his hardships and political passion, died of liver cancer. It was an irredeemable loss. For the first time since 1836, when he had fallen in love with her at the age of just eighteen, he found himself alone, deprived of his "greatest treasure,"[136] without the "face [that] reawakens the greatest and sweetest memories of [his] life."[137]

To avoid further compromising his own frail condition, he could not even be present at her funeral: "There was no gainsaying the doctor's interdict," he wrote sadly to his daughter Jenny. He thought of the words his wife had spoken to the nurse, shortly before her death, about some neglected formality: "We are no such external people."[138] Engels, however—a man Eleanor said was "of a kindness and devotion that baffle description"[139]—did attend the burial. In his graveside speech, he recalled: "If ever there was a woman whose greatest happiness lay in making others happy, this was she."[140]

Marx wrote to his daughter Jenny that it gave him "extraordinary happiness" to recall their trip to Paris that summer. Her mother had benefited greatly from the time she had spent with her and the children, and "the reliving of that time" had "distracted her" during the final weeks of the illness. He also said it was "a comfort" to him that "her strength gave out at the right time." The "highly unusual location" of the cancer meant that the pain had been "unbearable" only in "the very last days. . . . Even during her last hours there were no death agonies, [but] a gradual falling asleep, her eyes larger, lovelier, more luminous than ever."[141]

For Marx, the wrenching pain of this loss was compounded by physical suffering. The treatment he had to undergo was extremely painful, although he faced it in a stoical spirit. He wrote to his daughter Jenny:

> I still have to paint my chest, neck, etc., with iodine and, when regularly repeated, this produces a somewhat tiresome and painful inflammation of the skin. The said operation, which is only being performed to prevent a relapse during convalescence (now complete apart from a slight cough), is therefore doing me sterling service just at this moment. There is only one effective antidote for mental suffering, and that is physical pain. Set the end of the world on the one hand against a man with acute toothache on the other.[142]

His health became very precarious, as he wrote to his friend Becker: "I myself am still an invalid . . . so serious a grip had pleurisy combined with bronchitis gained over me that for a time, i.e. several days, the doctors doubted whether I would pull through."[143] He added to Danielson that at one point he "was very near "leaving this bad world." "The doctors," he added, "want to send me to the south of France or even to Algeria."[144] He was forced to stay in bed for a number of weeks, and in a letter to Sorge he spoke of being "confined to the house" and of "frittering away a certain amount of time on schemes for restoring [his] health."[145] Yet faced with the huge difficulties, Marx once again found the strength to pick himself up and resume work.

5. RETURN TO THE STUDY OF HISTORY

Between autumn 1881 and winter 1882, a large part of Marx's intellectual energies went into historical studies. He worked intensively on the *Chronological Extracts*, an annotated year-by-year timeline of world events from the first century BC on, summarizing their causes and salient features. It was the same method he had used for his *Notes on Indian History (664–1858)*, between autumn 1879 and summer 1880.

Once again he wanted to test whether his conceptions were well-founded in the light of major political, military, economic, and technological developments in the past. For some time, he had been aware that the schema of linear progression through the "Asiatic, ancient, feudal and modern bourgeois modes of production,"[146] which he had drawn in the "Preface" to *A Contribution to the Critique of Political Economy* (1859), was completely inadequate for an understanding of the movement of history, and that it was indeed advisable to steer clear of any philosophy of history. The frail state of his health prevented him from undertaking another encounter with the unfinished manuscripts of *Capital*. So he probably thought the time had come to turn his attention again to world history, particularly the key question of the relationship between the development of capitalism and the birth of modern states.[147] The completion of the two missing volumes of his *magnum opus* was left until the hoped-for recovery of his physical strength.

Apart from some minor sources he did not mention, Marx drew upon two main texts for his chronology. The first was the *History of the Peoples of Italy* (1825), by the Italian historian Carlo Botta (1766–1837), which was originally published in three volumes in French, since the author had had to flee Turin in 1814 to escape persecution at the hands of the Savoyard government and returned to Piedmont only after the defeat of Napoleon Bonaparte.[148] The second was the widely read and acclaimed *World History for the German People* (1844–1857), by Friedrich Schlosser (1776–1861), who in his lifetime had been considered the leading German historian.[149] Marx had both these books in his personal library—having probably inherited Schlosser's works from his friend Wilhelm Wolff (1809–1864)—and he jotted a number of observations and marginalia in the first two volumes of Botta's *History of the Peoples of Italy*.[150]

Marx filled four thick notebooks with notes on these two works,[151] in an even smaller, scarcely legible handwriting than usual. The covers bear the titles that Engels gave them when he was going through his friend's estate: "Chronological extracts. I: 96 to c. 1320; II: c. 1300 to c. 1470; III: c. 1470 to c. 1580; IV: c. 1580 to c. 1648."[152] Marx's summaries were written in German, English, and French, and sometimes interspersed with short comments. Many of these consist merely of corrections relating to dates or events. In other cases, however, Marx added critical considerations on significant figures or advanced his own interpretations of important historical events, from which we can infer his disagreement with the faith in progress and the moral judgments expressed by Schlosser. This new immersion in history did not stop with Europe but extended to Asia, the Middle East, the Islamic world, and the Americas.[153]

In the first notebook of his *Chronological Extracts*, mainly basing himself on Botta, Marx filled 143 pages with a chronology of some of the principal events between 91 BC and 1370 AD. Beginning with ancient Rome, he moved on to consider the fall of the Roman Empire, the rise of France, the historical importance of Charlemagne (742–814), the Byzantine Empire, and the various features and development of feudalism.

After the publication of *Capital, Volume I*, Marx had already occupied himself a number of times with the Middle Ages, and his knowledge of it had considerably increased in 1868, when he had taken a close interest in historical and agricultural questions and compiled notebooks of extracts from the works of various authors in those fields. Particularly important for him was the *Introduction to the Constitutive History of the German Mark, Farm, Village, Town and Public Authority* (1854) by the political theorist and legal historian Georg von Maurer (1790–1872).[154] Marx told Engels he had found Maurer's books "extremely significant," since they approached in an entirely different way "not only the primitive age but also the entire later development of the free imperial cities, of the estate owners possessing immunity, of public authority, and of the struggle between the free peasantry and serfdom."[155]

Marx attentively annotated everything that might be useful to him in analyzing taxation systems in various countries and epochs. He also took great interest in the special role of Sicily, on the margins of the Arab world and Europe, and in the Italian maritime republics and their important contribution to the development of mercantile capitalism. Finally, while consulting other books that helped him to integrate the information provided by Botta, Marx wrote many pages of notes on the Islamic conquest in Africa and the East, the Crusades, and the Baghdad and Mosul Caliphates.

In the second notebook, comprising 145 pages on the period from 1308 to 1469, Marx continued to transcribe notes on the final crusades in the "Holy Land." However, the most extensive part again concerned the Italian maritime republics and the economic advances in Italy, which Marx thought of as the beginning of modern capitalism.[156] Also drawing on Machiavelli, he summarized the main events in the political struggles of the Republic of Florence. At the same time, drawing on Schlosser's *World History for the German People*, Marx dwelled on the German political and economic situation in the fourteenth and fifteenth centuries, as well as the history of the Mongol Empire during and after the lifetime of Genghis Khan.[157]

In the third notebook, consisting of 141 pages, Marx dealt with the main political and religious conflicts of the period from 1470 to around 1580. He took a special interest in the clash between France and Spain, the tumultuous dynastic struggles of the English monarchy, and the life and influence of Girolamo

Savonarola (1452–1498). And, of course, he retraced the history of the Protestant Reformation, noting the support given to it by the emergent bourgeois class. A good part of his notes concern the figure of Martin Luther (1483–1546). Unlike Schlosser, he drew a highly negative portrait of him, trenchantly concluding that "this monk impede[d] everything progressive in the Reformation."[158]

Finally, in the fourth, 117-page notebook, Marx focused mainly on the numerous religious conflicts in Europe between 1580 and 1648. The longest section dealt with Germany before the outbreak of the Thirty Years War (1618–1648) and made a deep analysis of this period.[159] Marx dwelled on the roles of the Swedish king Gustavus Adolphus (1594–1632), Cardinal Richelieu (1585–1642), and Cardinal Mazarin (1602–1661). A final section was devoted to England following the death of Elizabeth I (1533–1603).[160]

Along with the four notebooks of extracts from Botta and Schlosser, Marx compiled another notebook with the same characteristics that was contemporaneous with the others and related to the same research. Here, basing himself on the *History of the Republic of Florence* (1875) by Gino Capponi (1792–1876), Marx built on the knowledge he had already gained about the years from 1135 to 1433. He also compiled further notes on the period from 449 to 1485, based on the *History of the English People* (1877) by John Green (1837–1883). The fluctuating state of his health did not allow him to advance any further, however. His notes stopped with the chronicles of the Peace of Westphalia, which put an end to the Thirty Years War in 1648.

When Marx's medical condition improved, he needed to do everything possible to eliminate "the danger of a relapse."[161] Accompanied by his daughter Eleanor, he moved on 29 December 1881 to Ventnor on the Isle of Wight, where he had been a few times before and was now advised to return, in the hope that "the warm climate and dry air there [would] rapidly complete his recovery."[162] Before leaving, he wrote to Jenny: "My dear child, the best service you can do me is to keep your chin up! I hope that I shall spend many more happy days with you and worthily fulfil my functions as a grandpa."[163]

He spent the first two weeks of 1882 in Ventnor. In order to go for walks without too much trouble, and to be "less dependent on the caprices of the weather," he had to wear a respirator "in case of need," which looked much like "a muzzle."[164] Even in these difficult circumstances, Marx never lost his ironical touch and wrote to Laura that "the vehemence with which the bourgeois papers in Germany have announced either [his] demise, or at any rate the inevitable imminence thereof" had "tickled [him] hugely."[165]

The days that Marx spent with Eleanor were far from easy. Weighed down by her existential problems, she was still deeply unsettled, unable to sleep and fearful that her nervous crisis might dramatically worsen. However great the affection they felt for each other, it was hard for them to communicate: he was "angry and anxious" and perceived her as "disagreeable and dissatisfied."[166]

Marx still managed to keep up with the main political events of the day. When the German chancellor, speaking in parliament, had been unable to ignore the deep distrust of government policy among German workers,[167] he wrote to Engels: "I regard it as a major victory, not only in Germany itself but vis-à-vis the outside world generally, that Bismarck should admit in the Reichstag that the German workers have to some extent 'given the thumbs down' to his state socialism."[168]

Marx's bronchitis was becoming chronic, however, and after his return to London family members discussed at length with Dr. Donkin about the climate that would provide the best conditions for him to get better. Rest in a warm place was advisable for a complete recovery; the Isle of Wight had not worked. Gibraltar was ruled out because Marx would have needed a passport to enter the territory, and as a stateless person he was not in possession of one. The Bismarckian empire was covered in snow and anyway still forbidden to him, while Italy was out of the question, since, as Engels put it, "the first proviso where convalescents are concerned is that there should be no harassment by the police."[169]

With the support of Dr. Donkin and Paul Lafargue, Marx's son-in-law, Engels convinced the patient to head for Algiers, which at the time enjoyed a good reputation among English people who could afford to escape the rigors of winter.[170] As Marx's daughter Eleanor later recalled, what pushed Marx into making this unusual trip was his old obsession: to complete *Capital*. She wrote:

> His general state keeps getting worse. If he had been more egoistic, he would have simply allowed things to take their course. But for him one thing stood above all else: devotion to the cause. He wanted to see his great work through to the end and therefore agreed once more to make a journey to recover his health.[171]

Marx left for the Mediterranean on 9 February, stopping on the way at Argenteuil. When his health did not improve, he decided after scarcely one week to continue alone to Marseilles, having persuaded Eleanor that it was unnecessary for her to accompany him. To Engels he confided: "Not for anything in the world would I have the girl think she is to be sacrificed as an old man's 'nurse' on the altar of family."[172]

After crossing the whole of France by train, he reached the great Provençal seaport on 17 February. He immediately obtained a ticket for the first ship bound for Africa,[173] and the next day, on a windy wintry afternoon, he was in the harbor queuing up with other passengers to go on board. He had a couple of suitcases crammed with heavy clothing, medicines, and a few books. At 5:00 p.m., the steamer *Said* left for Algiers, where Marx would stay for seventy-two days. This was the only time in his life that he spent outside Europe.[174]

4

THE MOOR'S LAST JOURNEY

1. THE TRIP TO ALGIERS AND REFLECTIONS
ON THE ARAB WORLD

After a stormy thirty-four-hour crossing, Marx reached his destination on 20
February. The next day he wrote to Friedrich Engels, and a week later he recalled that his "*corpus delecti*" had been "frozen to the marrow." He found an
ideally situated room, with a port view, at the Hôtel-Pension Victoria, in the
Upper Mustapha zone. It was a "magical panorama," which allowed him to appreciate the "wonderful combination of Europe and Africa."[1]

The only person who knew the identity of the newly arrived polyglot gentleman was Albert Fermé (1840–1904), a justice of the peace and follower of
Charles Fourier (1772–1837), who had landed in Algiers in 1870 after a period of
imprisonment on account of his opposition to the Second Empire. He was the
only real company Marx had there, serving as his guide on various excursions
and attempting to satisfy his curiosity about the new world.

As the days passed, however, Marx's health did not improve: he was still
troubled by the bronchitis, and an uncontrollable cough kept him awake at
night. The unusually cold, damp, and rainy weather—it was the worst winter
in ten years in Algiers—also favored another attack of pleurisy. "The only difference between my clothing in the Isle of Wight and my clothing in the city
of Algiers," he wrote to Engels, "is that in the villa I have up till now simply
replaced the rhinoceros greatcoat with my light greatcoat." He even contem-
plated moving 400 kilometers further south, to the village of Biskra on the

edge of the Sahara, but his poor physical condition dissuaded him from such a taxing journey. He therefore embarked on a lengthy period of complicated treatment in Algiers.

Dr. Charles Stephann (1840–1906), the best in the city, prescribed sodium arsenate during the day and a codeine-based opiate syrup to help him sleep at night. He also ordered Marx to reduce physical exertion to a minimum and to abstain from "real intellectual work except some reading for [his] distraction." Nevertheless, on 6 March the cough became even more violent and brought about repeated hemorrhaging. Marx was therefore forbidden to leave the hotel and even to engage in conversation: "rest, solitude and silence" were now "duties incumbent on [him] as a citizen."[2] At least, he wrote to Engels, "Dr. Stephann, like my dear Dr. Donkin [in London], does not forget the cognac."[3]

The most painful treatment proved to be a course of ten vesicatories, a therapy popular at the time that used agents to blister the skin in order to release subcutaneous toxins. Marx managed to complete these with the help of a young pharmacist. Little by little, by repeatedly painting his chest and back with collodion and opening the resulting blisters, Mr. Maurice Casthelaz (?) succeeded in drawing off the excess fluid from his lungs.

Not surprisingly, Marx began to regret his chosen destination: as he wrote to Paul Lafargue, "from the moment of [his] departure for Marseilles" there had been "the finest weather in both Nice and Menton," two other possibilities he had considered.[4] In the second half of March, he confided to his daughter Jenny: "In this foolish, ill-calculated expedition, I am now just arrived again at that standard of health when I possessed it on leaving" London. He also told her that he had had his doubts about travelling such a long way, "but that Engels and Bryan Donkin fired each other mutually into African furor, neither one nor the other getting any special information"[5] about the weather that year. In his view, "the thing was to inform oneself before starting on such a wild goose chase."[6]

On 20 March, Marx wrote to Lafargue that the treatment had been stopped for the time being, since there was no longer "a single dry place either on [his] back or [his] chest." The sight of his body reminded him of "a kitchen garden in miniature planted with melons." To his great relief, however, his sleep was "gradually returning": "someone who has not suffered from insomnia cannot appreciate that blissful state when the terror of sleepless nights begins to give way."[7]

On the other hand, Marx's breathing was more labored as a result of the nocturnal drawing of blisters, the need to remain bandaged, and the strict ban on scratching. Having learned that the weather in France had been "wonderful" since his departure from London, and bearing in mind the initial prediction of a rapid cure, he wrote to Engels that "a man ought never [to] delude himself by too sanguine views!"[8] Clearly there was "some way to go to *sana mens in sano corpore*."[9]

Marx's suffering was not only bodily. He felt lonely and wrote on 16 March to his daughter Jenny: "Nothing could be more magical than the city of Algiers, unless it be the countryside outside that city . . . ; it would be like the Arabian Nights—given good health—with all my dear ones (in particular not forgetting my grandsons)."[10] And on 27 March he added that he would have liked "by magic" to have Johnny, the eldest, there too—"to wonder . . . at Moors, Berbers, Turks, negroes, in one word this Babel and costumes (most of them poetic) of this oriental world, mixed with the 'civilized' French etc. and the dull Britons."[11]

To Engels, a comrade with whom he was used to sharing everything, he wrote of "an occasional bout of profound melancholy, like the great Don Quixote." His thoughts kept returning to the loss of his life-companion: "You know that few people are more averse to demonstrative pathos; still, it would be a lie [not] to confess that my thoughts are to a great part absorbed by reminiscence of my wife, such a part of my best part of life!"[12] One distraction from the pain of mourning was the spectacle of nature around him. Early in April he wrote that there was "wonderful moonlight on the bay," and he could "never stop feasting [his] eyes on the sea in front of [his] balcony."[13]

Marx also suffered from the enforced lack of serious intellectual activity. Since the start of the trip, he had been aware that it would be "a time-wasting operation," but he had eventually agreed to it when he realized that the "accursed disease" also "impairs one's intellect."[14]

He told Jenny that "any working" was "out of the question" in Algiers—even "the correction of *Capital* for a [third German] edition."[15] As to the current political situation, he limited himself to reading the telegraphic reports of a small local paper, *The Little Settler* [*Le Petit Colon*], and the only workers' sheet received from Europe, *The Equality* [*L'Égalité*], about which he noted sarcastically that "you can't call it a newspaper."[16]

Marx's letters of spring 1882 show that he was "eager to be again active and to drop that invalid's stupid job,"[17] "a pointless, arid, not to say expensive, existence."[18] To Lafargue he even said he was so busy doing nothing that he felt close to imbecility[19]—which suggests a fear on his part that he was no longer capable of taking up his usual existence where he had left off.

This progression of unfavorable events did not allow Marx to get to the bottom of Algerian reality, nor—as Engels foresaw—was it really possible for him to study the characteristics of "common ownership among the Arabs."[20] In 1879 he had already taken an interest in the land question in French-ruled Algeria, in the course of his studies in ethnology, landed property, and precapitalist societies. In that circumstance, Marx had transcribed from Kovalevsky's *Communal Landownership: The Causes, Course, and Consequences of Its Decline* that the "individualization of land ownership" would bring huge benefits to the invaders, but it would also favor the "political aim" of "destroying the foundation of this society."[21]

On 22 February 1882, an article in the Algiers daily *The News* [*L'Akhbar*] documented the injustices of the newly crafted system. Theoretically, any French citizen at that time could acquire a concession of more than 100 hectares of Algerian land, without even leaving his country, and he could then resell it to a native for 40,000 francs. On average, the *colons* sold every parcel of land they had bought for 20–30 francs at the price of 300 francs.[22]

Owing to his ill health, Marx was unable to return to these problems; nor was the article in *The News* brought to his attention. But his permanent desire for knowledge did not fade even in the most adverse circumstances. After exploring the area around his hotel, where housing reconstruction was under way on a vast scale, he noted that "although the workers engaged in this activity are healthy people and local residents they go down with fever after the first three days. Part of their wages, therefore, consists of a daily dose of quinine supplied by the employers."[23]

Marx made a number of interesting observations in his sixteen letters from the southern rim of the Mediterranean,[24] some of which display a still partly colonial vision. The ones that really stand out are those dealing with social relations among Muslims.

Marx was profoundly struck by the bearing of the Arabs: "Even the poorest Moor," he wrote, "surpasses the greatest European comedian in the art of wrapping himself in his hood and showing natural, graceful and dignified attitudes."[25] Noting how their social classes mixed, he wrote to his daughter Laura in mid-April that he had observed a group of Arabs playing cards, "some of them dressed pretentiously, even richly," others in, for once I dare call it blouses, sometime of white woollen appearance, now in rags and tatters." For a "true Muslim," he commented:

Such accidents, good or bad luck, do not distinguish Mahomet's children. Absolute equality in their social intercourse, not affected; on the contrary, only when demoralized, they become aware of it; as to the hatred against Christians and the hope of an ultimate victory over these infidels, their politicians justly consider this same feeling and practice of absolute equality (not of wealth or position but of personality) a guarantee of keeping up the one, of not giving up the latter. (Nevertheless, they will go to rack and ruin without a revolutionary movement.)[26]

Marx also marveled at the scant presence of the state:

In no town elsewhere, which is at the same time the seat of the central government, is there such *laisser faire, laisser passer*; police reduced to a bare minimum; unparalleled lack of embarrassment in public; the Moorish element is responsible for this. For Muslims there is no such thing as subordination; they are neither "subjects" nor "citizens" [*administrés*]; no authority, save in politics, something which Europeans have totally failed to understand.[27]

Marx scornfully attacked the Europeans' violent abuses and constant provocations, and, not least, their "bare-faced arrogance and presumptuousness vis-à-vis the 'lesser breeds,' [and] grisly, Moloch-like obsession with atonement" with regard to any act of rebellion. He also emphasized that, in the comparative history of colonial occupation, "the British and Dutch outdo the French." In Algiers itself, he reported to Engels, his friend the judge Fermé had regularly seen in the course of his career "a form of torture . . . to extract confessions from Arabs, naturally done . . . (like the English in India) by the 'police.'"

When, for example, a murder is committed by an Arab gang, usually with robbery in view, and the actual miscreants are in the course of time duly apprehended, tried and executed, this is not regarded as sufficient atonement by the injured colonist family. They demand into the bargain the "pulling in" of at least half a dozen innocent Arabs. . . . When a European colonist dwells among the "lesser breeds," either as a settler or simply on business, he generally regards himself as even more inviolable than handsome William I.[28]

Marx returned to the theme in another context, when he told Engels of the brutality of the French authorities toward "a poor, thieving Arab, a poor, multiple assassin by profession." Shortly before his execution, he learned that "he wasn't going to be shot but guillotined! This, in defiance of prior arrangements!" Nor was that all:

> His relatives had expected the head and body to be handed over to them so that they could sew the former to the latter and then bury the "whole." Which it is not! Howls, imprecations and gnashing of teeth; the French authorities dug their heels in, the first time they had done so! Now, when the body arrives in paradise, Mohammed will ask, "Where have you left your head? Or, how did the head come to be parted from its body? You're not fit to enter paradise. Go and join those dogs of Christians in hell!" And that's why his relations were so upset.[29]

Along with these political and social observations, Marx's letters also include material on Arab customs. In one, he told his daughter Laura a story that had greatly appealed to his practical side:

> A ferryman is ready and waiting, with his small boat, on the tempestuous waters of a river. A philosopher, wishing to get to the other side, climbs aboard. There ensues the following dialogue:
> Philosopher: Do you know anything of history, ferryman?
> Ferryman: No!
> Philosopher: Then you've wasted half your life!
> And again: The Philosopher: Have you studied mathematics?
> Ferryman: No!
> Philosopher: Then you've wasted more than half your life.
> Hardly were these words out of the philosopher's mouth when the wind capsized the boat, precipitating both ferryman and philosopher into the water.
> Whereupon, Ferryman shouts: Can you swim?
> Philosopher: No!
> Ferryman: Then you've wasted your whole life.
> And Marx added to Laura: "That will tickle your appetite for things Arabic."[30]

After more than two months of suffering, Marx's condition improved and he was at last able to return to France. First, however, he had a final surprise for Engels: "Apropos; because of the sun, I have done away with my prophet's

LEFT: The last photograph of Karl Marx, take by E. Dutertre in Algiers in 1882. IISH Collection BG A9/383.
RIGHT: A photomontage showing how Marx may have looked after having his hair cut and his beard shaved off. Creator and origins unknown.

beard and my crowning glory but (in deference to my daughters) had myself photographed before offering up my hair on the altar of an Algerian barber."[31] This would be the last snapshot of him. It is utterly unlike the granite profile to be found on the squares of "actually existing socialism," which the regimes of the day ordered to represent him. His moustache, rather like his ideas, has not lost the colour of youth—and his smiling face, for all life's trials and disappointments, still appears kindly and unassuming.[32]

2. A REPUBLICAN IN THE PRINCIPALITY

Bad weather continued to pester Marx. During his "last days in Africa,"[33] his health was sorely tested by the arrival of the sirocco, and the crossing to Marseilles—where he landed on 5 May, on his sixty-fourth birthday—was particularly rough. As he wrote later to Eleanor, "a violent storm . . . turned [his] cabin into a veritable wind tunnel." And once at their destination, the steamer did not actually enter the harbor, so that the passengers had to be taken off by boat, spending "several hours in a cold, draughty customs-hall-cum-purgatory until the time came for them to depart for Nice." These tribulations, he quipped, "more or less threw [his] machine out of gear" and "precipitated [him] into the hands of an Aesculapius" as soon as they reached Monte Carlo.[34]

The trusted Aesculapius was Dr. Kunemann (1828–?), an excellent doctor from Alsace who specialized in lung diseases.[35] It was discovered that the bronchitis had become chronic and, to Marx's "horror," that "the pleurisy had returned."[36] All the moving around had done further damage, and Marx used his customary literary references to joke about it with Engels: "Fate" would seem on this occasion to have displayed an alarming consistency—almost, one might say, as in the tragedies of Amandus Müllner" (1774–1829), where "fate" does indeed play an important role in human existence. Another course of four vesicatories was therefore necessary, and these took place between 9 and 30 May.

Since he had to get better before continuing on his way, Marx spent three weeks in the principality of Monaco. His descriptions of the atmosphere there mix shrewdness with social criticism: for example, he compared Monte Carlo to Gérolstein, the imaginary statelet in which Jacques Offenbach (1819–1880) placed his opera *The Grand Duchess of Gérolstein* (1867).

Marx went a few times to the reading room at the famous casino, which offered a good selection of international newspapers. But he told Engels that his "*table d'hôte* companions at the Hôtel de Russie" and, more generally, the public in the city were "more interested in what goes on in the Casino's gaming rooms." His letters from this period alternate between amused observations about people he came across—for example, "a son of Albion, sulky, ill-tempered and bewildered . . . because he had lost a certain number of yellow boys, whereas he had been absolutely intent on 'copping' the same"—and mordant comments such as: "He couldn't understand that not even British boorishness is able 'to bully' fortune."[37]

The most trenchant description of this alien world was offered to his daughter Eleanor, in a letter written shortly his departure:

> At the *table d'hôte*, in the cafés, etc., almost the only topic that is talked or whispered about is the roulette and the *trente et quarante* tables. Every now and again something is won, as for instance 100 francs by a young Russian lady (wife of a Russian diplomat-cum-agent) . . . , who, in return, loses 6,000 frs, while someone else can't keep enough for the journey home; others gamble away the whole of large family fortunes; very few

take away a share of the plunder—few of the gamblers, I mean, and those that do are almost without exception rich. There can be no question of intelligence or calculation here; no one can count with any probability on being favoured by "chance" unless he can venture a considerable sum.[38]

The frenzy in the air was not confined to the gaming rooms or the evening hours; it pervaded the whole city and entire day of those who visited it. For example, there was a kiosk right next door to the casino.

This is daily adorned with a placard, not printed, but handwritten and signed with the initials of the quill-pusher; for 600 francs he will provide, in black and white, the secret of the science of winning a million francs with a 1,000. . . . Nor, or so it is said, is it by any means rare for people to fall victim to this confidence trick. Indeed, most of the gamblers, both male and female, believe there is a science in what are pure games of chance; the ladies and gentlemen sit outside the said Café de Paris, in front of, or on the seats in, the wonderful garden that belongs to the casino, heads bent over little [printed] tables, scribbling and doing sums, while one of them may earnestly expound to another "what system" he prefers, whether one should play in series, etc., etc. It's like watching a bunch of lunatics.[39]

In short, it became clear to Marx that "the economic basis of Monaco-Gerolstein is the casino; if it were to close tomorrow it would be all up with Monaco-Gerolstein—the whole of it!" Without it not even Nice, "the rendez-vous in the winter months of the quality and of fortune-hunters alike, could continue to subsist as a fashionable centre. . . . And withal, how childish is the casino by comparison with the Bourse!"

After the last in the series of vesicatories, Dr. Kunemann discharged Marx and gave him permission to continue his journey. But he did advise him to stop off "in Cannes for a day or two" to allow the wounds to "dry out," after which he could move on up to Paris. Once in the exclusive French resort, Marx drew up a balance-sheet of his time on the Côte d'Azur:

I have spent an entire month vegetating in this lair of aristocratic idlers or adventurers. Nature superb, in other respects a dreary hole; . . . no plebeian "masses" here, apart from the hotel and café waiters, etc., and domestics, who belong to the *Lumpenproletariat*.[40]

The weather continued to do its worst and to weigh heavily on him. During the three days in Cannes, there was an exceptionally "strong (if warm) wind and eddies of dust," talk of which filled "the Riviera's local press." Marx responded with self-irony, joking to Engels that "Nature, too, can evince a certain philistine humour (after the manner, already humorously anticipated in the Old Testament, of the serpent feeding on dust, cf. the dusty diet of Darwin's worms)."

In the same letter, Marx dwelled on the doctor's final recommendations: "to eat well and amply even if it goes against the grain, and 'accustom' oneself to so doing; [to] drink 'decent' stuff and go for drives, etc. . . . [to] think as little as possible, etc." He could not fail to remark that "having followed these 'directions,' I am well on the way to 'idiocy,' and for all that have not rid myself of the bronchial catarrh. A consoling thought for me is that it was bronchitis that sent old Garibaldi to his 'eternal rest.'" In any case, he was convinced that "at a certain age it becomes completely indifferent how one is 'launched into eternity.'"[41]

On 7 June, some four months after his departure from London, Marx was finally in a position to take the train back to his daughter's house in Argenteuil. He advised her not to bother about his arrival—"Till now, I have always found that nothing has done me more harm than people, at the station, waiting for me"—and not to tell any of the comrades, even Lafargue, that he was expected. He still needed "absolute quietness,"[42] and, as he said to Engels too, "he felt it [was] still necessary . . . to have as little "intercourse with people" as possible."[43] The giant was weary and felt he was close to the end of the road. The words he wrote to Jenny were much the same as those of any other mortal: "By 'quietness' I mean the 'family life,' 'the children's noise,' that 'microscopic world' more interesting than the 'macroscopic.'"[44]

Back in Argenteuil, Marx compared his existence to that of a prisoner out on leave, since he always had to "report to the doctor nearest to the place where [he took] up [his] abode."[45] The Longuets' family doctor, Gustave Dourlen, knew Marx well and advised him "for a few weeks" to "try the sulphurous waters of Enghien[-les-Bains],"[46] a nearby locality where he would be able to consult a Dr. Feugier (?).

The still-unsettled weather did not allow Marx to start the cure at once; it also contributed to a very painful "attack of rheumatism in the region of [his] hips."[47] Only in the first few days of July could he take up the advice and travel to the sulphurous baths, from which he benefited greatly. As he told Engels, the operations had to be repeated regularly:

The air in the inhalation room is murky with sulphurous vapours; 30–40 minutes' spell here; every 5 minutes, at a special table, one inhales steam laden with specially pulverised sulphur (from one of the pipes (zinc) with stopcocks); each man encased in rubber from head to foot; after which they march in file round the table; innocent scene from Dante's *Inferno*.[48]

In the afternoon, after he had returned from the baths and rested for a while, he regularly went for "a walk and pottering about with the children, with consequences more detrimental to one's faculties of sight and hearing (let alone thought) than were ever experienced even by the Hegel of the *Phenomenology*."

Despite all the efforts, the bronchial catarrh "had by no means croaked its last," and the doctors advised him to continue the cure until the middle of August. In general, however, his condition had improved, so that early in the month he even had a meeting with some leaders of the Parisian workers' movement, including José Mesa (1840–1904), Paul Lafargue, Gabriel Deville (1854–1940), and Jules Guesde. It was the first time for months that he had agreed to anything like this, and although it "went off well" he wrote to Engels that it was "always the livelier talk and/or chatter which told on him—after the event."[49]

On 20 August Marx completed his "last perambulation in the inhalation chamber." At the final consultation, Dr. Feugier told him that "the pleuritic rubbing remain[ed] in status quo; an altogether predictable circumstance" and advised him, in agreement with Dr. Dourlen, to go to Lake Geneva, "whence the weather reports have so far been favourable," in the hope that "the last traces of [his] bronchial catarrh might depart of their own accord there."[50]

This time, not being able "to set forth on this hazardous journey alone," he was accompanied by his daughter Laura, to whom he joked—comparing himself to the Ismaelite Rashīd ad-Dīn Sinān (1132/1135–1192), the head of the Assassins sect that played an important role during the Crusades—that it was "more or less [her] duty to accompany the old man of the mountain."[51]

Before he left for Switzerland, Marx received a letter from a Parisian correspondent for various German newspapers, who said that, "as [Marx's] humble and obedient servant," he would like to conduct an interview with him, since "people in all circles of German 'society' were anxious to have official news of [his] health." "Of course," he informed Engels, in English, "I did not reply to that softsawder penman."[52]

The first stage of the journey, undertaken only by day "to obviate any pretext for a relapse,"[53] took them as far as Lausanne. Marx arrived with a cold, which he had caught at a meeting in Paris with Joseph Roy, the French translator of *Capital*. Despite the favorable weather forecasts, it was "wet and relatively cold" there. "First question I asked the waiter," he told Engels, "[was] 'How long has it been raining here?' Reply: 'Only been wet for 2 days' (i.e., since the day I left Paris). It's funny!"[54]

The final destination was the town of Vevey, on the northeast shore of Lake Geneva. Marx wrote to Engels that he was "still coughing," but that everything was going well: "We are living in the Land of Cockaigne."[55] He sorely missed Engels's company and tried to persuade him to come out from London and join him. But Engels was busy dealing with all kinds of practical matters, so that he could continue underwriting Marx's recurrent need for treatment: "I'd be damned glad if I could come over and see you, but were anything to happen to me, even temporarily, all our financial arrangements would be thrown out of gear. There's not a soul here to whom I could give power of attorney or entrust what are really rather complicated cash transactions."[56] Marx understood and once more expressed his gratitude: "Your altruistic concern for me is unbeliev-able, and I am often secretly ashamed."[57]

At the end of September, after he had returned to Jenny's home in Argenteuil, Marx again visited Dr. Dourlen to ask for permission "to cross the Channel."[58] He found Marx "enormously improved [and] well on the way to ridding [himself] of this persistent catarrh." But he ordered him not to spend more than a fortnight in London, or "3 weeks if the weather [was] really fine"; the "winter campaign," as he called it, would have to "start early in the Isle of Wight." Still, Marx joked to the friend awaiting him in England, "If the French government . . . knew of my pres-ence here . . . it might, even without Dr. Dourlen's permission, send me packing."[59]

Despite this terrible period he went through in the year following his wife's death, Marx tried to pursue his researches whenever he could. Being unable to resume the unfinished work on *Capital*, he did his best to keep up-to-date on various scientific and economic subjects. Among the highlights were his ex-cerpts from Édouard Hospitalier's (1853–1907) book *Modern Physics: The Main Applications of Electricity* [*La physique moderne. Les principales applications de l'électricité*] (1882) and his interest in "the development of discoveries made in the field of electricity,"[60] including the work of Marcel Deprez (1843–1918). Reviewing the reasons for these studies, Engels recalled:

Science was for Marx a historically dynamic, revolutionary force. However great the joy with which he welcomed a new discovery in some theoretical science whose practical application perhaps it was as yet quite impossible to envisage, he experienced quite another kind of joy when the discovery involved immediate revolutionary changes in industry and in historical development in general.[61]

Marx also occupied himself with ecology. Already in April 1880 he had studied the essay "Human Labour and Unity of Force" (1880), published in *Socialist Review* by Sergei Podolinsky (1850–1891), a Ukrainian socialist he had come to know in 1872 through their mutual friend Pyotr Lavrov (1823–1900). Podolinsky sent the manuscript of his article to Marx, underlining that the "first stimulus"[62] for his work had come from the reading of *Capital*, and that he was "particularly impatient" to know its author's opinion. Podolinsky's aim was to show that socialism was the form of social organization most suited to utilize solar energy for the satisfaction of human needs. He therefore wrote to Marx that he felt obligated to make an "attempt to bring surplus labour and current physical theories into harmony."[63] In reality, as Engels wrote in a long letter to Marx on the subject in December 1882,[64] Podolinsky had discovered that "human labour is capable of retaining solar energy on the earth's surface and harnessing it for a longer period than would otherwise have been the case." However, "all the economic deductions he [drew] from this [were] wrong."[65] For Engels, Podolinsky "went astray . . . because he tried to find in the field of natural science fresh evidence of the rightness of socialism and hence confused the physical with the economic."[66]

The correspondence between Engels and Marx shows how attentive they always were to new research on environmental issues. Although, toward the end of 1882, Marx lacked the strength to reply to Engels's detailed missive, he again began to study *Outlines of Human Physiology with Reference to Health Care and the Doctor's Practical Needs* (1868) by Johannes Ranke (1836–1916), probably with a view to going more deeply into Podolinsky's ideas.[67] In the excerpts he made in 1880 from Podolinsky's article, from which we can see that he did not underestimate the importance of such matters, he had focused more on thermodynamics. On the two principles of the concept of entropy introduced by Rudolf Clausius (1822–1888) in his *Mechanical Theory of Heat* (1864), he had noted: "The energy of the universe is constant. The entropy of the universe tends towards a maximum."[68]

In this last phase of his life, Marx's openness to the natural sciences, particularly zoology and biology, as well as ecology, was certainly stimulated by his friendship with Edwin Ray Lankester (1847–1929), a fellow at Exeter College, Oxford, and curator of the Grant Museum of Zoology.[69] Not only did Lankester read *Capital* "with the greatest pleasure and profit"[70] and initiate a prolific intellectual exchange with Marx; he also felt very close to him at a human level and helped him to find suitable doctors to address the terrible health problems that continued to rain down on the family.

3. "WHAT IS CERTAIN IS THAT I AM NOT A MARXIST"

In London, the days passed quickly. On 9 October, Marx wrote to his daughter Laura that his cough was "still tiresome" and that he had "to throw it off completely if [he was] to become altogether fit for action again."[71] The arrival of autumn brought damp and cloudy weather. Dr. Donkin, who was now looking after Marx again, advised him to move back to the Isle of Wight. First, he spent a whole day with Engels—who wrote to Lafargue: "Yesterday Marx dined with me and in the evening we all had supper at his house, after which we sat together drinking rum until one o'clock."[72] Then, on 30 October, he took the train for Ventnor.

Marx's condition soon worsened again, however, because of rheumatism "very close to the former seat of [his] iterated pleurisy."[73] This forced him to get to know a local doctor, James Williamson (?), who prescribed medication with a "quinine, morphia and chloroform" base.[74] Moreover, "in order not to be too dependent on capricious variations in wind and temperature when loitering out of doors," he was "again forced to carry a respirator with [him], in case of need." Thus, after his "long period of intellectual twilight,"[75] Marx still found it impossible to devote himself to the third German edition of *Capital*. On 10 November, he wrote to his daughter Eleanor: "Under the circumstances I have not yet got down to any real work, though I have been occupying myself with one thing and another by way of preparation."[76]

Engels kept him up-to-date about the situation in London: "All is well at your house, but the beer everywhere is rotten; only the German stuff in the West End is any good."[77] But Marx could not reciprocate with positive news of his own. The cough had grown worse and an annoying hoarseness had developed on top of it. He was therefore "condemned to remain in [his] room . . . until the inflammation had passed."[78]

On 14 December, he wrote to his daughter Laura that he had "been confined to the house for the past fortnight because of a tracheal catarrh," adding that he "lived the life of a hermit." He saw no one other than Dr. Williamson,[79] who, in view of the "damp and rainy" weather, forbade him to go out "until the next fine day."[80]

Nevertheless, Marx did not fail to comment as best he could on current events and the positions of the leaders of the French workers' movement. He was "troubled" by some of the latter's "ultra-revolutionary turns of phrase, having always regarded these as 'hot air'—a speciality our people would be well-advised to leave to the so-called anarchists who are, in fact, props of the existing order, not creators of disorder."[81]

Similarly, Marx did not spare those who proved incapable of maintaining an autonomous class position, and he warned that it was absolutely necessary for the workers to oppose the institutions and rhetoric of the state. When Joseph Cowen (1829–1900), a member of Parliament and president of the Cooperative Congress—Marx considered him "the best of the English parliamentarians"— justified the British invasion of Egypt,[82] Marx expressed his total disapproval to Eleanor.

Above all, he railed at the British government: "Very nice! In fact, there could be no more blatant example of Christian hypocrisy than the 'conquest' of Egypt—conquest in the midst of peace!" But Cowen, in a speech on 8 January 1883 in Newcastle, expressed his admiration for the "heroic exploit" of the British and the "dazzle of our military parade"; nor could he "help smirking over the entrancing little prospect of all those fortified offensive positions between the Atlantic and the Indian Ocean and, into the bargain, an 'African-British Empire' from the Delta to the Cape." It was the "English style," characterized by "responsibility" for the "home interest." In foreign policy, Marx concluded, Cowen was a typical example of "those poor British bourgeois, who groan as they assume more and more 'responsibilities' in the service of their historic mission, while vainly protesting against it."[83]

Marx also took a close interest in the economic side of what was happening in Egypt, as we can see from his eight pages of excerpts from "Egyptian Finance" (1882), an article by Michael George Mulhall (1836–1900) that appeared in the October issue of the London *Contemporary Review*. His own notes concentrated on two aspects. He reconstructed the financial blackmail operated by Anglo-German creditors after the Ottoman viceroy of Egypt, Ismail Pasha (1830–1895), had dramatically plunged the country into debt. Moreover, he sketched the oppressive taxation system devised by Ismail Pasha that extracted a terrible price from the population, showing particular attention to, and solidarity with, the forced dislocation of many Egyptian peasants.[84]

Marx also resumed study of the principal texts on the continuing social and political changes in Russia. In autumn 1882, as we can see from one of his very last books of excerpts,[85] he again occupied himself with the dynamics that were transforming the economy of that country. This notebook contains a list entitled "Russian on my shelves," probably already partly compiled in 1881 and covering publications in that language that Marx had in his personal library. This makes it arguable that he intended to go more deeply into these matters if he had sufficient time and strength. In particular, Marx studied recently published Russian works on the new social-economic relations following the land reform and abolition of serfdom in 1861. These included: *The Peasantry in the Age of Empress Catherine II* (1881), by Vasilii Semevskii (1848–1916); *The Artels in Russia* (1881), by Andrei Isaev (1851–1924); *Rural Common Land in Arkhangel Province* (1882), by Gerard Mineiko (1832–1888); and *The Fate of Capitalism in Russia* (1882), an interesting collection of articles that the economist and sociologist Vasilii Vorontsov (1847–1918) had published in *Otechestvennye Zapiski* since 1879. Vorontsov was one of the first Russian scholars to have discovered the importance of Marx's work, and partly thanks to his reading of *Capital* he distanced himself from Mikhailovsky's critique of the division of labor.[86] Vorontsov also occupied himself with the vexed question of how socialists should relate to economic backwardness, and in his book he argued that Russian industry should use "all the forms which have been created in the West, and, therefore, can develop very rapidly without passing at snail's pace through all the successive stages." Opting for the thesis of the so-called privileges of backwardness, Vorontsov argued that nations "which are latecomers to the arena of history" benefit from the "accumulated historical experience of other countries" and do not have to make strenuous efforts to reach instinctively what those others have already achieved. They could do it "consciously," not "groping in the dark but knowing what should be avoided."[87]

In addition to these volumes published in the early 1880s, Marx studied older works such as *The Peasant Question in the Age of Alexander II* (1862) by Aleksandr Skrebitzkii (1827–1915), and *On the Periphery and in the Capital* (1870) by Fyodor Elenev (1827–1902), who used the *nom de plume* Skaldin. He also began rereading the *Unaddressed Letters* of Chernyshevsky, which, though written in 1862, were published in London because of the Russian censorship, and only in 1874 thanks to an initiative of Pyotr Lavrov.[88]

Alongside all this reading, Marx's most important work concerning Russia was the manuscript "Notes on the Reform of 1861 and the Related Development in Russia" that he wrote between the end of 1881 and October 1882.[89]

These pages on the repercussions of the abolition of serfdom drew heavily on information contained in Danielson's "Sketches of Our Post-Reform Social Economy," but Marx also consulted other writings and numerous official publications, including statistics and economic data. His own text was divided into four parts, corresponding to the main questions of interest to him: I. Preparations for the Reform; II. Three work periods of the drafting commissions; III. Zemstvo; and IV. Russia. The ongoing changes in Russia continued to fascinate him until he had sufficient energy to devote to research.

During this period, some articles published in St. Petersburg "show[ed] the great run of [Marx's] theories in that country," and he told his daughter Laura that "nowhere was [his] success more delightful" to him, since "it [gave him] the satisfaction that [he was damaging] a power, which, besides England, [was] the true bulwark of the old society."[90]

On the other hand, no one escaped Marx's criticism. After the birth of the French Workers' Party, in September 1882, he raged to Engels about the husbands of his two elder daughters: "Longuet as the last Proudhonist and Lafargue as the last Bakuninist! The devil take them!"[91] And in a similar vein, he more than once attacked those who claimed to be following his ideas, wittily noting: "What is certain is that I am not a Marxist [*Ce qu'il y a de certain c'est que moi, je ne suis pas Marxiste*]."[92]

4. LEAVING THE STAGE

Marx could not closely follow developments in the European workers' movement, nor make further progress with his theoretical work. Although he had made every effort to get "fighting fit" again, and although he asked Eleanor to bring some books during her visit at the end of the year—the "*Physiology* by Ranke [and Edward] Freeman's (1823–1892) rotten little book (*History of Europe*) (1876), . . . in lieu of a chronological table"[93]—the shakiness of his health and worries about his daughter Jenny's physical condition after the birth of her latest child helped to make his situation increasingly desperate.

On 6 January, he reported to Dr. Williamson that, on rising, he had "got suddenly into a spasmodic cough, gasping, wrestling as if it were with suffocation." He was in no doubt about the significance of this sudden turn. The previous afternoon, he had received a letter with terrible news about his firstborn: "I knew of course that her illness was serious, but I was not prepared to hear that it passes now through a critical phasis."[94]

He also confessed to Engels that he thought he had "been going to choke," and that "nowadays, any sort of nervous excitement immediately grip[ped] [him] by the throat."[95] To Eleanor he wrote:

> I believe it was due to nervous irritation—my anxiety over Jennychen! . . . I would have hastened to Argenteuil at once, but for the possibility of saddling the child with the extra burden of a sick visitor! For no one can guarantee that the journey would [not] have punished me with a relapse such as I have so far fortunately escaped. All the same, it's hard not being able to go and see her.[96]

Marx, then, was enduring another "long confinement to the house";[97] the "semi-permanent cough," which was "tiresome enough," combined with "daily bouts of vomiting" to make the situation almost unbearable for him.[98] But it did not seem completely out of the question that he would recover his health. To Eleanor he complained that his state "frequently ma[de] work impossible," but he also said that "the doctor believes—he still believes and that is something!—he can rid me of this torment (with the help of a little remedy he has just prescribed). Those who will live will see."

However, the death of his beloved Jenny on 11 January, from cancer of the liver, erased any such hopes. Coming on top of his wife's death, this latest blow struck at a man already gravely ill and marked by hardships. Eleanor's later narrative is unique testimony to his state at the time:

> We had received a letter from the Moor . . . , in which he wrote that Jenny's health was finally improving and that we—Helene [Demuth] and I—should not be worried. We got the telegram announcing Jenny's death barely an hour after this letter. I left at once for Ventnor. I have lived through many sad hours, but none like that one. I felt I was taking my father his death sentence. In the long hours of that harrowing journey, I continued to wrack my brains thinking of how I should tell him the news. But there was no need to say anything: my face gave me away. The Moor immediately said: "Our little Jenny is dead!"—and he wanted to leave for Paris straight away, to help with holding the babies. I wanted to stay with him, but he brooked no opposition. I had been in Ventnor for just half an hour, and I was already on my way back to London with a sad and heavy heart, only to leave then at once for Paris. For the good of the babies, I did as the Moor wished.[99]

On 13 January, Marx too hurriedly set off for London. Before he left the Isle of Wight, he explained to Dr. Williamson that the reason was "the fatal news of the death of [his] oldest daughter," adding: "I find some relief in a grim headache. Physical pain is the only 'stunner' of mental pain."[100] These were the last words he would ever put on paper.

Thanks to Engels's correspondence, however, we are able to reconstruct many details of the last weeks of Marx's life. From a letter to Bernstein, we learn that after his return from Ventnor, Marx was "confined to the house with bronchitis—so far, luckily, only a mild attack."[101] And on 8 February, he further wrote to Bernstein that "for the past three weeks" Marx had been "so hoarse that he [could] barely speak."[102] At the time, Bernstein was the leader of German social democracy with whom Engels kept most regularly in touch, both because of his role as director of the journal *The Social Democrat* [*Der Socialdemocrat*] and because of the earlier conflicts between Engels and Wilhelm Liebknecht (1826–1900).

On 16 February, Engels wrote to Laura: "Latterly he [Marx] has had very bad sleepless nights which have broken down his intellectual appetite, so that he began to read, instead of novels, publisher's catalogues." And the next day, he added that it was "anyhow a good sign" that Marx had "given up the catalogues and returned to Frédéric Soulié[103] [1800–1847]," one of the most popular French writers before 1848. Still, Engels remained apprehensive: "The worst is that his case is so complicated that while the most pressing things, the breathing organs, have to be attended to, and now and then a sleeping draft is to be given, other things have to be neglected, for instance the stomach."[104]

At the end of the month, Engels sent another update to Bernstein: "Marx is still incapable of work, keeps to his room and reads French novels. His case seems to be a very complicated one."[105] The following week he noted to August Bebel that Marx's health was "still not really making the progress it should."[106] Finally, on 10 March, he wrote to Laura after a checkup by Dr. Donkin: "[He] saw Moor yesterday evening and I am glad to say gave a far more favorable account of his health than a fortnight ago. He said Moor was decidedly not worse, but better, if anything, than then." However, Marx was "still getting weaker, on account of the difficulty of swallowing," and that "we must force him to eat and drink."[107]

Things soon took a turn for the worse, as Marx's body went into rapid decline and he developed an abscess on the lung. Engels began to worry that the end was truly nigh for his lifelong friend: "Every morning for the past six weeks, as I turned the corner, I was mortally afraid that the blinds might have been lowered." What he feared soon came to pass, at 2.45 p.m. on 14 March 1883.[108]

The most complete account, in the most moving words, is the one he gave to Friedrich Sorge, the comrade who had become secretary of the International Working Men's Association after it moved to the United States in 1872:

> Yesterday, at half past two in the afternoon, his best time for receiving visitors, I arrived to find the household in tears; it seemed as if he was nearing his end. . . . There had been a slight haemorrhage, followed, however, by a sudden collapse. Our good old Lenchen, who has looked after him better than a mother would after her child, went upstairs, came down again: he was half asleep, she said, and invited me to come up with her. When we went in, he lay there sleeping, never to wake again. His pulse and breathing had stopped. In the space of two minutes he had passed away painlessly and peacefully.[109]

For all the pain at the loss of his dearest friend, Engels saw at once the implications of Marx's irreversible condition:

> All events, however terrible they may be, that come about with natural inevitability, bear within them their own consolation. So it was here. The art of medicine might, perhaps, have been able to secure for him a few years of vegetable-like existence, the life of a helpless creature, not dying suddenly but inch by inch, a triumphant testimony to the skill of the doctors. But that is something our Marx could never have stood. To live with so many uncompleted works before him, with the tantalising desire to complete them and the impossibility of doing so—that would have been a thousand times more bitter for him than the gentle death that overtook him. "Death is not a misfortune for the one that dies but for the one that survives," as he used to say with Epicurus. And to see this powerful man of genius continue to vegetate, a total wreck, for the greater glory of medicine and as a laughing-stock for the philistines whom, at the height of his powers, he had so often felled to the ground—no! A thousand times better that it should be as it is, a thousand times better that we should bear him the day after tomorrow to the grave in which his wife lies sleeping.[110] And after all that had gone before, with which not even the doctors are as familiar as I am, there could, in my view, have been only one choice.[111] Be that as it may.

Mankind is the poorer for the loss of this intellect—the most important intellect, indeed, which it could boast today. The movement of the proletariat will continue on its course but it has lost its focal point, the point to which Frenchmen, Russians, Americans and Germans would automatically turn at moments of crisis, on every occasion receiving clear, indisputable advice such as only genius and consummate expertise can give. Local bigwigs and lesser luminaries, if not imposters, will be given a free hand. Ultimate victory remains assured, but the digressions, the temporary and local aberrations—already so inevitable—will now proliferate as never before. Well, we have got to see it through[112]—what else are we here for? But we're not going to lose heart, for all that—not by a long chalk.[113]

This is just what happened after Marx's death, as so many others raised his banners. From Latin America to the Far East, in trade union offices on the impoverished periphery or great halls of prestigious universities, tens of millions of workers and students would read his writings, gaining from them an understanding of the condition of the oppressed, finding inspiration to engage in fresh struggles and to organize strikes, social movements, and political parties. They would fight for bread and roses, against injustice and for freedom, and in so doing would keep Marx's theories fully actual.

In the course of this long process—during which Marx was studied in depth, transformed into an icon, embalmed in official manuals, misunderstood, censured, pronounced dead, and from time to time discovered anew—there were some who turned his ideas on their head, with doctrines and practices that he would have resolutely combated in his lifetime. Others, however, enriched his ideas, brought them up-to-date, and drew out some of the problems and contradictions in them, with the same kind of critical spirit that he himself adopted and would have greatly appreciated.

Those who look through Marx's writings again today, or who turn to them for the first time, cannot but be fascinated by the capacity of his social-economic analyses to explain the world. Nor can they fail to be impressed by the message that radiates incessantly from the whole of his work: organize the struggle to end the bourgeois mode of production and to achieve the emancipation of the workers of the world from the domination of capital.

CHRONOLOGY, 1881–1883

1881

January–late June	During these months in London, Marx finished some summaries he had begun in late 1880 of works by H. Morgan, J. Money, J. Phear, and H. Maine. The *Ethnological Notebooks* containing this material amount to approximately two hundred pages. At the same time, he occupied himself with differential calculus in the *Mathematical Notebooks*. From the second half of February until 8 March he wrote the preliminary drafts and the letter to Vera Zasulich on the rural commune in Russia.
Last week in June to approx. 19 July	Stay in Eastbourne with his wife Jenny von Westphalen.
20–25 July approx.	Return to London and preparations for departure to France.
26 July to 16 August	Visit to eldest daughter Jenny Longuet in the Paris suburb of Argenteuil, together with his wife and Helene Demuth.
17 August to 28 December	Return to London. Immersion in deep historical studies and extensive extracts from works by F. Schlosser and C. Botta. The result was the *Chronological Extracts*, a huge annotated synthesis of more than 550 pages dealing with the main

	political events from 91 BC to the Treaty of West-phalia in 1648. While caring constantly for his sick wife, he spent his spare time reading recent books on Russia and resumed his mathematical studies. After mid-October, attacks of pleurisy and bronchitis immobilized him for roughly two months.
2 December	Death of his wife.
29–31 December	Journey to Ventnor on the Isle of Wight with his youngest daughter Eleanor, in search of a milder climate.

1882

1–15 January	Stay in Ventnor continued.
16 January to 8 February	Back in London to consult doctors about the most effective treatment for his condition. On 21 January, Marx and Engels completed the preface to the Russian edition of the *Manifesto of the Communist Party*.
9–16 February	Departure for Algeria. Still accompanied by Eleanor, he stopped off at his daughter Jenny's in Argenteuil.
17 February	Marx continued the trip alone. Having crossed France, he stayed one night in Marseilles.
18–19 February	Crossing to Africa on the steamship *Said*: destination Algiers.
20 February to 2 May	Stay in Algerian capital, where a recurrence of his old bronchitis and an attack of pleurisy forced him into another two long months of painful treatment.
3–4 May	Return crossing to France, following an improvement in his medical condition.
5 May	Landed in Marseilles on his sixty-fourth birthday; visited Nice briefly.
6 May to 3 June	Stay in Monte Carlo, made necessary by another worsening of his health and the need to undergo further treatment.

4–7 June	Brief visit to Cannes, following his doctor's advice, before the journey from Marseilles to Paris.
8 June to 22 August	Visit to his daughter Jenny in Argenteuil. From early July to 20 August, a course of thermal treatment in Enghien-les-Bains.
23 August to 27 September	Trip to Switzerland with his daughter Laura. A brief stay in Lausanne, then four weeks at Vevey on Lake Geneva. Stopped off in Geneva on the return journey.
28 September to 6 October	Back in France. Stayed with his daughter Laura in Paris, then briefly at Jenny's home in Argenteuil.
7 October	Return to England.
8–29 October	Again in London for three weeks, he compiled extracts from texts on economics and anthropology. He also worked on a manuscript on post-1861 Russia.
30 October to 31 December	Another period in Ventnor, where he tried with great difficulty to regain his health and resume work.

1883

1–12 January	Further stay in Ventnor, where on the 12th he received news of his daughter Jenny's death.
13 January to 13 March	Grief-stricken, he immediately returned to London. His condition suddenly grew worse because of a lung abscess. With his little remaining strength, he consulted book catalogues and read French novels.
14 March	Died of heart failure caused by pulmonary tuberculosis, at home.

NOTES

Introduction

1. Boris Nicolaevsky and Otto Maenchen-Helfen, *Karl Marx: Man and Fighter* (London: Pelican Books, 1976), IX.

2. One of the recent works marking this renaissance is Marcello Musto, ed., *The Marx Revival: Essential Concepts and New Interpretations* (Cambridge: Cambridge University Press, 2020).

3. On the vicissitudes of the publication history of Marx's work, see Marcello Musto, "The Rediscovery of Karl Marx," *International Review of Social History* 52, no. 3 (2007): 477–498.

4. Karl Marx, "Afterword to the Second German Edition," in Marx, *Capital, Volume I*, MECW, 35:17; "Nachwort zur zweiten Auflage," in Marx, *Das Kapital. Erster Band*, MEW, 23:15.

5. Karl Marx, "Provisional Rules of the International Working Men's Association," MECW, 20:14; "Provisorische Statuten der Internationalen Arbeiter-Assoziation," MEW, 16:14.

6. Karl Marx, *Critique of the Gotha Programme*, MECW, 24:87; *Kritik des Gothaer Programms*, MEW, 19:21.

7. Cf. the section "Chronology of Marx's Writings," in Marcello Musto, *Another Marx: Early Manuscripts to the International* (London: Bloomsbury, 2018), 7–11.

8. Cf. Maximilien Rubel, *Marx, critique du marxisme* (Paris: Payot, 1974), 439–440.

9. One of the most striking examples of this division of labor is Franz Mehring's request to Rosa Luxemburg that she write the section on *Capital, Volumes II and III*, for his book *Karl Marx: The Story of His Life* (Ann Arbor: University of Michigan Press, 1962): see "Author's Introduction," XIII.

10. On the excessive weight that many exegetes have given to Marx's early writings, see Marcello Musto, "The Myth of the 'Young Marx' in the Interpretations of the *Economic and Philosophic Manuscripts of 1844*," *Critique* 43, no. 2 (2015): 233–260.

11. See, for example, Mehring, chap. 15, "The Last Decade," in *Karl Marx*, 501–532; Otto Rühle, "The Evening and the End," in *Karl Marx: His Life and Work* (New York: Routledge, 2011), 359–370; Karl Vorländer, chap. 19, "Relations to the Social Movement," and chap. 20, "The Final Period of Suffering—Death—Marx's Personality," in

Karl Marx (Leipzig: F. Meiner, 1929), 248–260 and 261–278; Boris Nicolaevsky and Otto Maenchen-Helfen, chap. 21, "The Last Ten Years," in *Karl Marx: Man and Fighter*, 392–407; and David McLellan, chap. 8, "The Last Decade," in *Karl Marx: His Life and His Thought* (London: Macmillan, 1973), 412–451. Even Maximilien Rubel, justly famed for his close textual studies, did not go beyond the limits of his predecessors in *Karl Marx. Essai de biographie intellectuelle* (Paris: Rivière, 1957), 416–434. In Maximilien Rubel, *Marx: Life and Works* (London: Macmillan, 1980), the French scholar wrote that "the last ten years of Marx's life were like a slow agony" during which "his activity [was] limited to correspondence and a few articles." But he added: "Nevertheless—even in a period so poor in published work—Marx filled about 50 notebooks, almost exclusively devoted to extracts from his reading. His 'literary bulimia' yielded nearly 3,000 pages of microscopic writing. To this should be added, finally, 'tons' of statistical material which, at his death, left Engels dumbfounded" (ibid., 100).

12. Biographies published in recent years exemplify how, even since the resumption of the MEGA^2 project, the work of the "late Marx" has been overlooked by the vast majority of scholars. Jonathan Sperber's insignificant *Karl Marx: A Nineteenth-Century Life* (New York: Liveright, 2013) simply ignored Marx's late writings. Gareth Stedman Jones's lengthy *Karl Marx: Greatness and Illusion* (Cambridge, MA: Harvard University Press, 2016) examined the whole period from 1872 to 1883 only in a short epilogue, while devoting five chapters (170 pages) to Marx's early life (1818–1844), when he published only two journal articles and had just initiated the study of political economy, and three chapters (150 pages) to the time frame 1845–1849. In Sven-Eric Liedman's 750-page *A World to Win: The Life and Works of Karl Marx* (London: Verso, 2018), there are only two very short sections dedicated to what Marx did after the *Critique of the Gotha Programme*. One of them—a superficial analysis of Morgan's *Ancient Society* (Liedman, *A World to Win*, 507–513)—is strangely located before the consideration of writings like *Herr Vogt* (published in 1860) and Marx's participation in the International Working Men's Association (1864–1872). The choice of a nonchronological order impedes a clear understanding of Marx's theoretical evolution during the final phase of his life. Common to all three of these biographies is a scant attention to the secondary literature. Finally, this tendency is not absent from Gregory Claeys's very interesting work *Marx and Marxism* (London: Penguin, 2018), in which everything that happened between 1872 and 1883 is compressed into the brief chapter "Marx's Mature System," despite the fact that the late Marx had very little that can be described as systematic (ibid., 203–215).

13. An important milestone will be the publication of the volume edited by David Smith, *Marx's World: Global Society and Capital Accumulation in Marx's Late Manuscripts* (New Haven, CT: Yale University Press, forthcoming 2021).

14. Rubel, *Karl Marx. Essai de biographie intellectuelle*, 3.

Prelude: "Struggle!"

1. See the chapter "John Swinton, Crusading Editor," in Sender Garin, *Three American Radicals: John Swinton, Charles P. Steinmetz, and William Dean Howells* (Boulder, CO: Westview Press, 1991), 1–41.

2. See the police report "Declaration by Karl Marx on His Naturalisation in England," MECW, 24:564.

3. See Karl Marx to Friedrich Sorge, 27 September 1877, MECW, 45:278; MEW, 34:296.

4. Karl Marx to Ferdinand Domela Nieuwenhuis, 27 June 1880, MECW, 46:16; MEW, 34:447.

5. Karl Marx to Nikolai Danielson, 12 September 1880, MECW, 46:30; MEW, 34:463.

6. Ibid.; ibid.

7. Karl Marx, "[Account of an Interview with John Swinton, Correspondent of *The Sun*]," 6 September 1880, MECW, 24:585; as John Swinton, "Account of an Interview with Karl Marx: Published in the 'Sun,'" MEGA^2, I/25:442–443.

8. Ibid., MECW, 24:583; ibid., MEGA^2, I/25:442.

9. Ibid.; ibid.

10. Ibid., MECW, 24:584; ibid.

11. Ibid., MECW, 24:585; ibid., MEGA^2, I/25:443.

Chapter 1: New Research Horizons

1. For a description of Marx's previous study at No. 1 Maitland Park Road, see Paul Lafargue, in *Reminiscences of Marx and Engels*, ed. Institute of Marxism-Leninism (Moscow: Foreign Languages Publishing House, 1957), 73–74.

2. See Hans-Peter Harstick, Richard Sperl, and Hanno Strauß, "Einführung," in *Die Bibliotheken von Karl Marx und Friedrich Engels*, Karl Marx and Friedrich Engels, MEGA^2, IV/32:73. This volume of more than 730 pages, which is the fruit of seventy-five years of research, includes an index of 1,450 books (2,100 volumes)—two-thirds of the total belonging to Marx and Engels (2,100 books in 3,200 volumes)—as well as a listing of all the book pages to which he appended notes. It also contains references to Marx's marginal comments on 40,000 pages of 830 texts.

3. The "blue books," so called because of their blue binding, were reports by parliamentary commissions on social issues and aspects of industrial life in various countries. Marx made great use of them for his work on *Capital*.

4. "Account of Karl Marx's Interview with the *Chicago Tribune* Correspondent," *Chicago Tribune*, 5 January 1879, MECW, 24:569; "Interview mit dem Grundleger des modernen Sozialismus. Besondere Korrespondenz der 'Tribune,'" 5 Januar 1879, MEW, 34:508–509.

5. Lafargue, in *Reminiscences of Marx and Engels*, ed. Institute of Marxism-Leninism, 73–75. On Marx's vast literary interests and knowledge, see Siebert S. Prawer, *Karl Marx and World Literature* (London: Verso, 2011), in particular 384–385.

6. Lafargue, in *Reminiscences of Marx and Engels*, ed. Institute of Marxism-Leninism, 73.

7. Karl Marx to Laura and Paul Lafargue, 11 April 1868, MECW, 43:10; MEW, 32:545.

8. Karl Marx, *A Contribution to the Critique of Political Economy*, MECW, 29:264; *Zur Kritik der politischen Ökonomie*, MEW, 13:9.

9. A year after Marx's death, Engels wrote to Laura Lafargue on 16 February 1884: "We have got the old 'storehouse' at last cleared out, found a whole lot of things that have to be kept, but about half a ton of old newspapers that it is impossible to sort. . . . Amongst the manuscripts there is the first version of *Capital* (1861–63) and there I find several hundred pages: *Theories of Surplus Value*," MECW 47:104.

10. Lafargue, in *Reminiscences of Marx and Engels*, ed. Institute of Marxism-Leninism, 74.

11. Henry Hyndman, *The Record of an Adventurous Life* (London: Macmillan, 1911), 250.

12. Lafargue, in *Reminiscences of Marx and Engels*, ed. Institute of Marxism-Leninism, 73.

13. See Asa Briggs and John Callow, *Marx in London: An Illustrated Guide* (London: Lawrence and Wishart, 2008), 62–65.

14. Marian Comyn, "My Recollections of Marx," *The Nineteenth Century and After* 91 (1922): 165.

15. In July 1870, as joint inheritor of the sewing-thread producer, Ermen & Engels, Friedrich Engels sold his share in the business and received sufficient capital to guarantee a decent living for himself and the Marx family.

16. Karl Marx to Nikolai Danielson, 19 February 1881, MECW, 46:61; MEW, 35:154.

17. Karl Kautsky, in *Gespräche mit Marx und Engels*, ed. Hans Magnus Enzensberger (Frankfurt: Insel, 1973), 556.

18. Marian Comyn, "My Recollections of Marx," 163.

19. Cf. Karl Marx to Jenny Longuet, 11 April 1881, MECW, 46:82; MEW, 35:178.

20. Cf. Marian Comyn, "My Recollections of Marx," 161.

21. Karl Marx to Jenny Longuet, 11 April 1881, MECW, 46:82; MEW, 35:178.

22. "Sir Mountstuart Elphinstone Grant Duff's Account of a Talk with Karl Marx: From a Letter to Crown Princess Victoria," 1 February 1879, MECW, 24:580; "Sir Mountstuart Elphinstone Grant Duff, Account of a Talk with Karl Marx: Aus einem Brief an Kronprinzessin Victoria," MEGA² I/25:438.

23. Edward Bernstein, *My Years of Exile* (London: Leonard Parsons, 1921), 156.

24. Kautsky, in *Gespräche mit Marx und Engels*, ed. Enzensberger, 556.

25. Ibid., 558.

26. Ibid., 556.

27. Marian Comyn, "My Recollections of Marx," 161.

28. Karl Marx to Nikolai Danielson, 19 February 1881, MECW, 46:60; MEW, 35:154.

29. Ibid., MECW, 46:61; ibid.

30. These were the diminutives that Marx used for his three grandsons: Jean, Henri (1878–1883), and Edgar Longuet (1879–1950). The youngest later recalled that his grandfather "played with children as if he were a child himself, without worrying in the slightest that it might undermine his authority. In the local streets he was called 'Papa Marx.' He always carried sweets in his pocket to give to children. Later, he transferred

this love to his grandchildren." Edgar Longuet, in *Gespräche mit Marx und Engels*, ed. Enzensberger, 579. August Bebel (1840–1913) recalled that Marx "knew how to play with the two grandchildren and how much love he had for them" (August Bebel, ibid., 528); Wilhelm Liebknecht noted that "for Marx the company of children was a need: it was at once refreshing and restorative" (Wilhelm Liebknecht, in ibid., 541); and Hyndman also observed that "children liked him and he played with them as friends" (Hyndman, *Adventurous Life*, 259).

31. Karl Marx to Jenny Longuet, 11 April 1881, MECW, 46:81; MEW, 35:177.

32. Karl Marx to Jenny Longuet, 29 April 1881, MECW, 46:89; MEW, 35:186.

33. Karl Marx to John Swinton, 2 June 1881, MECW, 46:93; MEW, 35:191.

34. Friedrich Engels to Jenny Longuet, 31 May 1881, MECW, 46:77; MEW, 35:188.

35. Karl Marx to Jenny Longuet, 6 June 1881, MECW, 46:95; MEW, 35:194.

36. Karl Marx to Nikolai Danielson, 19 September 1879, MECW, 45:409; MEW, 34:409. Marx's letters to Kovalevsky have not been preserved because a colleague of the Russian historian destroyed them for fear that the police would find them in a raid.

37. See Lawrence Krader, *The Asiatic Mode of Production: Sources, Development and Critique in the Writings of Karl Marx* (Assen: Van Gorcum, 1975), 343.

38. Karl Marx, "Excerpts from M. M. Kovalevskij (Kovalevsky), *Obschinnoe zemlevladenie. Prichiny, khod i posledstviya ego razlozheniya* [Communal landownership: The causes, course and consequences of its decline]," in Lawrence Krader, *The Asiatic Mode of Production: Sources, Development and Critique in the Writings of Karl Marx*, 28 (Assen: Van Gorcum, 1975); "Exzerpte aus M. M. Kovalevskij. Obschinnoe zemlevladenie (Der Gemeindelandbesitz)," in Karl Marx, *Über Formen vorkapitalistischer Produktion. Vergleichende Studien zur Geschichte des Grundeigentums 1879–80*, 21–109. Frankfurt: Campus, 1977. A section of Marx's notes bearing on Kovalevsky, which includes some of the quotations given here, has not yet been translated into English.

39. Ibid., 29.

40. Ibid., 38. Kevin Anderson, *Marx at the Margins: On Nationalism, Ethnicity, and Non-Western Societies* (Chicago: University of Chicago Press, 2010), has suggested that the difference with India is partly due to the fact that "India was colonized in a later period by an advanced capitalist power, Britain, which actively tried to create individual private property in the villages" (ibid., 223–224).

41. Marx, "Excerpts from M. M. Kovalevsky, 388; "Exzerpte aus M. M. Kovalevskij," 82. Anderson, *Marx at the Margins*, related them to the significance of "India's communal forms" for Marx as "potential sites of resistance to colonialism and capital" (ibid., 233).

42. The act whereby a free man places himself in a relation of dependence (entailing certain obligations of service) on a superior power in return for "protection" or recognition of his property in land.

43. Cf. Marx, "Excerpts from M. M. Kovalevsky," 383; "Exzerpte aus M. M. Kovalevskij," 76.

44. Ibid., 376; ibid., 69. For an analysis of Kovalevsky's positions, and of certain differences with those of Marx, see the chapter "Kovalevsky on the Village Community and

Land-Ownership in the Orient," in Krader, *The Asiatic Mode of Production*, 190–213. Cf. Peter Hudis, "Accumulation, Imperialism, and Pre-Capitalist Formations: Luxemburg and Marx on the Non-Western World," *Socialist Studies* VI, no. 2 (2010): 84.

45.   According to Hans-Peter Harstick, "Einführung. Karl Marx und die zeitgenössische Verfassungsgeschichtsschreibung," in Marx, *Über Formen vorkapitalistischer Produktion*, Marx favored "a differentiated analysis of Asian and European history and directed his polemic . . . mainly against those who simply transposed social-structural concepts from the West European model to Indian or Asiatic social relations" (ibid., XIII).

46.   Marx, "Excerpts from M. M. Kovalevsky," 405; "Exzerpte aus M. M. Kovalevskij," 100. The words in parentheses are Marx's, while those between quotation marks are from the *Annales de l'Assemblée nationale du 1873*, VIII, Paris 1873, included in Kovalevsky's book.

47.   Marx, "Excerpts from M. M. Kovalevsky," 405; "Exzerpte aus M. M. Kovalevskij," 100–101.

48.   Ibid., 411; ibid., 107.

49.   Ibid., 412; ibid., 109.

50.   Ibid., 408 and 412; ibid., 103 and 108.

51.   Ibid., 412; ibid., 109.

52.   According to Krader, *The Asiatic Mode of Production*, the notes on Kovalevsky contain Marx's refutation of "the application of the theory of feudal society to India and Algeria" (ibid., 343).

53.   James White, *Marx and Russia: The Fate of a Doctrine* (London: Bloomsbury, 2018), 37–40.

54.   Karl Marx, *Notes on Indian History (664–1858)* (Honolulu: University Press of the Pacific, 2001), 58.

55.   Ibid., 165, 176, 180.

56.   Ibid., 155–156, 163.

57.   Ibid., 81.

58.   According to Anderson, *Marx at the Margins*, "these passages indicate a shift from [Marx's] 1853 view of Indian passivity in the face of conquest"; he "often ridicules or excises . . . passages from Sewell portraying the British conquest of India as a heroic fight against Asiatic barbarism." Since the articles on the Sepoy revolt, which Marx published in the *New-York Tribune* in 1857, his "sympathy" for the Indian resistance had "only increased" (ibid., 216, 218).

59.   Marx, *Notes on Indian History (664–1858)*, 163–164, 184.

60.   Karl Marx, "Exzerpte aus Werken von Lothar Meyer, Henry Enfield Roscoe, Carl Schorlemmer, Benjamin Witzschel, Wilhelm Friedrich Kühne, Ludimar Hermann, Johannes Ranke und Joseph Beete Jukes," MEGA², IV/31: 21–442.

61.   Marx, "Marginal Notes on Adolph Wagner's *Lehrbuch der politischen Ökonomie*," MECW, 24:546; "Randglossen zu Adolph Wagners *Lehrbuch der politischen Ökonomie*," MEW, 19:370.

62.   Ibid., MECW, 24:534; ibid., MEW, 19:358.

63. Ibid., MECW, 24:537; ibid., MEW, 19:361.

64. Ibid., MECW, 24:538; ibid., MEW, 19:362.

65. Adolph Wagner, *Lehrbuch der politischen Ökonomie* (Leipzig: Winter, 1879–1899), 45; quoted in Marx, "Marginal Notes," MECW, 24:533; MEW, 19:357.

66. Marx, "Marginal Notes," MECW, 24:535; MEW, 19:359.

67. Ibid., MECW, 24:546; ibid., MEW, 19:370.

68. Wagner, *Lehrbuch der politischen Ökonomie*, 45–46; quoted in Marx, "Marginal Notes," MECW, 24:535; MEW, 19:359.

69. Marx, "Marginal Notes," MECW, 24:536, ibid., MEW, 19:360.

70. Wagner, *Lehrbuch der politischen Ökonomie*, 45–46; quoted in Marx, "Marginal Notes," MECW, 24:535; ibid., MEW, 19:359.

71. Marx, "Marginal Notes," MECW, 24:535; ibid.

72. Wagner, *Lehrbuch der politischen Ökonomie*, 105; quoted in Marx, "Marginal Notes," MECW, 24:556; MEW, 19:380.

73. In 1918, in his *Karl Marx: The Story of His Life*, Franz Mehring (1846–1919) described the claim that Marx's final decade was "a slow death" as "greatly exaggerated" (ibid., 501). But he also asserted incorrectly that "since 1878 he had done nothing further to complete his main work" (ibid., 526). David Ryazanov (1870–1938) showed in 1923 that "although in 1881–1883 he lost some of his faculty for creative work, he never lost his appetite and capacity for research." David Ryazanov, "Neueste Mitteilungen über den literarischen Nachlaß von Karl Marx und Friedrich Engels," in *Archiv für die Geschichte des Sozialismus und der Arbeiterbewegung* 11 (1925): 386. In 1929, in his *Karl Marx* (Leipzig: F. Meiner, 1929), Karl Vorländer (1860–1928) stated that "for a man who matured so early, but who had suffered so many trials, physical old age set in earlier than for many others" (ibid., 248), adding that "from 1878 he felt more often and to an ever greater extent incapable of work" (ibid., 261). A decade later, Isaiah Berlin (1909–1997) echoed: "He wrote less and less, his style grew more crabbed and obscure." Isaiah Berlin, *Karl Marx: His Life and Environment* (London: Oxford University Press, 1963), 280. The last period of Marx's labors was certainly difficult, and often tortuous, but it was also very important theoretically.

74. Karl Marx to Nikolai Danielson, 19 February 1881, MECW, 46:61; MEW, 35:154.

75. This title was given posthumously by Lawrence Krader (1919–1998), the editor of these manuscripts. However, the content of these studies is more accurately related to anthropology, hence the title of the section in the present chapter.

76. The parts from Phear and Maine were included in Karl Marx, *The Ethnological Notebooks of Karl Marx*, ed. Lawrence Krader (Assen: Van Gorcum, 1972), 243–336; *Die ethnologischen Exzerpthefte*, ed. Lawrence Krader (Berlin: Suhrkamp, 1976), 361–500. Marx did not leave a precise dating of his work. Krader, the main researcher of these texts, argued that Marx first familiarized himself with Morgan's book and then compiled the excerpts—see "Addenda," in ibid., 87. See also Kautsky's testimony from his trip to London in March–June 1881 that "prehistory and ethnology were then intensively preoccupying Marx." Kautsky, *Gespräche mit Marx und Engels*, ed. Enzensberger, 552.

77. According to Maurice Bloch, *Marxism and Anthropology: The History of a Relationship* (London: Routledge, 1983), Marx wanted first of all "to reconstruct a general history and theory of society in order to explain the coming to be of capitalism." But he also had a "rhetorical" interest linked to the need for "examples and cases to show that the institutions of capitalism are historically specific and therefore changeable." However, this second "rhetorical use of anthropological material was never completely separate from the historical use, and the mixture of the two became . . . the source of many problems" (ibid., 10). Pierre Dardot and Christian Laval, *Marx, prénom Karl* (Paris: Gallimard, 2012), have written that "Marx's main effort in his final years was to give a new historical foundation to the perspective of communism, at the risk of seriously endangering a theoretical edifice constructed on the basis of the nineteenth-century evolutionist and progressivist *episteme*" (ibid., 667). Polemicizing against those who underrate the importance of Marx's last notebooks, Heather Brown argued in *Marx on Gender and the Family: A Critical Study* (Leiden: Brill, 2012) that they "contain some of his most creative attempts at working through the development of human society" (ibid., 147).

78. The gens was a unit "consisting of blood relatives with a common descent." see Henry Morgan, *Ancient Society* (New York: Henry Holt, 1877), 35.

79. Hyndman, *Adventurous Life*, 253–254.

80. Morgan, *Ancient Society*, 515.

81. Ibid., 472.

82. Marx, *The Ethnological Notebooks*, 115; *Die ethnologischen Exzerpthefte*, 153.

83. Ibid., 292; ibid., 430.

84. Ibid., 309; ibid., 456.

85. Ibid., 324; ibid., 479.

86. Ibid., 281; ibid., 417.

87. Morgan, *Ancient Society*, 469.

88. Marx, *The Ethnological Notebooks*, 120; *Die ethnologischen Exzerpthefte*, 160–161.

89. Ibid., 210; ibid., 302.

90. Karl Marx and Friedrich Engels, *Manifesto of the Communist Party*, MECW, 6:482; *Manifest der Kommunistischen Partei*, MEW, 4:462. In a note to the 1888 English edition of the *Manifesto of the Communist Party*, Engels wrote: "The inner organization of this primitive communistic society was laid bare, in its typical form, by Lewis Henry Morgan's crowning discovery of the true nature of the gens and its relation to the tribe. With the dissolution of the primeval communities, society begins to be differentiated into separate and finally antagonistic classes" (ibid.; ibid.).

91. Friedrich Engels, *The Origin of the Family, Private Property and the State*, MECW, 26:131; *Der Ursprung der Familie, des Privateigentums und des Staats*, MEW, 21:27.

92. Ibid., MECW, 26:173; ibid., MEW, 21:68.

93. Engels, *The Origin of the Family*, MECW, 26:173–174; MEW, 21:68. In this work, Engels actually published some of Marx's comments on Morgan's book.

94. Cf. Raya Dunayevskaya, *Rosa Luxemburg, Women's Liberation, and Marx's Philosophy of Revolution* (Chicago: University of Illinois Press, 1991): "Marx . . . showed that

the elements of oppression in general, and of women in particular, arose from within primitive communism, and not only related to change from 'matriarchy'" (ibid., 173).

95. Karl Marx, *The Ethnological Notebooks*, 121; *Die ethnologischen Exzerpthefte*, 161.

96. Cf. Brown, *Marx on Gender and the Family*: "In ancient Greece . . . women were clearly oppressed, but, for Marx, their mythology had the potential to illustrate to them . . . how much freer they could be" (ibid., 172).

97. Marx, *The Ethnological Notebooks*, 116; *Die ethnologischen Exzerpthefte*, 154. Brown, *Marx on Gender and the Family*, has diligently compiled many other considerations that attracted Marx's attention (ibid., 160ff.).

98. Ibid., 123, 104; ibid., 164, 136. See Maurice Godelier, *Perspectives in Marxist Anthropology* (London: Verso, 1977), 67–68, 101–102.

99. Morgan, *Ancient Society*, 551.

100. Ibid., 551–552.

101. The words in parentheses were added by Marx. See Marx, *The Ethnological Notebooks*, 139; *Die ethnologischen Exzerpthefte*, 190.

102. Morgan, *Ancient Society*, 551–552.

103. See Godelier, *Perspectives in Marxist Anthropology*, 124. For a critique of any possible "return to an original state of unity," see Daren Webb, *Marx, Marxism and Utopia* (Aldershot, UK: Ashgate, 2000), 113ff.

104. Engels wrongly believed that Morgan's political positions were very progressive. See, for example, Friedrich Engels to Friedrich Adolph Sorge, 7 March 1884, where he wrote that *Ancient Society* was "a masterly exposé of primitive times and their communism. [Morgan had] rediscovered Marx's theory of history all on his own, . . . drawing communist inferences in regard to the present day." MECW 47, 115–116. Marx never expressed himself in such terms. On the thought of the American anthropologist, see Daniel Moses, *The Promise of Progress: The Life and Work of Lewis Henry Morgan* (Columbia: University of Missouri Press, 2009).

105. Marx, *The Ethnological Notebooks*, 139; *Die ethnologischen Exzerpthefte*, 190. According to Krader: "Marx made it clear, as Morgan did not, that this process of reconstitution will take place on another level than the old, that it is a human effort, of man for and by himself, that the antagonisms of civilization are not static or passive, but are comprised of social interests which are ranged for and against the outcome of the reconstitution, and this will be determined in an active and dynamic way." Krader, "Introduction," in Marx, *The Ethnological Notebooks*, 14. As Maurice Godelier pointed out in *The Mental and the Material* (London: Verso, 2012), in Marx there was never any "idea of a primitive 'El Dorado.' He never forgot that in primitive "classless societies" there were "at least three forms of inequality: between men and women, between senior and junior generations, and between autochthons and foreigners" (ibid., 78).

106. See Krader, "Introduction," in Marx, *The Ethnological Notebooks*, 19.

107. In this work, Marx analyzed the "opposition" between "civil society" and "the state"; the state does not lie "within" society but stands "over against it." "In democracy the state as particular is merely particular. . . . The French have recently interpreted this as meaning that in true democracy the political state is annihilated. This is correct

insofar as the political state . . . no longer passes for the whole." Karl Marx, "A Contribution to the Critique of Hegel's Philosophy of Law," MECW, 3:30; "Kritik des Hegelschen Staatsrechts," MEW, 1:233.

108. Thirty years later, the critique is more sharply focused: "At the same pace at which the progress of modern industry developed, widened, intensified the class antagonism between capital and labour, the State power assumed more and more the character of the national power of capital over labour, of a public force organized for social enslavement, of an engine of class despotism." Karl Marx, *The Civil War in France*, MECW, 22:329; *Der Bürgerkrieg in Frankreich*, MEW, 17:336.

109. Marx, *The Ethnological Notebooks*, 329; *Die ethnologischen Exzerpthefte*, 487. Cf. Krader, "Introduction," in ibid., 59.

110. Marx, *The Ethnological Notebooks*, 329; *Die ethnologischen Exzerpthefte*, 487–488.

111. See Krader, "Introduction," in ibid., 37; and Christine Ward Gailey, "Community, State, and Questions of Social Evolution in Karl Marx's Ethnological Notebooks," in *The Politics of Egalitarianism*, ed. Jacqueline Solway (New York: Berghahn Books, 2006), 36.

112. Marx, *The Ethnological Notebooks*, 324; *Die ethnologischen Exzerpthefte*, 479.

113. See Fritjof Tichelman, "Marx and Indonesia: Preliminary Notes," in *Schriften aus dem Karl-Marx-Haus*, vol. XXX: *Marx on Indonesia and India* (Trier: Karl-Marx-Haus, 1983), 18. See also Engels's view of money: "It would be a good thing if someone were to take the trouble to throw light on the proliferation of state socialism, drawing for the purpose on an exceedingly flourishing example of the practice in Java. All the material is to be found in *Java, How to Manage a Colony* . . . . Here one sees how the Dutch have, on the basis of the communities' age-old communism, organized production for the benefit of the state and ensured that the people enjoy what is, in their own estimation, a quite comfortable existence; the consequence is that the people are kept in a state of primitive stupidity and the Dutch exchequer rakes in 70 million marks a year." Friedrich Engels to Karl Kautsky, 16 February 1884, MECW, 47:102–103.

114. Cf. Musto, "The Rediscovery of Karl Marx," 479–480.

115. See Alessandro Casiccia, "La concezione materialista della società antica e della società primitiva," in Henry Morgan, *La società antica* (Milan: Feltrinelli, 1970), XVII.

116. See Gailey, *Community, State, and Questions*, 35, 44.

117. Marx, "Exzerpte aus Werken von Lothar Meyer, Henry Enfield Roscoe, Carl Schorlemmer, Benjamin Witzschel, Wilhelm Friedrich Kühne, Ludimar Hermann, Johannes Ranke und Joseph Beete Jukes," MEGA^2, IV/31:443–463.

118. Karl Marx to Friedrich Engels, 11 January 1858, MECW, 40:244; MEW, 29:256.

119. Karl Marx to Friedrich Engels, 23 November 1860, MECW, 41:216; MEW, 30:113.

120. Karl Marx to Friedrich Engels, 20 May 1865, MECW, 42:159; MEW, 31:122.

121. Engels later recalled an interruption of a few years in Marx's work on *Capital*:

"There was another intermission after 1870, due mainly to Marx's ill health. As usual, Marx employed this time for studies; agronomics, rural relations in America and, especially, Russia, the money market and banking, and finally natural sciences such as geology and physiology, and above all independent mathematical works, form the content of the numerous excerpt notebooks of this period." Friedrich Engels, "Preface to the First German Edition," in Karl Marx, *Capital, Volume II*, MECW, 36:7.

122.   See Sofya Yanovskaya, "Preface to the 1968 Russian edition," in Karl Marx, *Mathematical Manuscripts* (London: New Park, 1983), IX. For an overview of some of the most interesting interpretations of Marx's studies on mathematics, see Pradip Baksi, ed., *Karl Marx and Mathematics: A Collection of Texts in Three Parts* (New Delhi: Aakar Books, 2019).

123.   A heated dispute arose between Newton and Leibniz, each accusing the other of plagiarism and advancing claims to have "got there first." See Alfred Rupert Hall, *Philosophers at War* (Cambridge: Cambridge University Press, 1980), 234.

124.   Marx, *Mathematical Manuscripts*, 35–106; *Mathematische Manuskript* (Kronberg: Scriptor 1974), 75–129.

125.   See Lucio Lombardo Radice, "Dai manoscritti matematici di K. Marx," *Critica Marxista-Quaderni*, no. 6 (1972): 273. In his manuscripts, Marx used the term "algebraic" for any expression not containing derivative or differential symbols and "symbolic" for expressions containing the figures peculiar to differential calculus, such as dx and dy.

126.   In defense of Newton and Leibniz, it should be pointed out that—with different contents and viewpoints—they created this method of calculation only as an algebraic expedient to solve some geometrical problems. They were not concerned to explain its foundations, which remained mysterious and undefined.

127.   Moreover, Marx's belief that mathematical symbolism should faithfully reflect actual processes in the real world may today be considered ingenuous by some.

128.   For a different opinion, see Yanovskaya, "Preface," XI–XII.

129.   Friedrich Engels to Karl Marx, 18 August 1881, MECW, 46:131–132; MEW, 35:23–25. In his speech at Marx's funeral, Engels pointed out the lasting significance of these studies: "In every single field in which Marx investigated . . . even in that of mathematics, he made independent discoveries." Frederick Engels, "Karl Marx's Funeral," MECW, 24:468.

130.   Karl Marx to Friedrich Engels, 22 November 1882, MECW, 46:380; MEW, 35:114.

131.   Karl Marx to Friedrich Engels, 31 May 1873, MECW, 44:504; MEW, 33:82. For examples of studies in the 1870s that advanced his work on *Capital, Volume Three*, see the voluminous manuscript of 1875: Karl Marx, "Mehrwertrate und Profitrate mathematisch behandelt," MEGA², II/14:19–150.

132.   See Alain Alcouffe, "Introduction," in *Les manuscrits mathématiques de Marx*, ed. Alain Alcouffe (Paris: Economica, 1985), 20–21.

133.   Originally scheduled for Zurich, the congress was eventually held in October, in the smaller town of Chur because of a police ban.

134. Karl Marx to Ferdinand Domela Nieuwenhuis, 22 February 1881, MECW, 46:66; MEW, 35:160.

135. Ibid.; ibid.

136. Ibid.; ibid.

137. Ibid., MECW, 46:66–67; ibid., MEW, 35:160–161.

138. Ibid., MECW, 46:67; ibid., MEW, 35:161.

139. Ibid.; ibid.

140. Henry George, *Progress and Poverty* (New York: Robert Schalkenbach Foundation, 2006), 224–225.

141. Karl Marx to Friedrich Sorge, 20 June 1881, MECW, 46:99–101; MEW, 35:199.

142. Karl Marx and Friedrich Engels, *Manifesto of the Communist Party*, MECW, 6:505; *Manifest der Kommunistischen Partei*, MEW, 4:481.

143. Karl Marx to John Swinton, 2 June 1881, MECW, 46:93; MEW, 35:191. For Engels too, the "state = socialism" equation was totally unacceptable. As he wrote to Bernstein, in March 1881: "It is nothing but self-interested misrepresentation on the part of the Manchester bourgeois to describe as 'socialism' all interference by the state with free competition: protective tariffs, guilds, tobacco monopoly, nationalization of branches of industry, the Overseas Trading Company, royal porcelain factory. That is something we should criticize, but not believe. If we do the latter and base a theoretical argument thereon, this will collapse together with its premises—simply upon its being proved, that is, that this alleged socialism is nothing but feudal reaction on the one hand and, on the other, a pretext for extortion, its secondary object being to turn as many proletarians as possible into officials and pensioners dependent on the state, and to organize, alongside the disciplined army of officials and military, a similar army of workers. Compulsory suffrage imposed by senior functionaries instead of by factory overseers—fine socialism that!" Friedrich Engels to Eduard Bernstein, 12 June 1881, MECW, 46:74.

144. Karl Marx, *The Poverty of Philosophy*, MECW, 6:203; *Das Elend der Philosophie*, MEW, 4:171.

145. Karl Marx to Friedrich Sorge, 20 June 1881, MECW, 46:100–101; MEW, 35:199–200.

146. Ibid., MECW, 46:101; ibid., MEW, 35:200.

147. Ibid.; ibid. See also Hyndman's testimony: "Marx looked it through and spoke of it with a sort of friendly contempt: 'The Capitalists' last ditch,' he said." Although Hyndman insisted on the positive impact of his journalistic style on the masses, Marx, perhaps a little envious of George's fame, "would not hear of this as a sound contention." He said that "the promulgation of error could never be of any good to the people: 'To leave error unrefuted is to encourage intellectual immorality. For ten who go farther, a hundred may very easily stop with George, and the danger of this is too great to run.'" Hyndman, *Adventurous Life*, 258–259.

148. Karl Marx to Friedrich Sorge, 20 June 1881, MECW, 46:101; MEW, 35:201. George's remarks on Marx are also interesting. After Marx's death, he stated that, although he had not read his writings, he felt "deep respect for a man whose life was devoted to efforts for the improvement of social conditions." in Philip S. Foner, ed.,

Karl Marx Remembered: Comments at the Time of His Death (San Francisco: Synthesis Publications, 1983), 101. The next year, however, in a letter to Hyndman, he stressed that Marx "lacked analytical power and logical habits of thought." Henry George, *An Anthology of Henry George's Thought*, ed. Kenneth C. Wenzer (Rochester, NY: University of Rochester Press, 1997), 175. In two letters to the chancellor of Massachusetts Institute of Technology, Francis Walker (1840–1897), he further described Marx as the "prince of muddleheads" and a "superficial thinker" (ibid., 78, 177). Roy Douglas has noted that "when Marx died in 1883 . . . there must have been dozens of Englishmen who had argued about Henry George for every one who had even heard of the Prussian Socialist." Roy Douglas, *Land, People and Politics: A History of the Land Question in the United Kingdom, 1878–1952* (London: Allison and Busby, 1976), 48. Things would change completely in the space of a few years.

149. Karl Marx to Nikolai Danielson, 19 February 1881, MECW, 46:62; MEW, 35:156.

150. Ibid., MECW, 46:63; ibid.

151. Karl Marx to Friedrich Sorge, 5 November 1880, MECW, 46:46; MEW, 34:478.

152. Cf. Selig Perlman, "The Anti-Chinese Agitation in California," in *History of Labour in the United States*, ed. John R. Commons et al., vol. 2 (New York: Macmillan, 1918), 254.

153. Henry George, "The Kearney Agitation in California," *The Popular Science Monthly* 17 (August 1880): 435. Marx's notes are contained in Karl Marx, IISH Amsterdam, *Marx-Engels Papers*, B 161.

154. David Smith, "Accumulation by Forced Migration: Insights from *Capital* and Marx's Late Manuscripts," in *Marx 201: Rethinking Alternatives*, ed. Marcello Musto (London: Palgrave, forthcoming 2020), observed of Marx's notes in his final years that "the glowing memory of the Paris Commune remained alive. . . . But Marx saw that labour is no solid crystal. Evidence of labour's contradictions was becoming increasingly salient, and urgent" (ibid.).

155. See Edward J. Renehan, *Dark Genius of Wall Street: The Misunderstood Life of Jay Gould, King of the Robber Barons* (New York: Basic Books, 2006); and Maury Klein, *The Life and Legend of Jay Gould* (Baltimore: Johns Hopkins University Press, 1997), 393.

156. Karl Marx to Nikolai Danielson, 19 February 1881, MECW, 46:63; MEW, 35:156–157.

157. Ibid.; ibid., MEW, 35:157.

158. Ibid.; ibid.

159. Ibid., MECW, 46:63–64; ibid.

160. Karl Marx to Jenny Longuet, 11 April 1881, MECW, 46:84; MEW, 35:180.

161. This famous phrase was reported by Gladstone's secretary. See Edgar J. Feuchtwanger, *Gladstone* (London: Allen Road, 1975), 146.

162. Karl Marx to Jenny Longuet, 11 April 1881, MECW, 46:84; MEW, 35:180.

163. Founded in 1879, the Irish National Land League was a political organization that defended the interests of Irish tenant farmers.

164. Karl Marx to Jenny Longuet, 11 April 1881, MECW, 46:84; MEW, 35:180–181. On Marx's reaction, see also Hyndman's recollection of a meeting with him at the time: "When speaking with fierce indignation of the policy of the Liberal Party, especially in regard to Ireland, the old warrior's small deep-sunk eyes lighted up, his heavy brows wrinkled, the broad, strong nose and face were obviously moved by passion, and he poured out a stream of vigorous denunciation." Hyndman, *Adventurous Life*, 247. On Gladstone's policies in 1880–1881, see Richard Shannon, *Gladstone*, vol. 2: *1865–1898* (Chapel Hill: University of North Carolina Press, 1999), 248–278. On his positions regarding Ireland, see Colin Matthew, *Gladstone: 1875–1898* (Oxford: Clarendon Press, 1995), 183–210; and James Camlin Beckett, *The Making of Modern Ireland 1603–1923* (London: Faber and Faber, 1981), 389–394.

165. Karl Marx to Jenny Longuet, 29 April 1881, MECW, 46:90; MEW, 35:187.

166. Karl Marx to Jenny Longuet, 11 April 1881, MECW, 46:84; MEW, 35:180.

167. Karl Marx to Jenny Longuet, 29 April 1881, MECW, 46:90; MEW, 35:187. In the last years of his life, Marx often used "John Bull," a name already in common usage, as a personification of Britain.

168. Ibid.; ibid.

169. Karl Marx to Jenny Longuet, 6 June 1881, MECW, 46:95; MEW, 35:194.

170. Karl Marx to Friedrich Sorge, 14 November 1879, MECW, 45:422; MEW, 34:422.

171. Engels revealed the background in a letter to Bernstein: "The themes for this were dictated to him [Guesde] by Marx, here in my own room, in the presence of Lafargue and myself. . . . [It was] a masterpiece of cogent reasoning, calculated to explain things to the masses in a few words. I have seldom seen its like and, even in this concise version, found it astonishing." Friedrich Engels to Eduard Bernstein, 25 October 1881, MECW, 46:148; MEW, 35:232.

172. Karl Marx, "Preamble to the Programme of the French Workers Party," MECW, 24:340; "Einleitung zum Programm der französischen Arbeiterpartei," MEW, 19:238.

173. Ibid.; ibid.

174. Jules Guesde and Paul Lafargue, "Le programme du Parti ouvrier," in Jules Guesde, *Textes Choisis, 1867–1882* (Paris: Éditions sociales, 1959), 118. On Guesde, see Jean-Numa Ducange, *Jules Guesde: The Birth of Socialism and Marxism in France* (London: Palgrave Macmillan, 2020).

175. Ibid.

176. Karl Marx, "Preamble to the Programme of the French Workers Party," MECW, 24:340; MEW, 19:238.

177. In November 1880, in a letter to her husband, Marx's eldest daughter, Jenny Longuet, had referred to the discussion between her father and Guesde: "As to the question of the fixation of a minimum salary, it may perhaps interest you to know that Papa did all he could to persuade Guesde to omit it from their programme, explaining to him that such a measure, if adopted, would, according to economical laws, produce the result of making of this fixed minimum *a maximum*. But Guesde stuck to it, on the

plea that it would give them a hold on the working classes if it did nothing else." Jenny Longuet to Charles Longuet, 23 November 1880, MECW, 46:474.

178. Karl Marx to Friedrich Sorge, 5 November 1880, MECW, 46:43–44; MEW, 34:475–476.

179. Ibid., MECW, 46:44; ibid., MEW, 34:476. Among the "stupidities," Marx included the suppression of inheritance (Point 12 in the Programme), an old Saint-Simonian demand, against which he had polemicized with Bakunin in the International Working Men's Association: "If the working class had sufficient power to abolish the right of inheritance, it would be powerful enough to proceed to expropriation, which would be a much simpler and more efficient process." Karl Marx, "On Inheritance," in *Workers Unite: The International 150 Years Later*, ed. Marcello Musto (London: Bloomsbury, 2014), 159.

180. Karl Marx to Friedrich Sorge, 5 November 1880, MECW, 46:43; MEW, 34:475.

181. The French questionnaire, with its brief introduction, was based on an original that Marx composed partly in English and partly in French: see Karl Marx, "Workers' Questionnaire," in MECW, 24:328–334; "Fragebogen für Arbeiter," MEW, 19:230–237.

182. See the "General Scheme of the Inquiry" which Marx drafted in 1867 and inserted into the "Instructions for the Delegates of the Provisional General Council: The Different Questions," MECW, 20:186–187; "Instruktionen für die Delegierten des Provisorischen Zentralrats zu den einzelnen Fragen," MEW, 16:192.

183. Karl Marx, "Workers' Questionnaire," MECW, 24:329; "Fragebogen für Arbeiter," MEW, 19:231.

184. Ibid., MECW, 24:329–330; ibid., MEW, 19:232–233.

185. Ibid., MECW, 24:331; ibid., MEW, 19:233.

186. Ibid., MECW, 24:334; ibid., MEW, 19:236.

187. See D. Lanzardo, "Intervento socialista nella lotta operaia. L'inchiesta operaia di Marx," *Quaderni Rossi* 5 (April 1965): 17. According to Maximilien Rubel, *Karl Marx. Essai de biographie intellectuelle* (Paris: Rivière, 1957), what differentiated Marx's questionnaire from others previously conducted in France was "its class character: the workers were invited to describe their economic and social situation in the first person and for their own ends" (ibid., 416–417). In Rubel's view, it was "a veritable workers' manual in political economy. . . . Marx's aim was to encourage French workers to become conscious of their social alienation" (ibid., 424).

188. Lafargue, in *Reminiscences of Marx and Engels*, ed. Institute of Marxism-Leninism, 72.

189. Karl Marx to Jenny Longuet, 11 April 1881, MECW, 46:81–82; MEW, 35:177–188. In fact, Engels did not prove to be so keen on Kautsky; he much preferred the other young mind in the German party, Bernstein. As he reported to August Bebel—the German socialist leader whom both he and Marx held in greatest esteem—Bernstein "has real tact and grasps things straight away; the exact opposite of Kautsky, who's an honest guy but a pedant. He's a born quibbler, in whose hands complex matters don't become simple, but simple things become complicated." According to Engels, "in longer articles, more suitable for a journal, he will sometimes be able to produce something

really good, but with the best will in the world he won't be able to conquer his own nature. It's stronger than he is. In a newspaper, a doctrinaire of this kind is a real disaster." This was why Engels did what he could—and succeeded—to persuade Bernstein to continue editing the weekly *The Social Democrat* [*Der Sozialdemokrat*]. Friedrich Engels to August Bebel, 25 August 1881, MECW, 46:137.

190. That is, followers of Jules Grévy (1807–1891), president of the Republic and figurehead of the opportunist republicans.

191. Karl Marx to Friedrich Engels, 9 August 1881, MECW, 46:117; MEW, 35:17.

192. Karl Marx to Friedrich Engels, 18 August 1881, MECW, 46:133–134; MEW, 35:27–28.

193. Lafargue, in *Reminiscences of Marx and Engels*, Institute of Marxism-Leninism, 73.

Chapter 2: Controversy over the Development of Capitalism in Russia

1. This was the name of the castle where Alexander III took refuge after his father's assassination in 1881.

2. Karl Marx and Friedrich Engels, "Preface to the Second Russian Edition of the *Manifesto of the Communist Party*," MECW, 24:426; "Vorrede zur zweiten russischen Ausgabe des *Manifests der Kommunistischen Partei*," MEW, 19:296. For a complete collection of the writings and letters of Marx and Engels on Russia, see Maximilien Rubel, ed., *Karl Marx / Friedrich Engels: Die russische Kommune* (Munich: Hanser, 1972).

3. In 1858 Marx wrote: "The movement for the emancipation of the serfs in Russia strikes me as important in so far as it indicates the beginning of an internal development that might run counter to the country's traditional foreign policy." Karl Marx to Friedrich Engels, 29 April 1858, MECW, 40:310; MEW, 29:324. At the time, serfs made up approximately 38 percent of the population in Russia.

4. See Henry Eaton, "Marx and the Russians," *Journal of the History of Ideas* 41, no. 1 (1980): 89, where all the Russian citizens he met or corresponded with are listed in alphabetical order.

5. Karl Marx, "Letter to *Otechestvennye Zapiski*," MECW, 24:199; "Brief an die Redaktion der 'Otetschestwennyje Sapiski,'" MEW, 19:108.

6. According to Paul Lafargue, Engels told Marx that he would "willingly burn the papers relating to the rise of property in Russia, as they had prevented him for many years from finishing *Capital*." Paul Lafargue, "Frederick Engels," *The Social Democrat* 9, no. 8 (1905): 487.

7. See the information included in the volume *Die Bibliotheken von Karl Marx und Friedrich Engels*, MEGA², IV/32:184–187. For a reconstruction of Marx's discovery of Chernyshevsky's work, see "Entstehung und Überlieferung," in Karl Marx, *Exzerpte und Notizen: Februar 1864 bis Oktober 1868, November 1869, März, April, Juni 1870, Dezember 1872*, MEGA², IV/18, 1142–1144.

8. See Richard Pipes, "Narodnichestvo: A Semantic Inquiry," *Slavic Review* XXIII, no. 3 (1964): 421–458. Andrzej Walicki, *Controversy over Capitalism: Studies in the Social Philosophy of the Russian Populists* (Oxford: Clarendon Press, 1969), 27, located

the birth of populism in 1869, around the time of the publication of the *Historical Letters* (1868–1870) by Pyotr Lavrov (1823–1900), *What Is Progress?* (1869) by Nikolai Mikhailovsky (1842–1904), and *The Condition of the Working Class in Russia* (1869) by Vasilii Bervi-Flerovsky (1829–1918).

9.   Karl Marx to Sigfrid Meyer, 21 January 1871, MECW, 44:105; MEW, 33:173.

10.   Karl Marx to Nikolai Danielson, 18 January 1873, MECW, 44:469; MEW, 33:599.

11.   Karl Marx to Nikolai Danielson, 12 December 1872, MECW, 44:457; MEW, 33:549.

12.   Karl Marx, "Afterword to the Second German Edition," in Marx, *Capital, Volume I*, MECW, 35:15; "Nachwort zur zweiten Auflage," Marx, *Das Kapital, Erster Band*, MEW, 23:21.

13.   Nikolai Chernyshevsky, "Kritika filosofskikh preubezhdenii protiv obshchinnogo vladeniya" [Critique of philosophical prejudices against communal ownership of the land], in Chernyshevsky, *Sobranie sochinenii*, vol. 4 (Moscow: Ogonyok, 1974), 402. A very short selection of excerpts from this text is available in Nikolai Chernyshevsky, "A Critique of Philosophical Prejudices against Communal Ownership," in *Late Marx and the Russian Road*, ed. Teodor Shanin (London: Routledge, 1984), 182–190; these have been consulted for the present translation and cited hereafter, when available.

14.   Ibid., 404–405.

15.   Ibid., 406; Chernyshevsky, "A Critique of Philosophical Prejudices," 182.

16.   Ibid.; ibid.

17.   See Marco Natalizi, *Il caso Černyševskij* (Milan: Bruno Mondadori, 2006), 55. On Chernyshevsky's interaction with his cultural milieu, see Norman G. O. Pereira, *The Thought and Teachings of N. G. Černyševskij* (The Hague: Mouton, 1975).

18.   Marx had already made similar criticisms of Herzen's theses in "A Contribution to the Critique of Political Economy," MECW, 29:275; "Zur Kritik der politischen Ökonomie," MEW, 13:20. In *Roots of Revolution: A History of the Populist and Socialist Movements in Nineteenth Century Russia* (New York: Alfred A. Knopf, 1960), Franco Venturi correctly points out that Chernyshevsky did not consider the *obshchina* "as a typically Russian institution, a characteristic of the Slav spirit . . . but only as a survival in Russia of forms of social organization which elsewhere had now disappeared" (ibid., 148).

19.   Chernyshevsky, "Kritika filosofskikh preubezhdenii," 371.

20.   For Venturi, *Roots of Revolution*, this was the central theme of Chernyshevsky's discussion of the peasant commune: "The obshchina should be revivified and transformed by Western Socialism; it should not be portrayed as a model and symbol of Russia's mission" (ibid., 160).

21.   Walicki, *Controversy over Capitalism*, argues that for Chernyshevsky capitalism represented "great progress relative to precapitalist forms of society"; his "enemy number one" was not "capitalism but Russian backwardness" (ibid., 20). According to Natalizi, *Il caso Černyševskij*, Chernyshevsky "was far from being an adversary of bourgeois progress in Russia. If we had to use a label for him, he was a Westernizer" (ibid., 3).

22.   Chernyshevsky, "Kritika filosofskikh preubezhdenii," 372.

23. Ibid., 391.

24. According to Walicki, *Controversy over Capitalism*, Chernyshevsky wanted "to skip the 'intermediate stages of development' or at least enormously reduce their length. His main argument for the commune was a dialectical conception of progress, claiming that the first stage of any development is, as a rule, similar in form to the third; thus, primitive communal collectivism is similar in form to the developed collectivism of a socialist society" (ibid., 18).

25. Chernyshevsky, "Kritika filosofskikh preubezhdenii," 402.

26. Alexander Herzen, *The Russian People and Socialism: An Open Letter to Jules Michelet* (London: Weidenfeld and Nicolson, 2011), 199. On the idea of "freedom from the weight of the past," see Walicki, *Controversy over Capitalism*, 116–117.

27. On the life of the Russian revolutionary, see Jay Bergman, *Vera Zasulich: A Biography* (Stanford, CA: Stanford University Press, 1983).

28. Vera Zasulich, "A Letter to Marx," in Shanin, *Late Marx and the Russian Road*, 98–99.

29. Ibid.

30. Ibid. Martin Buber, *Paths in Utopia* (Syracuse, NY: Syracuse University Press, 1996), commented: "The decision as to which of the two was the historical truth was left in Marx's hands" (ibid., 91).

31. Walicki, *Controversy over Capitalism*, rightly observed that Marx's studies of Morgan's *Ancient Society* "enabled him to look afresh at Russian Populism, which was by then the most significant attempt 'to find what is newest in the oldest'" (ibid., 192).

32. Karl Marx and Friedrich Engels, *Manifesto of the Communist Party*, MECW, 6:514; *Manifest der Kommunistischen Partei*, MEW, 4:489.

33. Ibid., MECW, 6:488; ibid., MEW, 4:466.

34. Ibid., MECW, 6:490; ibid., MEW, 4:468.

35. Ibid., MECW, 6:496; ibid., MEW, 4:473–474.

36. Karl Marx, "Speech at the Anniversary of the *People's Paper*," MECW, 14:655; "Rede auf der Jahresfeier des *People's Paper*," MEW, 12:3.

37. Karl Marx, *Outlines of the Critique of Political Economy*" [*Grundrisse*], MECW, 28:337; *Grundrisse der Kritik der politischen Ökonomie*, MEW, 42:323. For a commentary on this complex text, see Marcello Musto, ed., *Karl Marx's Grundrisse: Foundations of the Critique of Political Economy 150 Years Later* (London: Routledge, 2008).

38. Karl Marx, *Capital, Volume I*, MECW, 35:749; *Das Kapital, Erster Band*, MEW, 23:790–791.

39. Ibid., MECW, 35:750; ibid., MEW, 23:790.

40. Ibid.; ibid.

41. Ibid., MECW, 35:336; ibid., MEW, 23:351.

42. Ibid., MECW, 35:340; ibid., MEW, 23:354.

43. Ibid., MECW, 35:338; ibid., MEW, 23:353.

44. Ibid., MECW, 35:588; ibid., MEW, 23:618. See also Marx's letter of 7 December 1867, where he provided Engels with a synthesis of the main arguments he wanted to see mentioned in a review of *Capital* that his friend was then preparing. He described

his work as a demonstration that "present society, economically considered, is pregnant with a new, higher form." Following a risky comparison between his own discoveries and Charles Darwin's (1809–1882) theory of evolution, he further suggested that his book showed "there is hidden progress even where modern economic relations are accompanied by frightening direct consequences," and that, "owing to this critical approach of his," he had "perhaps, in spite of himself, sounded the death-knell to all socialism, that is, to utopianism, for evermore." Finally, among the sentences suggested to Engels he reemphasized the profound conviction that, "whereas Mr. Lassalle hurled abuse at the capitalists and flattered the backwoods Prussian squirearchy, Mr. Marx, on the contrary, shows the historical necessity of capitalist production." Karl Marx to Friedrich Engels, 7 December 1867, MECW, 42:494; MEW, 31:404.

45. Marx, *Grundrisse*, MECW, 29:94; MEW, 42:604.

46. Ibid., MECW, 29:87; ibid., MEW, 42:598.

47. Ibid., MECW, 29:94; ibid., MEW, 42:604.

48. Ibid., MECW, 28:418; ibid., MEW, 42:402.

49. Ibid., MECW, 28:465; ibid., MEW, 42:446.

50. Ibid.; ibid.

51. Marx, *Capital, Volume I*, MECW, 35:122; MEW, 23:126.

52. Ibid., MECW, 35:507; ibid., MEW, 23:528.

53. Karl Marx, "Instructions for the Delegates of the Provisional General Council: The Different Questions," MECW, 20:188; "Instruktionen für die Delegierten des Provisorischen Zentralrats zu den einzelnen Fragen," MEW, 16:193.

54. Marx, *Capital, Volume I*, MECW, 35:492; MEW, 23:514.

55. Ibid., MECW, 35:506; ibid., MEW, 23:528.

56. Ibid., MECW, 35:504–505; ibid., MEW, 23:526.

57. Ibid., MECW, 35:506; ibid., MEW, 23:528.

58. Ibid., MECW, 35:90–91; ibid., MEW, 23:94.

59. Karl Marx, "Notes on Bakunin's Book *Statehood and Anarchy*," MECW, 24:518; "Konspekt von Bakunins Buch Staatlichkeit und Anarchie," MEW, 18:633.

60. Karl Marx, "Critique of the Gotha Programme," MECW, 24:83; "Kritik des Gothaer Programms," MEW, 19:17.

61. Karl Marx, "Preamble to the Programme of the French Workers Party," MECW, 24:340; "Einleitung zum Programm der französischen Arbeiterpartei," MEW, 19:238.

62. Karl Marx, "Afterword to the Second German Edition," MECW, 35:17; "Nachwort zur zweiten Auflage," MEW, 23:25.

63. Karl Marx, "Marginal Notes on Adolph Wagner's *Lehrbuch der politischen Ökonomie*," MECW, 24:533; "Randglossen zu Adolph Wagners *Lehrbuch der politischen Ökonomie*," MEW, 19:357.

64. See James H. Billington, *Mikhailovsky and Russian Populism* (Oxford: Clarendon Press, 1958).

65. According to Walicki, *Controversy over Capitalism*, "Mikhailovsky did not deny that the guilds and the contemporary Russian *artels* had limited individual freedom and the possibilities of individual development; he thought, however, that the negative

consequences of this limitation had been less dangerous than the negative results of capitalist development. . . . Mikhailovsky concluded that it was utterly unjustified to say that capitalism 'had liberated the individual.' . . . There is no exaggeration in maintaining that among the authors whose books contributed most to Mikhailovsky's approval of such a view, the main part has been played by Marx" (ibid., 59–60).

66. Nikolai Mikhailovsky, "Karl Marks pered sudom g. Yu. Zhukovskogo" [Karl Marx before the tribunal of Mr. Yu. Zhukovsky], in Mikhailovsky, *Sochinenija*, vol. IV (St. Peterburg: B. M. Vol'f, 1897), 171, quoted from the translation in Walicki, *Controversy over Capitalism*, 146. This article followed the criticism of Marx that appeared in 1877 under the name of Yuri Zhukovsky in the journal *European Messenger* [*Vestnik Evropy*], and Nikolai Sieber's defense of *Capital* in *Otechestvennye Zapiski*. See Cyril Smith, *Marx at the Millennium* (London: Pluto, 1996), 53–55. In 1894, in an article he wrote for *Russian Wealth* [*Russkoe Bogatsvo*], Mikhailovsky restated what he had argued seventeen years earlier.

67. Karl Marx, "Nachtrag zu den Noten des ersten Buches," in Marx, *Das Kapital*, MEGA^2 II/5:625. This "Appendix to the Notes of Volume I" was eliminated from the reprint of 1872 and omitted from all translations of the work.

68. A recent example of this view may be found in White, *Marx and Russia*, which asserts that after the publication of *Capital* "Marx revise[d] his attitude to Herzen's conceptions, if not to Herzen himself" (ibid., 8).

69. Marx, "Letter to *Otechestvennye Zapiski*," MECW, 24:196; MEW, 19:107.

70. Alexander Herzen, "Revolution in Russia," in *The Herzen Reader*, ed. Kathleen Parthe (Evanston, IL: Northwestern University Press, 2012), 63.

71. Marx, "Letter to *Otechestvennye Zapiski*," MECW, 24:196; MEW, 19:107.

72. On Tkachev's ideas, see Venturi, *Roots of Revolution*, 389–428.

73. Friedrich Engels, "On Social Relations in Russia," MECW, 24:39–40.

74. In a message written in pencil on the cover of his copy of Tkachev's "Open Letter," Marx revealed his view on the contents of that text and commented that it was "so stupid that Bakunin may have contributed." Karl Marx to Friedrich Engels, February–March 1875, MECW, 45:59; MEW, 34:5. Maximilien Rubel noted that it was Marx himself who asked Engels to "publish a reply." Rubel, *Marx: Life and Works*, 105.

75. Engels, "On Social Relations in Russia," 45. Cf. Venturi, *Roots of Revolution*, 93–94.

76. Marx, "Letter to *Otechestvennye Zapiski*," MECW, 24:135; MEW, 19:108.

77. Marx, *Capital, Volume I*, MECW, 35:704–761; MEW, 23:741–802.

78. Marx, "Letter to *Otechestvennye Zapiski*," MECW, 24:200; MEW, 19:108. See also Karl Marx, *Le capital, Paris 1872–1875*, MEGA^2, II/7:634. This addition to the original 1867 edition, which Marx introduced when revising the French translation of his book, was not included by Engels in the fourth German edition of 1890, which later became the standard version for translations of *Capital*. In a footnote to Karl Marx, *Œuvres. Économie I* (Paris: Gallimard, 1963), Rubel called this "one of the important additions" (ibid., 1701, n. 1) to the part on "The So-Called Primitive Accumulation." The edition published by Engels states that the history of primitive accumulation

"assumes different aspects in different countries and runs through its various phases in different orders of succession, and at different historical epochs. In England alone, which we take as our example, has it the classic form." Marx, *Capital, Volume I*, MECW, 35:707; MEW, 23:744.

79. Marx "Preface to the First German Edition," MECW, 35:9; "Vorwort zur ersten Auflage," MEW, 23:15. In the French edition, Marx slightly restricted the scope of this phrase: "Le pays le plus développé industriellement ne fait que montrer à ceux qui le suivent sur l'échelle industrielle de leur propre avenir." K. Marx, *Le Capital*, MEGA², II/7:12. In his *Provincializing Europe: Postcolonial Thought and Historical Difference* (Princeton, NJ: Princeton University Press, 2000), Dipesh Chakrabarty misinterpreted this passage as a typical example of historicism that follows the principle of "first in Europe, then elsewhere" (ibid., 7). He further presented the "ambiguities in Marx's prose" as characteristic of those who regard "history as a waiting room, a period that is needed for the transition to capitalism at any particular time and place. This is the period to which . . . the third world is often consigned" (ibid., 65). At any event, Neil Lazarus, "The Fetish of 'the West' in Postcolonial Theory," in *Marxism, Modernity and Postcolonial Studies*, ed. Crystal Bartolovich and Neil Lazarus (Cambridge: Cambridge University Press, 2002), has rightly pointed out that "not all historical narrativization is teleological or 'historicist'" (ibid., 63).

80. Karl Marx, "Preface to the First German Edition," MECW, 35:8; "Vorwort zur ersten Auflage," MEW, 23:12.

81. "Report of a Speech by Karl Marx at the Anniversary Celebration of the German Workers' Educational Society in London, February 28, 1867," MECW, 20:415; "Aufzeichnung einer Rede von Karl Marx auf dem Stiftungsfest des Deutschen Bildungsvereins für Arbeiter in Londonam" 28. Februar 1867, MEW, 16:524.

82. Marx, "Letter to *Otechestvennye Zapiski*," MECW, 24:200; MEW, 19:111.

83. Ibid.; ibid., MEW, 19:108, 111.

84. Ibid., MECW, 24:200; ibid., MEW, 19:111.

85. Ibid.; ibid.

86. Ibid.; ibid., MEW, 19:111–112. White, *Marx and Russia*, found that the words attributed to Mikhailovsky constitute an "astonishing accusation." "Marx," he wrote, "had never regarded the development of capitalism as merely historical, merely empirical. He had conceived of capitalism as a universal system, the outward manifestation of man's inner species being. *Das Kapital* had limited itself to the development of capitalism on the historical plane only because Marx had been unable to discover the more essential and logic steps in the process" (ibid., 32). The recent publication of Marx's unfinished manuscripts and study notes, in the *Marx-Engels-Gesamtausgabe* (MEGA²), showed, on the contrary, how strongly he oriented himself to empirical research and historical analysis. In contrast to what many previous interpreters have maintained, these new materials definitively refute the idea that he was mainly driven by a new philosophy of history, or that he had obsessive recourse to the dialectical method.

87. See Pier Paolo Poggio, *L'Obščina. Comune contadina e rivoluzione in Russia* (Milan: Jaca Book, 1978), 148.

88.   Various attempts have been made to explain why Marx did not publish his reply to Mikhailovsky. When Engels forwarded it in 1885 to the editors of *The Northern Messenger* [*Severnii Vestnik*], he said that it had not been published "for reasons unknown to [him]." Friedrich Engels, "To the Editors of the *Severny Vestnik*," in MECW, 26:311. A year earlier, however, in a letter to Vera Zasulich, he had said: "This is the reply he wrote; it bears the stamp of a piece done for publication in Russia, but he never sent it to Petersburg for fear that the mere mention of his name might compromise the existence of the review which published his reply." Friedrich Engels to Vera Zasulich, 6 March 1884, MECW, 47:112. It should be noted that there is no proof that the journal would have really been in danger if it had hosted a text by Marx in its pages. Without having made the necessary checks in support of his thesis, Haruki Wada, "Marx and Revolutionary Russia," in *Late Marx*, ed. Teodor Shanin (London: Routledge, 1984), argued that "the true reason . . . was rather that Marx, after reading his letter again, saw something wrong with his critique of Mikhailovsky" (ibid., 60). White, *Marx and Russia*, pointed out that in the issue of *Otechestvennye Zapiski* following the one with Mikhailovsky's article, Sieber had reaffirmed that "the process formulated by Marx was universally obligatory" (ibid., 33). Sieber's belief that "capitalism was a universal phenomenon, encountered in every society at a certain stage of its development" (ibid., 45), is a telling example of how Marx was perceived in Russia.

89.   According to White, *Marx and Russia*, this "perception acquired considerable momentum and resilience, so that even when Marx's letter was eventually published it was difficult to shake" (ibid., 33). On the relationship between populism and Marxism in Russia, see also Richard Pipes, *Struve: Liberal on the Left, 1870–1905* (Cambridge, MA: Harvard University Press, 1970); and the recent Vesa Oittinen, *Marxism, Russia, Philosophy* (London: Palgrave, 2020), esp. chap. 3.

90.   See Buber, *Paths in Utopia*: "His exertions to give the right answer are of a thoroughness and scrupulosity worthy of admiration. Already before this he had occupied himself with the same knotty problem, and now he attacked it afresh with especial intensity. Again and again we see him cancelling one formulation of great delicacy and precision only to seek another still more adequate. Although but a series of fragmentary sketches, these notes seem to me the most important attempt that has been made to grasp synthetically the theme of the Russian village community" (ibid., 91).

91.   Karl Marx, "Drafts of the Letter to Vera Zasulich: Second Draft," MECW, 24:360; "Brief von V. I. Sassulitsch: Zweiter Entwurf," MEW, 19:396.

92.   Ibid.; ibid.

93.   Karl Marx, "Drafts of the Letter to Vera Zasulich: First Draft," MECW, 24:349; "Brief von V. I. Sassulitsch: Erster Entwurf," MEW, 19:384–385.

94.   Karl Marx, "Drafts of the Letter to Vera Zasulich: Third Draft," MECW, 24:365; " Brief von V. I. Sassulitsch: Dritter Entwurf," MEW, 19:402.

95.   Marx, "Second Draft," MECW, 24:361; MEW, 19:397.

96.   See also Teodor Shanin, "Late Marx: Gods and Craftsmen," in *Late Marx*, ed. Teodor Shanin (London: Routledge, 1984), 16.

97.   Marx, "Second Draft," MECW, 24:361; MEW, 19:397.

98. Karl Marx, "The Future Results of British Rule in India," MECW, 12:217–218; "Die künftigen Ergebnisse der britischen Herrschaft in Indien," MEW, 9:221.

99. Ibid., MECW, 12:221; ibid., MEW, 9:224.

100. Ibid., MECW, 12:222; ibid., MEW, 9:226.

101. See, for example, Edward Said, *Orientalism* (London: Routledge, 1995), 153–156. Said (1935–2003) not only argued that "Marx's economic analyses are perfectly fitted . . . to a standard Orientalist undertaking," but also insinuated that they depended on the "age-old distinction between Orient and Occident" (ibid., 154). In reality, Said's reading of Marx's work was one-sided and superficial. The first to bring out the flaws in his interpretation was Sadiq Jalal al-Azm (1934–2016), who, in the article "Orientalism and Orientalism in Reverse," *Khamsin* 8 (1980), wrote: "This account of Marx's views and analyses of highly complex historical processes and situations is a travesty. . . . There is nothing specific to either Asia or the Orient in Marx's body of work" (ibid., 14–15). With regard to "productive capacities, social organization, historical ascendancy, military might and technological development, . . . Marx, like anyone else, knew of the superiority of modern Europe over the Orient. But to accuse him . . . of turning this contingent fact into a necessary reality for all time is simply absurd (ibid., 15–16). Similarly, Aijaz Ahmad, in *Theory: Classes, Nations, Literatures* (London: Verso, 1992), well demonstrated how Said "decontextualized quotations from Marx's work, with little sense for what the passage in question represented, simply in order to slot them into his 'Orientalist archive'" (ibid., 231, 223). Against the idea of Marx's supposed Eurocentrism, see also Irfan Habib, "Marx's Perception of India," in *Karl Marx on India*, ed. Iqbal Husain (New Delhi: Tulika, 2006), XIX–LIV. On the limitations of Marx's journalistic articles of 1853, see Kolja Lindner, "Marx's Eurocentrism: Postcolonial Studies and Marx's Scholarship," *Radical Philosophy* 161 (2010): 27–41.

102. For Eric Hobsbawm, introduction to *Pre-Capitalist Economic Formations* by Karl Marx (London: Lawrence & Wishart, 1964), "Marx's increasing preoccupation with primitive communalism" was related to "his growing hatred of and contempt for capitalist society. . . . It seems probable that Marx, who had earlier welcomed the impact of Western capitalism as an inhuman but historically progressive force on the stagnant pre-capitalist economies, found himself increasingly appalled by this inhumanity" (ibid., 50).

103. Marx, "Third Draft," MECW, 24:365; MEW, 19:402.

104. Ibid., MECW, 24:368; ibid., MEW, 19:405.

105. Ibid., MECW, 24:367; ibid.

106. Marx, "Second Draft," MECW, 24:361; MEW, 19:397.

107. Ibid., MECW, 24:362; ibid.

108. Marx, "First Draft," MECW, 24:352; MEW, 19:388–389.

109. Marx, "Second Draft," MECW, 24:362; MEW, 19:398.

110. Marx, "Third Draft," MECW, 24:368; MEW, 19:405.

111. Marx, "First Draft," MECW, 24:349; MEW, 19:385.

112. Ibid., MECW, 24:357; ibid., MEW, 19:392.

113. Ibid., MECW, 24:351; ibid., MEW, 19:388.

114. Marx, "Second Draft," MECW, 24:362; MEW, 19:398.

115. Marx, "Third Draft," MECW, 24:366; MEW, 19:403.

116. Marx, "First Draft," MECW, 24:353; MEW, 19:389–390.

117. See the interpretations of Wada, "Marx and Revolutionary Russia," 60, where it is argued that the drafts showed a "significant change since the publication of *Capital* in 1867." Similarly, Enrique Dussel, *El último Marx (1863–1882) y la liberación latino-americana* (Mexico City: Siglo XXI, 1990), spoke of a "change of course" (260, 268–269); and Tomonaga Tairako, "Marx on Capitalist Globalization," *Hitotsubashi Journal of Social Studies* 35 (2003), has argued that Marx "change[d] his perspective on the global revolution carried out by the working class" (ibid., 12). Other authors have suggested a "third-worldist" reading of the late Marx, in which the revolutionary subject is no longer factory workers but the masses in the countryside and the periphery. Reflections and various interpretations on these questions may also be found in Umberto Melotti, *Marx and the Third World* (London: Palgrave, 1977); Kenzo Mohri, "Marx and 'Under-development,'" *Monthly Review* 30, no. 11 (1979), 32–43; and Jean Tible, *Marx Selvagem* (São Paulo: Autonomia Literária, 2018).

118. See Marian Sawer's excellent work *Marxism and the Question of the Asiatic Mode of Production* (The Hague: Martinus Nijhoff, 1977), 67: "What happened, in the 1870s in particular, was not that Marx changed his mind on the character of the village communities, or decided that they could become the basis of socialism as they were; rather, he came to consider the possibility that the communities could be revolutionized not by capitalism but by socialism. . . . He does seem to have entertained seriously the hope that with the intensification of social communication and the modernization of production methods the village system could be incorporated into a socialist society. In 1882 this still appeared to Marx to be a genuine alternative to the complete disintegration of the *obshchina* under the impact of capitalism." See also Gianni Sofri, *Il modo di produzione asiatico. Storia di una controversia marxista* (Turin: Einaudi, 1969): "In the final years of his life, the study of social conditions in Russia led him to accept that, under certain conditions, it might be possible to pass to a higher form of communism by skipping the capitalist stage. Bearing in mind that Russia appeared to him a 'semi-Asiatic' country more advanced than India and China, a gradual evolution of Marx's thinking on this point seems undeniable" (ibid., 70).

119. Marx, "Third Draft," 367; MEW, 19:403–404. After the emancipation of 1861, the peasantry was able to acquire land, but only by paying compensation in the form of tribute.

120. Ibid.; ibid., MEW, 19:404.

121. Marx, "First Draft," MECW, 24:355; MEW, 19:393.

122. Ibid., 354; ibid., MEW, 19:390–391.

123. Ibid.; ibid., MEW, 19:391.

124. Marx, "Third Draft," MECW, 24:368; MEW, 19:404.

125. Ibid.; ibid., MEW, 19:405.

126. Cf. Venturi, "Introduzione," in Venturi, *Il populismo russo. Herzen, Bakunin, Cernysevskij*, vol. I (Turin: Einaudi, 1972): "In short, Marx ended up accepting the ideas

of Chernyshevsky" (ibid., XLI). This is similar to Walicki's view in *Controversy over Capitalism*: "The reasoning of Marx bears much resemblance to Chernyshevsky's *Critique of Philosophical Prejudices against the Communal Ownership of the Land*." If the populists had been able to read the preliminary drafts of the letter to Zasulich, "they would no doubt have seen in them an invaluable, authoritative justification of their hopes" (ibid., 189).

127. Marx, "First Draft," MECW, 24:358; MEW, 19:391.

128. Ibid., MECW, 24:356; ibid., MEW, 19:390–391.

129. Ibid.; ibid., MEW, 19:392.

130. The *artel* form of cooperative association, originally of Tatar origin, was based on blood ties and attended to the collective responsibility of its members toward the state and third parties.

131. Marx, "First Draft," MECW, 24:356; MEW, 19:389.

132. Ibid., MECW, 24:353; ibid., MEW, 19:390.

133. The *volost* was a traditional administrative subdivision in Imperial Russia.

134. Marx, "First Draft," MECW, 24:353; MEW, 19:390.

135. Ibid., MECW, 24:359–360; ibid., MEW, 19:395.

136. Marx and Engels, "Preface to the Second Russian Edition," MECW, 24:426; MEW, 19:296.

137. According to Walicki, *Controversy over Capitalism*, the short text from 1882 "reaffirm[ed] the thesis that socialism has a better chance in the highly developed countries, but at the same time it assume[d] that the economic development of backward countries may be essentially modified under the influence of international conditions" (ibid., 180).

138. *Narodnaya Volya*, 5 February 1882, reprinted in *Literatura partii Narodnoi Voli* (Paris: Société nouvelle de librairie et d'édition, 1905), 558.

139. Karl Marx, "Letter to Vera Zasulich," MECW, 24:370; "Marx an V. I. Sassulitsch," MEW, 19:242.

140. Marx was referring to the secret organization that split from Land and Freedom [*Zemlya i Volya*], in 1879 and opted for "terrorist" struggle.

141. Marx, "Letter to Vera Zasulich," MECW, 24:370; MEW, 19:242.

142. Ibid.; ibid., MEW, 19:242–243.

143. Ibid., MECW, 24:370–371; ibid.

144. Ibid., MECW, 24:371; ibid., MEW, 19:243.

145. According to Álvaro García Linera, *Forma valor y forma comunidad* (Buenos Aires: Prometeo, 2010), "one of the tragic errors of twentieth-century Marxism was its propensity to convert real history and living events into selfless servants of the history of philosophy" (ibid., 229). See also Étienne Balibar, *The Philosophy of Marx* (London: Verso, 1995), 108ff.; and Daniel Bensaïd, *Marx for Our Times: Adventures and Misadventures of a Critique* (London: Verso, 2002), in particular the chapter "A New Way of Writing History" 9–39.

146. Karl Marx to Vera Zasulich, 8 March 1881, MECW, 46:71; MEW, 35:166.

147. David Ryazanov, who first discovered and published the preliminary drafts of the letter, maintained that Marx did not answer Zasulich as he would have wished

because of his reduced capacity for work: see Ryazanov, "The Discovery of the Drafts," in *Late Marx*, ed. Teodor Shanin (London: Routledge, 1984), 129. It is a view shared by Rubel in *Marx, critique du marxisme* (Paris: Payot, 2000), 104. Much more convincing is Venturi, "Introduzione," for whom the drafts of the reply to Zasulich "show in the liveliest manner his doubts and hesitations regarding the central problem of Populism" (ibid., XLI). Poggio, *L'Obščina*, argued that Marx hesitated "to state a forceful position on an issue whose political and theoretical implications made it so explosive" (ibid., 157). And Walicki, *Controversy over Capitalism*, rightly observed that, although "the possible role of the peasant commune as a mainspring of Russia's social regeneration was, no doubt, curiously exaggerated," the drafts contain "many penetrating insights which undermined the nineteenth-century method of interpreting social change in terms of a lawful 'natural' process" (ibid., 194).

148. Zasulich and Plekhanov went so far as to conceal Marx's letter, for evident political reasons. It was published only in 1924, more than forty years after it was written.

149. Friedrich Engels to Nikolai Danielson, 24 February 1893, MECW, 50:112; MEW, 39:38.

150. According to Venturi, "Introduzione," "with the great spurt of industrialization in the late nineteenth century, Marx's doubts seemed for the moment to fall away, while a new and rigid vision of bourgeois development came to assert itself" (ibid., XLIV).

151. Venturi, *Roots of Revolution*, observed that the Land and Freedom militants "did not share Marx's views on the working classes, though they admitted the broad outlines of his examination of the development of bourgeois society. And they did not believe in a Socialism which would come into being when capitalist development reached its end" (ibid., 622).

152. Venturi, *Roots of Revolution*, 661–662. Cf. Samuel H. Baron, "Lo sviluppo del capitalismo in Russia nel pensiero di Plechanov," in *Storia del marxismo contemporaneo*, ed. Istituto Giangiacomo Feltrinelli (Milan: Feltrinelli, 1974), 426–450.

153. The revolutionary Vera Figner (1852–1942) claimed that the name of the old Land and Freedom organization was distributed between the two movements that arose out of its ashes: Black Repartition took the idea of "land" and People's Will that of "freedom," since the Russian word *volya* could mean both will and freedom. See Walicki, *Controversy over Capitalism*, 103.

154. Cited in Venturi, *Roots of Revolution*, 679.

155. Ibid., 681.

156. Ibid., 671.

157. Ibid.; Karl Marx to Friedrich Sorge, 5 November 1880, MECW, 46:45–46; MEW, 34:478.

158. Karl Marx to Jenny Longuet, 11 April 1881, MECW, 46:83; MEW, 35:179.

159. On Marx's sympathy for Russian populism, see the testimony of Nikolai Morozov (1854–1946), who recollected a conversation in December 1880 when Marx said that he was very interested in People's Will and that its "struggle against the autocracy

seemed to him . . . a kind of fairy tale, a story from a fantasy novel." Nikolai Morozov, in *Reminiscences of Marx and Engels*, ed. Institute of Marxism-Leninism, 302.

160. Karl Marx to Jenny Longuet, 11 April 1881, MECW, 46:83; MEW, 35:179.

161. In *Le repliche della storia. Karl Marx tra la Rivoluzione francese e la critica della politica* (Turin: Bollati Boringhieri, 1989), Bruno Bongiovanni argued that "we should not underestimate the horizon of international politics in Marx's intellectual trajectory . . . in relation to Russia.""Marx's works in their entirety" allow us to infer that he envisaged the following sequence of events: "war against Russia, military defeat of Russia, Russian revolution (not socialist but Jacobin), absence (temporary or permanent?) of the reactionary gendarme of Europe, socialist transformation in Europe . . . , return of revolution in Russia, and then—but only then—the possibility that the *obshchina* could be used in the transition to socialism." (ibid., 201–202). However, what Bongiovanni defined as "the mechanism of the development of revolution" became weaker in the reflections of the late Marx. The revolution is not bound by the force of circumstance to begin in Europe and reach Russia only in a "second round" (ibid., 212).

162. Although Bongiovanni placed too much emphasis on the word "irreversibly," he rightly states that "in the final analysis, *Gemeinschaft* [community] cannot be miraculously transubstantiated into socialism without the irreversibly emancipatory presence of *Gesellschaft* [society]" (ibid., 189).

Chapter 3: The Travails of "Old Nick"

1. This expression was first used in 1846 with reference to the division between Marx and the German communist Wilhelm Weitling (1808–1871) and was subsequently used in the 1852 Cologne trials against communists. Cf. Rubel, *Marx, critique du marxisme*, 26.

2. This term appeared for the first time in 1854. See Georges Haupt, *Aspects of International Socialism, 1871–1914* (Cambridge: Cambridge University Press, 1986), 2.

3. Henry Hyndman later remarked: "In 1880 it is scarcely too much to say that Marx was practically unknown to the English public, except as a dangerous and even desperate advocate of revolution, whose organization of the International had been one of the causes of the horrible Commune of Paris, at which all decent respectable people shuddered and thought of with horror." Hyndman, *Record of an Adventurous Life*, 249–250.

4. Karl Kautsky, in Benedict Kautsky, ed., *Friedrich Engels' Briefwechsel mit Karl Kautsky* (Vienna: Danubia, 1955), 32.

5. Friedrich Engels to Eduard Bernstein, 25 October 1881, MECW, 46:146; MEW, 35:230.

6. Ibid.; ibid., MEW, 35:229–230.

7. Ibid., MECW, 46:149; ibid., MEW, 35:232–233.

8. Ibid., MECW, 46:149–150; ibid., MEW, 35:233.

9. Karl Marx to Charles Longuet, 4 January 1881, MECW, 46:55; MEW: 35:148.

10. Ibid.; ibid.

11. Johann Most, *Kapital und Arbeit. Ein populärer Auszug aus "Das Kapital" von Marx* (Chemnitz 1873), MEGA², II/8:735–800.

12. Carlo Cafiero, *"Il Capitale" di Carlo Marx brevemente compendiato da Carlo Cafiero. Libro Primo: Sviluppo della Produzione Capitalistica* (Milan: E. Bignami e C., 1879).

13. Ferdinand Domela Nieuwenhuis, *Kapitaal en Arbeid* (The Hague, 1881).

14. Ibid., 3.

15. Karl Marx to Ferdinand Domela Nieuwenhuis, 22 February 1881, MECW, 46:65; MEW, 35:159.

16. Ibid., MECW, 46:66; ibid., MEW, 35:160.

17. "Account of Karl Marx's Interview with the *Chicago Tribune* Correspondent," *Chicago Tribune*, 5 January 1879, MECW, 24:577; "Interview mit dem Grundleger des modernen Sozialismus Besondere Korrespondenz der *Tribüne*," MEW, 34:515.

18. Friedrich Engels to Karl Kautsky, 1 February 1881, MECW, 46:56; MEW, 35:150.

19. Ibid., MECW, 46:57; ibid.

20. Ibid.; ibid.

21. Karl Marx to Nikolai Danielson, 19 February 1881, MECW, 46:61; MEW, 35:155.

22. Karl Marx to Friedrich Sorge, 15 December 1881, MECW, 46:161; MEW, 35:247.

23. Karl Marx to Jenny Longuet, 7 December 1881, MECW, 46:158; MEW, 35:243.

24. Karl Marx to Nikolai Danielson, 13 December 1881, MECW, 46:161; MEW, 35:246.

25. Marx's correspondence contains a couple of references to Hyndman, before and after the end of their relations, which show that he always had a critical view of him. On 11 April 1881, he wrote to Jenny Longuet: "The day before yesterday . . . we were invaded by Hyndman and his wife, both of whom have too much staying-power. I quite like the wife on account of her brusque, unconventional and determined manner of thinking and speaking, but it's amusing to see how admiringly she hangs on the lips of her complacent chatterbox of a husband!" Karl Marx to Jenny Longuet, 11 April 1881, MECW, 46:82; MEW, 35:178. A few months after their final quarrel, Marx commented: "Many evenings this fellow has pilfered from me, in order to take me out and to learn in the easiest way." Karl Marx to Friedrich Sorge, 15 December 1881, MECW, 46:163; MEW, 35:248.

26. Henry Hyndman, *England for All* (New York: Barnes & Noble, 1974), XXXVIII; partially in Karl Marx to Friedrich Sorge, 15 December 1881, MECW, 46:163; MEW, 35:248.

27. Karl Marx to Henry Hyndman, 2 July 1881, MECW, 46:103; MEW, 35:203. This is the draft of the letter that Marx kept in his files. Hyndman said that he "unfortunately destroyed most of Marx's letters at the time of [their] difference." Hyndman, *Adventurous Life*, 259–260. Jenny Marx foresaw everything when she wrote to her daughter Laura Lafargue from Eastbourne on 2 July 1881: "On Saturday, the pale-eyed Hyndman received his blow on the head. He is not likely to prop up the letter on his looking-glass,

although, for all its pungency, it was so wittily worded that anger was barely perceptible. I think Mohr was rather happy in this opus." in Yvonne Kapp, *Eleanor Marx: Family Life 1855–1883*, vol. 1 (London: Virago, 1979), 211.

28. Karl Marx to Henry Hyndman, 2 July 1881, MECW, 46:102; MEW, 35:202.

29. Karl Marx to Friedrich Sorge, 15 December 1881, MECW, 46:163; MEW, 35:248.

30. Ibid. Subsequently, Hyndman also contacted Engels, who wrote back: "I shall be very happy to make your personal acquaintance as soon as you shall have set yourself right with my friend Marx whom I see you can now afford to quote." Friedrich Engels to Henry Hyndman, ca. 31 March 1882, MECW, 46:228. Marx commented: "It serves the laddie right that your note should have annoyed him, especially since he took these liberties with me only because he was counting on my own inability, for 'considerations of propaganda,' to compromise him in public." Karl Marx to Friedrich Engels, 8 April 1882, MECW, 46:234.

31. Karl Marx to Henry Hyndman, 2 July 1881, MECW, 46:103; MEW, 35:203.

32. See Emile Bottigelli, "La rupture Marx-Hyndman," *Annali dell'Istituto Giangia-como Feltrinelli* III (1961): "The reasons for the breach were not only personal or related to the ambitions of a frustrated writer. . . . They were a theoretical position whereby Marx announced to the Democratic Federation and one of its principal founders that he had no truck with that initiative" (ibid., 625).

33. Henry Hyndman to Karl Marx, 25 February 1880, IISH Amsterdam, *Marx-Engels Papers*, C 261, C 262. Most of Hyndman's letters have never been published; some are quoted in Chushichi Tsuzuki, *H. M. Hyndman and British Socialism* (London: Oxford University Press, 1961), including the present that was mentioned at p. 34.

34. Karl Marx to Henry Hyndman, 8 December 1880, MECW, 46:49; MEW, 34:482.

35. Ibid.; ibid., MEW, 34:482–483.

36. See Mountstuart Elphinstone Grant Duff's (1829–1906) report of a meeting with Marx at the beginning of 1879. The English nobleman asked a provocative question: "Well, I said, supposing that your Revolution has taken place and that you have your Republican form of Government—it is still a long long way to the realization of the special ideas of yourself and our friends. Doubtless, he answered, but all great movements are slow. It would merely be a step to better things as your Revolution of 1688 was—a mere stage on the road." "Sir Mountstuart Elphinstone Grant Duff's Account of a Talk with Karl Marx: From a Letter to Crown Princess Victoria," MECW, 24:580.

37. John Rae, "The Socialism of Karl Marx and the Young Hegelians," *The Contemporary Review* XL (July–December 1881): 587–607.

38. Karl Marx to Friedrich Sorge, 15 December 1881, MECW, 46:162; MEW, 35:247–248.

39. E. Belfort Bax, "Leaders of Modern Thought XXIII: Karl Marx," *Modern Thought* 3, no. 2 (1881): 349, 354.

40. Karl Marx to Friedrich Sorge, 15 December 1881, MECW, 46:163; MEW, 35:248–249.

41. Friedrich Engels, "Preface to the English Edition," in Marx, *Capital, Volume I*, MECW, 35:35.

42. Karl Marx, "Das Kapital. Zweites Buch. Der Zirkulationsprozeß des Kapitals. Zu benutzende Textstellen früherer Darstellungen (Manuskript I bis IV)," MEGA², II/11:525–548.

43. Karl Marx, "Das Kapital. Zweites Buch. Der Zirkulationsprozeß des Kapitals. Erster Abschnitt (Fragmente II)," MEGA², II/11:550–697.

44. Marx, "Das Kapital. Zweites Buch. Der Zirkulationsprozeß des Kapitals. (Manuskript VIII)," MEGA², II/11:698–828.

45. See Teinosuke Otani, Ljudmila Vasina, and Carl-Erich Vollgraf, "Einführung," MEGA², II/11:881.

46. Karl Marx to Friedrich Engels, 18 July 1877, MECW, 45:242; MEW, 34:48.

47. Karl Marx to Friedrich Engels, 25 July 1877, MECW, 45:251; MEW, 34:59.

48. Karl Marx to Friedrich Sorge, 27 September 1877, MECW, 45:276; MEW, 34:294.

49. The reference is to *Theories of Surplus-Value*; cf. Marcello Musto, *Another Marx: Early Manuscripts to the International* (London: Bloomsbury, 2018), 137–149.

50. Karl Marx to Sigmund Schott, 3 November 1877, MECW, 45:287; MEW, 34:307.

51. The words "third section" refer to the studies of the early 1860s on the history of economic theories. The second section consists of the writings that Engels later published as Volumes II and III of *Capital*. (See Karl Marx to Ludwig Kugelmann, 13 October 1866, MECW, 42:328; MEW, 31:534). It should be noted, however, that Marx's account to Schott of the state of his manuscripts did not fully correspond to reality. Carl-Erich Vollgraf, in *Marx's Further Work on Capital*, has rightly said that sizable parts of *Theories of Surplus-Value* did not yet contain Marx's own "fully elaborated interpretation," and that many pages were "not well thought out [and] pedantic" (ibid., 62).

52. Karl Marx to Sigmund Schott, 29 March 1878, MECW, 45:304; this letter, written in English, was not included in the MEW volumes and has not yet been published in those of MEGA².

53. Ibid. See also Karl Marx, IISH Amsterdam, *Marx-Engels Papers*, B 140, B 141, and B 146. On Marx's view of Kaufman, see also Karl Marx to Nikolai Danielson, 10 April 1879, MECW, 45:358; MEW, 34:374.

54. Karl Marx to Thomas Allsop, 28 April 1878, MECW, 45:307. This letter, written in English, was not included in the MEW volumes and has not yet been published in those of MEGA².

55. Karl Marx to Nikolai Danielson, 28 November 1878, MECW, 45:346; MEW, 34:362.

56. Karl Marx to Friedrich Sorge, 4 April 1876, MECW, 45:115; MEW, 34:179.

57. Karl Marx to George Rivers, 24 August 1878, MECW, 45:317; MEW, 34:339.

58. Karl Marx to Nikolai Danielson, 15 November 1878, MECW, 45:344; MEW,

34:359. Cf. the considerations on California in Marx's letter to Friedrich Sorge, 5 November 1880, MECW, 46:46; MEW, 34:478; see Chap. 1 of this book, p. 41–42.

59. See Vollgraf, *Marx's Further Work on Capital*, 64–65.

60. Karl Marx, "Exzerpte und Notizen zur Geologie, Mineralogie und Agrikulturchemie. März bis September 1878," MEGA², IV/26:3–94.

61. Ibid., 139–679.

62. Friedrich Engels, "Marx, Heinrich Karl," MECW, 27:341.

63. Eleanor Marx to Carl Hirsch, 8 June 1878, MECW, 45:449.

64. Karl Marx to Friedrich Engels, 18 September 1878, MECW, 45:329; MEW, 34:83.

65. "Account of Karl Marx's Interview with the *Chicago Tribune* Correspondent," *Chicago Tribune*, 5 January 1879, MECW, 24:569; MEW, 34:509.

66. Ibid., MECW, 24:572; ibid., MEW, 34:511.

67. Ibid., MECW, 24:573; ibid., MEW, 34:511.

68. Ibid.; ibid.

69. Ibid., MECW, 24:576–577; ibid., MEW, 34:514.

70. Ibid., MECW, 24:573; ibid., MEW, 34:512.

71. Ibid., MECW, 24:569; ibid., MEW, 34:509.

72. "Sir Mountstuart Elphinstone Grant Duff's Account of a Talk with Karl Marx (from a Letter to Crown Princess Victoria)," MECW, 24:581; "Sir Mountstuart Elphinstone Grant Duff, Account of a Talk with Karl Marx: Aus einem Brief an Kronprinzessin Victoria," MEGA² I/25:441.

73. Karl Marx to Nikolai Danielson, 15 November 1878, MECW, 45:343; MEW, 34:358.

74. Karl Marx to Nikolai Danielson, 10 April 1879, MECW, 45:354; MEW, 34:370.

75. Ibid., MECW, 45:355; ibid., MEW, 34:372.

76. Ibid., MECW, 45:358; ibid., MEW, 34:375.

77. Ibid., MECW, 45:356; ibid., MEW, 34:373.

78. Ibid.; ibid.

79. Karl Marx to Ferdinand Domela Nieuwenhuis, 27 June 1880, MECW, 46:16; MEW, 34:447.

80. Karl Marx to Nikolai Danielson, 10 April 1879, MECW, 45:356; MEW, 34:372.

81. On Marx's trips to Karlsbad, see Egon Erwin Kisch, *Karl Marx in Karlsbad* (Berlin: Aufbau, 1953); and Marcello Musto, *Karl Marx. Biografia intellettuale e politica 1857–1883* (Turin: Einaudi, 2018), 153–159.

82. Karl Marx to Nikolai Danielson, 10 April 1879, MECW, 45:353; MEW, 34:370.

83. Karl Marx to Jenny Longuet, 19 August 1879, MECW, 45:372; MEW, 34:388.

84. Karl Marx to Friedrich Engels, 25 August 1879, MECW, 45:376; MEW, 34:96.

85. Karl Marx to Friedrich Sorge, 19 September 1879, MECW, 45:410; MEW, 34:410.

86. Karl Marx to Friedrich Engels, 10 September 1879, MECW, 45:388; MEW, 34:107.

87. Karl Marx to Nikolai Danielson, 19 September 1879, MECW, 45:409; MEW, 34:409.

88. According to Michael Heinrich, "*Capital* after the MEGA: Discontinuities, Interruptions, and New Beginnings," *Crisis & Critique* III, no. 3 (2016): 92–138. Marx understood that, "in connection with credit and crisis theory, it was no longer possible to abstract from the role of the state, and particularly from the national banks and public credit, and neither could one abstract from the role of international trade, exchange rates and international credit flows." Marx also thought that his earlier engagement with "technological questions, which formed the basis for *Capital, Volume I*, was no longer sufficient given the enormous advances" in recent years. (Ibid., 132).

89. Friedrich Engels to Johann Philipp Becker, 19 December 1879, MECW, 45:432; MEW, 34:432.

90. Marx to Laura Lafargue, 18 December 1871, MECW, 44:283; MEW, 33:363.

91. Marx to Maurice Lachâtre, 18 March 1872, MECW, 44:344; MEW, 33:434.

92. Marx to Nikolai Danielson, 28 May 1872, MECW, 44:385; MEW, 33:477.

93. Jenny Marx to Ludwig Kugelmann, 3 May 1872, MECW, 44:578; MEW, 33:700.

94. Jenny Marx to Ludwig and Gertrud Kugelmann, 27 June 1872, MECW, 44:582.

95. Engels to Ludwig Kugelmann, 1 July 1873, MECW, 44:515.

96. Karl Marx to Friedrich Sorge, 27 September 1877, MECW, 45:276; MEW, 34:295.

97. Karl Marx, *Le Capital, Paris 1872–1875*, MEGA2, II/7.

98. Karl Marx, "Afterword to the French Edition," MECW, 35:24.

99. Karl Marx to Friedrich Sorge, 27 September 1877, MECW, 45:276; MEW, 34:295.

100. Karl Marx to Nikolai Danielson, 15 November 1878, MECW, 45:343; MEW, 34:358.

101. Karl Marx to Nikolai Danielson, 28 November 1878, MECW, 45:346; MEW, 34:362. For a list of the additions and modifications in the French translation that were not included in the third and fourth German editions, see Karl Marx, *Das Kapital. Kritik der politischen Ökonomie. Erster Band, Hamburg 1867*, MEGA^{2,} II/5:732–783.

102. The editorial work that Engels undertook after his friend's death to prepare the unfinished parts of *Capital* for publication was extremely complex. The various manuscripts, drafts and fragments of Volumes II and III, written between 1864 and 1881, correspond to approximately 2,350 pages of the MEGA^2. Engels successfully published Volume II in 1885 and Volume III in 1894. However, it must be borne in mind that these two volumes emerged from the reconstruction of incomplete texts, often consisting of heterogeneous material. They were written in more than one period in time and thus include different, and sometimes contradictory, versions of Marx's ideas. Unfinished though it remained, those who today want to use essential theoretical concepts for the critique of the capitalist mode of production still cannot dispense with reading Marx's *Capital*.

103. See, for example, Marx to Danielson, 13 December 1881: "In the first instance I must first be restored to health, and in the second I want to finish off the second volume. . .

as soon as possible. . . . I will arrange with my editor that I shall make for the 3d edition only the fewest possible alterations and additions. . . . When these 1,000 copies forming the third edition are sold, then I may change the book in the way I should have done at present under different circumstances." MECW, 46:161–162; MEW, 35:264.

104. "Moor" was how Marx was known in the family and among his closest comrades. As Engels remembered: "he was never called Marx there, or even Karl, but only Moor, just as each of us had his own nickname; indeed, at the point where nicknames ceased so too did the closest intimacy. Moor had been his nickname since his university days and on the *New Rhenish Newspaper* he was always called Moor. If I had addressed him in any other way he would have thought something was amiss that needed putting right." Friedrich Engels to Theodor Cuno, 29 March 1883, MECW, 46:466. Similarly, August Bebel later wrote: "Marx's wife and daughters always called him 'Moor,' as if he had no other name. The nickname derived from his once jet-black hair and beard, which contrary to his mustache, had turned white." August Bebel, in *Gespräche mit Marx und Engels*, ed. Enzensberger, 528. Also, Bernstein recalled: "I wanted to wish goodbye, but Engels insisted: 'No, no, come with me to the Moor.' 'To the Moor?' I said. 'But who is he?' 'Marx. Who else?,'" replied Engels in a tone that signified that one must as a matter of course know whom he meant. Edward Bernstein, *My Years of Exile*, 154. For a complete list of the many diminutives used in the Marx family, see Olga Meier, ed., *The Daughters of Karl Marx: Family Correspondence 1866–1898* (New York: Harcourt Brace Jovanovich, 1982), XIII.

105. Friedrich Engels to Jenny Longuet, 17 June 1881, MECW, 46:97; MEW, 45:196–197.

106. Karl Marx to Friedrich Sorge, 20 June 1881, MECW, 46:98; MEW, 35:198.

107. Friedrich Engels to Karl Marx, 7 July 1881, MECW, 46:104; MEW, 35:5.

108. Karl Marx to Laura Lafargue, 13 April 1882, MECW, 46:238; MEW, 35:305. In this letter, Marx told his daughter how he fondly remembered her "faithful daily visits so cheering to that crosspatch, Old Nick." See also Kapp, *Eleanor Marx*, 218.

109. As quoted in ibid. The most complete collection of Jenny Marx's correspondence is available in Angelika Limmroth and Rolf Hecker, eds., *Jenny Marx. Die Briefe* (Berlin: Karl Dietz, 2014).

110. Karl Marx to Jenny Longuet, 22 July 1881, MECW, 46:106; MEW, 35:206.

111. Karl Marx to Friedrich Engels, 27 July 1881, MECW, 46:107; MEW, 35:7.

112. The first letter with this signature was in the year of the publication of *Capital*. See Karl Marx to Laura Marx, 13 May 1867, MECW, 42:376; MEW, 31:549. Among all the trashy claims about Marx, some of them tinged with antisemitism or racism, one of the most absurd is that "he had the devil's view of the world, and the devil's malignity; sometimes he seemed to know that he was accomplishing works of evil." Robert Payne, *Marx: A Biography* (New York: Simon & Schuster, 1968), 317. In the same tradition is the farcical *Was Marx a Satanist?* (Glendale, CA: Diane Books, 1979), by the American (former Romanian) priest Richard Wurmbrand. Marx, for his part, used "Old Nick" in a gently jocular vein. On 25 September 1869, for example, he wrote to Laura Lafargue: "I regret that I cannot celebrate at home the birthday of my dear clear bird's eye, but Old

Nick's thoughts are with you. Thou art enclosed in my heart." Karl Marx to Laura Lafargue, 25 September 1869, MECW, 43:355; MEW, 32:632. Again, on 4 February 1871, after Laura gave birth to a son, he wrote to Paul Lafargue: "Embrace little Schnappy on my part and tell him that Old Nick feels highly elated at the two photograms of his successor." Karl Marx to Paul Lafargue, 4 February 1871, MECW, 44:112; MEW, 33:176.

113.   Karl Marx to Friedrich Engels, 27 July 1881, MECW, 46:109; MEW, 35:8.

114.   Friedrich Engels to Karl Marx, 29 July 1881, ibid.; MEW, 35:9.

115.   Generous as ever, Engels replied at once: "As regards the paltry £30, don't let it give you any grey hairs. . . . Should you need more, however, let me know and I shall make the cheque larger." Friedrich Engels to Karl Marx, 6 August 1881, MECW, 46:113; MEW, 35:14.

116.   Karl Marx to Friedrich Engels, 3 August 1881, MECW, 46:110; MEW, 35:11.

117.   Ibid.; ibid., MEW, 35:11–12. Marx gave them signs of life only a few days later: "I have been here for nearly a fortnight; haven't visited Paris or any of my acquaintances. My wife's condition has permitted neither the one nor the other." Karl Marx to Carl Hirsch, 6 August 1881, MECW, 46:115; MEW, 35:207.

118.   Karl Marx to Friedrich Engels, 9 August 1881, MECW, 46:116; MEW, 35:16.

119.   Marx wrote the same to Laura in London: "Mama is in a serious condition as a result of her growing weakness. It was therefore my intention (as we shall only be able to travel by easy stages this time) to set off at all costs at the end of the week, and I informed the patient accordingly. Yesterday, however, she thwarted my plan by sending out our washing." Karl Marx to Laura Lafargue, 9 August 1881, MECW, 46:118; MEW, 35:208.

120.   Karl Marx to Friedrich Engels, 9 August 1881, MECW, 46:116; MEW, 35:16.

121.   Yvonne Kapp surmises that Eleanor's "problem was twofold and acute": she was trying to break off her secret engagement to Lissagaray, whom the family had never accepted, and at the same time she "longed to make a career for herself on the stage." Kapp, *Eleanor Marx*, 227.

122.   Karl Marx to Jenny Longuet, 18 August 1881, MECW, 46:135; MEW, 35:218. To Engels he wrote that Dr. Donkin thought it "a miracle . . . that a collapse of this kind hadn't happened before." Karl Marx to Friedrich Engels, 18 August 1881, MECW, 46:133; MEW, 35:27.

123.   Karl Marx to Jenny Longuet, 18 August 1881, MECW, 46:135; MEW, 35:219.

124.   Karl Marx to Friedrich Engels, 19 August 1881, MECW, 46:136; MEW, 35:29.

125.   Karl Marx to Karl Kautsky, 1 October 1881, MECW, 46:143; MEW, 35:226.

126.   Karl Marx to Minna Kautsky, 1 October 1881, MECW, 46:143–144; MEW, 35:227.

127.   Karl Marx to Karl Kautsky, 1 October 1881, MECW, 46:143; MEW, 35:226.

128.   Paul Lafargue, in *Reminiscences of Marx and Engels*, ed. Institute of Marxism-Leninism (Moscow: Foreign Languages Publishing House, 1957), 75.

129.   "You must not leave the children. It would be the merest madness and would cause Papa more anxiety than your being here could give him pleasure or do him good—much as we all wish you were here." Quoted in Kapp, *Eleanor Marx*, 219.

130.   Friedrich Engels to Eduard Bernstein, 25 October 1881, MECW, 46:150; MEW, 35:233. Marx himself wrote to Becker in December: "So serious a grip had pleurisy combined with bronchitis gained over me that for a time, i.e. several days, the doctors doubted whether I would pull through." Karl Marx to Johann Philipp Becker, 10 December 1881, MECW, 46:159; MEW, 35:244.

131.   Friedrich Engels to Johann Philipp Becker, 4 November 1881, MECW, 46:151.

132.   Friedrich Engels to Eduard Bernstein, 30 November 1881, MECW, 46:155.

133.   Engels was jubilant: "Never has a proletariat conducted itself so magnificently. In England, after the great defeat of 1848, there was a relapse into apathy and, in the end, resignation to bourgeois exploitation, with the proviso that the trades union fought individual battles for higher wages." Friedrich Engels to Eduard Bernstein, 30 November 1881, MECW, 46:152–153.

134.   Quoted in Kapp, *Eleanor Marx*, 219.

135.   Ibid., 219–220. Marx later wrote to Danielson that it had been so bad not to be able to see his wife "during 3 out of the last 6 weeks of her life," even though they had been "in two rooms contiguous with each other." Karl Marx to Nikolai Danielson, 13 December 1881, MECW, 46:160; MEW, 35:245.

136.   Karl Marx to Jenny Marx, 15 December 1863, MECW, 41:499; MEW, 30:643. On the life of Jenny Marx and her relationship with Marx, see Mary Gabriel, *Love and Capital: Karl and Jenny Marx and the Birth of a Revolution* (New York: Little, Brown, 2011). Another recent publication is *Angelika Limmroth, Jenny Marx. Die Biographie* (Berlin: Dietz, 2018), while the more dated works include Luise Dornemann, *Jenny Marx: Der Lebensweg einer Sozialistin* (Berlin: Dietz, 1971); and Heinz Frederick Peters, *Red Jenny: A Life with Karl Marx* (New York: St. Martin's, 1986).

137.   Karl Marx to Jenny Marx, 21 June 1856, MECW, 40:56; MEW, 29:535.

138.   Karl Marx to Jenny Longuet, 7 December 1881, MECW, 46:156; MEW, 35:240.

139.   Kapp, *Eleanor Marx*, 219.

140.   Ibid., 221.

141.   Karl Marx to Jenny Longuet, 7 December 1881, MECW, 46:156–157; MEW, 35:240–241.

142.   Ibid., MECW, 46:156; ibid., MEW, 35:240.

143.   Karl Marx to Johann Philipp Becker, 10 December 1881, MECW, 46:159; MEW, 35:244.

144.   Karl Marx to Nikolai Danielson, 13 December 1881, MECW, 46:160; MEW, 35:245.

145.   Karl Marx to Friedrich Sorge, 15 December 1981, MECW, 46:162; MEW, 35:247.

146.   Karl Marx, *A Contribution to the Critique of Political Economy*, MECW, 29:263; *Zur Kritik der Politischen Ökonomie*, MEW, 13:9.

147.   See Michael Krätke, "Marx and World History," *International Review of Social History* 63, no. 1 (2018), which in its reconstruction of these four notebooks argued that Marx conceived the birth of modern states as a process related to "the development of

trade, agriculture, mining, fiscalism, and spatial infrastructure" (ibid., 123). Krätke also argued that Marx compiled these notes in the long-held belief that he was "giving the socialist movement a solid, social-scientific foundation instead of a political philosophy" (ibid., 92).

148.   On the life of the Italian historian, see Scipione Botta, *Vita privata di Carlo Botta. Ragguagli domestici ed aneddotici raccolti dal suo maggior figlio* (Florence: G. Barbera, 1877).

149.   On the intellectual biography of Schlosser, see Michael Gottlob, *Geschichtsschreibung zwischen Aufklärung und Historismus. Johanna von Müller und Friedrich Christoph Schlosser* (Frankfurt: Peter Lang, 1989), esp. section IV.

150.   See Bruno Kaiser, *Ex libris Karl Marx und Friedrich Engels. Schicksal und Verzeichnis einer Bibliothek* (Berlin: Dietz, 1967), 36–37. Cf. MEGA², IV/32:158, 586–587.

151.   There is no reference to these studies in Marx's correspondence, and so it is difficult to date them precisely. The editors of the *Marx-Engels-Werke* provisionally placed the excerpts between "late 1881 and late 1882" (MEW, 19:621–622), while Rubel, in his *Marx: Life and Works*, 121, stated that they "undoubtedly" date from late 1881. The first hypothesis is too general, but the second does not seem altogether accurate, since Marx, having done the bulk of the work in 1881, most probably continued to press on with the project at certain points in 1882. One can assume this from the different styles of underlining in the manuscripts, as well as from Marx's letter of 23 December 1882 to his daughter Eleanor (see Chap. 4, n. 81). It is therefore arguable that these notebooks (IISH Marx-Engels Papers, B 157, B 158, B 159, B 160) belong to Marx's only two periods of intellectual activity in the last eighteen months of his life, as he moved between London and the Isle of Wight: from autumn 1881 to 9 February 1882, and from early October 1882 to 12 January 1883. What is certain is that he did not work on the historical chronology during the eight months of 1882 that he spent in France, Algeria, and Switzerland.

152.   In some cases, the contents of the notebooks differ slightly from the dates indicated by Engels. The only part to have been published comprises approximately a sixth of the total of the third and fourth notebooks, most of the pages being taken from the latter. These materials appeared in 1953, in an anthology lacking textual references prepared by Wolfgang Harich: Marx-Engels-Lenin-Stalin, *Zur deutschen Geschichte* (Berlin: Dietz, 1953). Eight years later, the title changed to Karl Marx and Friedrich Engels, *Über Deutschland und die deutsche Arbeiterbewegung*. The sections drawn from the *Chronological Extracts* are included in *Band 1: Von der Frühzeit bis zum 18. Jahrhundert* (Berlin: Dietz, 1973): 285–516.

153.   Krätke, "Marx and World History," has argued that "Marx gave no room to Euro-centrism; he considered world history in no way synonymous with 'European history'" (ibid., 104).

154.   See the recently published Karl Marx, "Exzerpte aus Georg Ludwig von Maurer: Einleitung zur Geschichte der Mark-, Hof-, Dorf- und Stadt-Verfassung und der öffentlichen Gewalt," MEGA², IV/18:542–559, 563–577, 589–600.

155.   Karl Marx to Friedrich Engels, 25 March 1868, MECW, 42:557; MEW, 32:51. On Marx's study of Maurer's work, see Tomonaga Tairako, "A Turning Point in Marx's

Theory on Pre-Capitalist Societies—Marx's Excerpt Notebooks on Maurer in Mega IV/18–," *Hitotsubashi Journal of Social Studies* 47, no. 1 (January 2016): 1–10; and Kohei Saito, *Karl Marx's Ecosocialism: Capital, Nature, and the Unfinished Critique of Political Economy* (New York: Monthly Review Press, 2017), 264–265.

156. Krätke, "Marx and World History," maintained that Marx situated "the beginnings of modern capitalism" in the "economic development of the Italian city republics at the end of the thirteenth century" (ibid., 111).

157. Krätke has argued that the fall of the Mongol state "invite[d] Marx to reflect on the limits of political power over vast territories" (ibid., 112).

158. Karl Marx, IISH Amsterdam, *Marx-Engels Papers*, B 159, 113. This brief comment of Marx's is reported in Krätke, "Marx and World History," 114.

159. The parts of these extracts published in Harich's edition in 1953 amounted to more than ninety pages: see Karl Marx and Friedrich Engels, *Über Deutschland und die deutsche Arbeiterbewegung*, 424–516.

160. Krätke, "Marx and World History," stated that the fourth notebook of the *Chronological Extracts* shows "the strength of Marx as a historically well-informed social scientist, who easily alternates from the inner development of specific countries to major European and international politics without, however, losing sight of the economic foundations of the whole" (ibid., 6).

161. Friedrich Engels to Karl Marx, 8 January 1882, MECW, 46:174; MEW, 35:32.

162. Friedrich Engels to Ferdinand Domela Nieuwenhuis, 29 December 1881, MECW, 46:167; MEW, 35:253.

163. Karl Marx to Jenny Longuet, 17 December 1881, MECW, 46:131; MEW, 35:251.

164. Karl Marx to Friedrich Engels, 5 January 1882, MECW, 46:171; MEW, 35:30.

165. Karl Marx to Laura Lafargue, 4 January 1882, MECW, 46:170; MEW, 35:256.

166. Eleanor Marx to Jenny Longuet, 8 January 1882, in Meier, *The Daughters of Karl Marx*, 145–146. On the whole episode, see Kapp, *Eleanor Marx*, 225–228. On 4 January, Marx wrote to Laura: "My companion eats practically nothing; suffers badly from nervous tics; reads and writes all day long . . . , seemingly endures staying with me simply out of a sense of duty, as a self-sacrificing martyr." Karl Marx to Laura Lafarge, 4 January 1882, MECW, 46:169; MEW, 35:255.

167. See the stenographic records of Reichstag debates, *Stenographische Berichte über die Verhandlungen des Reichstags* (Berlin, 1882), 1:486. Bismarck's speech followed his electoral defeat in the great industrial centers of Germany.

168. Karl Marx to Friedrich Engels, 15 January 1882, MECW, 46:183; MEW, 35:39.

169. Friedrich Engels to Eduard Bernstein, 25 January 1882, MECW, 46:186–187; MEW, 35:265. In his view, "Italy [could] hold out fewer guarantees than anywhere else—save, of course, Bismarck's empire." See also Karl Marx to Pyotr Lavrov, 23 January 1882, MECW, 46:184; MEW, 35:262.

170. See Gilbert Badia, "Marx en Algérie," in Karl Marx, *Lettres d'Alger et de la Côte d'Azur* (Paris: Le Temps des Cerises, 1997), 17.

171. Eleanor Marx, in *Gespräche mit Marx und Engels*, ed. Enzensberger, 577–578.

172. Karl Marx to Friedrich Engels, 12 January 1882, MECW, 46:176; MEW, 35:34-35. On Eleanor Marx and her special relationship with her father, besides Kapp, *Eleanor Marx*, see also Chushichi Tsuzuki, *The Life of Eleanor Marx, 1855-1898: A Socialist Tragedy* (Oxford: Clarendon Press, 1967); Eva Weissweiler, *Tussy Marx: Das Drama der Vatertochter* (Cologne: Kiepenheuer & Witsch, 2002); and most recently, Rachel Holmes, *Eleanor Marx: A Life* (London: Bloomsbury, 2014).

173. See Karl Marx to Friedrich Engels, 17 February 1882: "No question of passports and such like. Nothing is entered on the passengers' tickets save Christian and surnames." MECW, 46:200; MEW, 35:42.

174. The trip to the Algerian capital has not received much attention from Marx's biographers. Even Jacques Attali, himself born in Algiers, devoted only half a page to it in his *Karl Marx, ou l'Esprit du monde* (Paris: Librairie Arthème-Fayard, 2005), 410; despite some inexactitudes about Marx's stay, he noted that he was ignorant of the Oran uprising between summer 1881 and spring 1883. Marlene Vesper's *Marx in Algier* (Bonn: Pahl-Rugenstein Nachfolger, 1995) traced with great precision all the events that Marx witnessed at first hand during his visit to Algiers. Also of interest is René Gallissot, ed., *Marxisme et Algérie* (Paris: Union générale d'éditions, 1976). The novel by Hans Jürgen Krysmanski, *Die letzte Reise des Karl Marx* (Frankfurt: Westend, 2014), was originally intended as the screenplay for a film on Marx's stay in Algiers, but was never produced because of a lack of funding.

Chapter 4: The Moor's Last Journey

1. Karl Marx to Friedrich Engels, 1 March 1882, MECW, 46:213-214; MEW, 35:44, 45.

2. Karl Marx to Jenny Longuet, 16 March 1882, MECW, 46:219; MEW, 35:291.

3. Karl Marx to Friedrich Engels, 1 March 1882, MECW, 46:215; MEW, 35:46.

4. Karl Marx to Paul Lafargue, 20 March 1882, MECW, 46:221; MEW, 35:293. He added: "But there was this insistent idea—for which I was not responsible—of the African sun and the wonder-working air out here!" (ibid.; ibid.).

5. Karl Marx to Jenny Longuet, 16 March 1882, MECW, 46:218; MEW, 35:289-290.

6. Karl Marx to Jenny Longuet, 27 March 1882, MECW, 46:224; MEW, 35:295. He added: "Between us: Though in the Isle of Wight the weather was unfavourable, but still my health improved so greatly that people wondered. . . . At London, on the contrary, Engels' excitement . . . in fact has upset me: I felt, I could no longer stand it; hence my impatience to get from London away on any condition whatever! People may kill someone out of real most sincere love; with all that nothing more dangerous in such cases for a reconvalescent!" (ibid.; MEW, 35: 295-296)

7. Karl Marx to Paul Lafargue, 20 March 1882, MECW, 46:221-222; MEW, 35:293-294.

8. Karl Marx to Friedrich Engels, 1 March 1882, MECW, 46:215; MEW, 35:46.

9. Karl Marx to Friedrich Engels, 28-31 March 1882, MECW, 46:226; MEW, 35:51.

10. Karl Marx to Jenny Longuet, 16 March 1882, MECW, 46:219; MEW, 35:290.

11. Karl Marx to Jenny Longuet, 27 March 1882, MECW, 46:225; MEW, 35:296.

12. Karl Marx to Friedrich Engels, 1 March 1882, MECW, 46:213, 215; MEW, 35:44, 46.

13. Karl Marx to Friedrich Engels, 4 April 1882, MECW, 46:229; MEW, 35:52.

14. Karl Marx to Pyotr Lavrov, 23 January 1882, MECW, 46:184; MEW, 35:262.

15. Karl Marx to Jenny Longuet, 27 March 1882, MECW, 46:225; MEW, 35:296. In October 1881, the publisher Otto Meissner had asked Marx to make any necessary corrections or additions to Volume I of his *magnum opus*, in preparation for a new edition.

16. Karl Marx to Paul Lafargue, 20 March 1882, MECW, 46:221; MEW, 35:293.

17. Karl Marx to Jenny Longuet, 6–7 April 1882, MECW, 46:230; MEW, 35:298.

18. Karl Marx to Friedrich Engels, 20 May 1882, MECW, 46:210; MEW, 35:65.

19. See Paul Lafargue to Friedrich Engels, 19 June 1882, in Frederick Engels, Paul Lafargue, and Laura Lafargue, *Correspondence*, vol. 1: 1868–1886 (Moscow: Foreign Languages Publishing House, 1959), 87.

20. Cf. Friedrich Engels to Eduard Bernstein, 22–25 February 1882, MECW, 46:210–211; MEW, 35:285. Lafargue was later certainly exaggerating when he said that "Marx has come back with his head full of Africa and the Arabs; he took advantage of his stay in Algiers to devour its library; it seems to me that he has read a great number of works on the condition of the Arabs." Paul Lafargue to Friedrich Engels, 16 June 1882, in Engels, Lafargue, and Lafargue, *Correspondence*, 83. As Badia has pointed out, it is much more likely that Marx was unable to "learn much about the social and political situation in the French colony," although his "letters from Algiers testify to his many-sided curiosity." in Badia, "Marx en Algérie, 13.

21. Marx, "Excerpts from M. M. Kovalevsky," 412; "Exzerpte aus M. M. Kovalevskij," 109.

22. See Vesper, *Marx in Algier*, 33–34, which reproduced passages from the article "The Concessions" in the local daily.

23. Karl Marx to Paul Lafargue, 20 March 1882, MECW, 46:220; MEW, 35:292. Marx added that "the same practice can be observed in various places in South America." Ibid.; ibid.

24. This total refers only to his surviving correspondence. In reality, Marx wrote more letters, including some to his daughter Eleanor, but these have been lost over time: "He wrote me long letters from Algiers. Many of these I no longer possess, since at his request I sent them on to Jenny and she gave only a few back to me." Eleanor Marx, in *Gespräche mit Marx und Engels*, ed. Enzensberger, 578.

25. Karl Marx to Jenny Longuet, 6–7 April 1882, MECW, 46:231–232; MEW, 35:300.

26. Karl Marx to Laura Lafargue, 13–14 April 1882, MECW, 46:242; MEW, 35:308.

27. Ibid., MECW, 46:238; ibid., MEW, 35:305.

28. Karl Marx to Friedrich Engels, 8 April 1882, MECW, 46:234; MEW, 35:54.

29. Karl Marx to Friedrich Engels, 18 April 1882, MECW, 46:246–247; MEW, 35:57–58.

30. Karl Marx to Laura Lafargue, 13–14 April 1882, MECW, 46:243; MEW, 35:311.

31. Karl Marx to Friedrich Engels, 28 April 1882, MECW, 46:249; MEW, 35:60.

32. Marx himself said that, although he had not had "one day of complete repose" in the eight weeks before the photograph, he was "still putting a good face on things." Ibid; ibid. Engels was very happy with what his friend had told him. "He had his photograph taken in Algiers," he wrote to Bebel, "and is looking quite his old self again." Friedrich Engels to August Bebel, 16 May 1882, MECW, 46:259; MEW, 35:322. Cf. Vesper, *Marx in Algier*, 130–135.

33. Karl Marx to Friedrich Engels, 8 May 1882, MECW, 46:253; MEW, 35:61.

34. Karl Marx to Eleanor Marx, 28 May 1882, MECW, 46:267; MEW, 35:327.

35. Cf. Karl Marx to Friedrich Engels, 5 June 1882, MECW, 46:272; MEW, 35:69.

36. Karl Marx to Friedrich Engels, 20 May 1882, MECW, 46:262; MEW, 35:64. Marx did not write to his daughters of this development, since "it would alarm them unnecessarily." ibid., MECW, 46:264; ibid., MEW, 35:65.

37. Karl Marx to Friedrich Engels, 8 May 1882, MECW, 46:254; MEW, 35:62.

38. Karl Marx to Eleanor Marx, 28 May 1882, MECW, 46:268; MEW, 35:328.

39. Ibid., MECW, 46:269; ibid., MEW, 35:329. The English engineer Joseph Jaggers (1830–1892) did discover a way of breaking the bank—not by any scientific system, however, but simply by studying a mechanical dysfunction. In 1873, he realized that one roulette wheel was more unbalanced than the others, so that it came up with nine numbers more often than others. He managed to win one and a half million francs, before the casino became aware of the defect and repaired it without difficulty.

40. Karl Marx to Friedrich Engels, 5 June 1882, MECW, 46:272; MEW, 35:68.

41. Ibid., MECW, 46:274; ibid., MEW, 35:69–70.

42. Karl Marx to Jenny Longuet, 4 June 1882, MECW, 46:271; MEW, 35:330.

43. Karl Marx to Friedrich Engels, 5 June 1882, MECW, 46:274; MEW, 35:70. The literary reference here is to a work by Adolph von Knigge (1752–1796), entitled precisely *On Intercourse with People* (1788).

44. Karl Marx to Jenny Longuet, 4 June 1882, MECW, 46:272; MEW, 35:330.

45. Karl Marx to Friedrich Engels, 9 June 1882, MECW, 46:275; MEW, 35:71.

46. Ibid.; ibid. As Engels reported, "his further movements . . . depend entirely upon the doctors." Friedrich Engels to Friedrich Sorge, 20 June 1882, MECW, 46:278; MEW, 35:332.

47. Karl Marx to Friedrich Engels, 24 June 1882, MECW, 46:284; MEW, 35:74. On the foul weather that troubled him even back at his daughter's house in Argenteuil, see Lafargue's remarks: "The Parisians are in despair; they have never had a June like this; one might think oneself in England, it is so horrid. Marx puts up with the bad weather; he told me that wherever he went, as soon as he sat down to table, there was a general grumble about the weather, so fine yesterday, so wretched today. 'It is my fault,' Marx answered; 'I bring the bad weather with me.' If he had lived in the Middle Ages, he would have been burnt for a sorcerer." Paul Lafargue to Friedrich Engels, 16 June 1882, in Engels, Lafargue, and Lafargue, *Correspondence*, 85.

48. Karl Marx to Friedrich Engels, 4 July 1882, MECW, 46:290–291; MEW, 35:75.

49. Karl Marx to Friedrich Engels, 3 August 1882, MECW, 46:296–298; MEW, 35:76, 78.

50. Karl Marx to Friedrich Engels, 21 August 1882, MECW, 46:308; MEW, 35:83. Shortly afterwards, Engels wrote to Jenny: "We have every reason to be content with what progress he has made under the very unfavorable weather that has persecuted him so tenaciously, and after three pleurisies, two of which were so severe. . . . A little more Enghien or Cauterets for his remnant of bronchitis and then a climatic cure on high ground in the Alps or Pyrenees will then set him completely up again ready for work." Friedrich Engels to Jenny Longuet, 27 August 1882, MECW, 46:315–316; MEW, 35:354.

51. Karl Marx to Laura Lafargue, 17 June 1882, MECW, 46:277; MEW, 35:331.

52. Karl Marx to Friedrich Engels, 24 August 1882, MECW, 46:310; MEW, 35:85–86.

53. Karl Marx to Friedrich Engels, 21 August 1882, MECW, 46:308; MEW, 35:83.

54. Karl Marx to Friedrich Engels, 24 August 1882, MECW, 46:310; MEW, 35:85.

55. Karl Marx to Friedrich Engels, 4 September 1882, MECW, 46:317; MEW, 35:91.

56. Friedrich Engels to Karl Marx, 12 September 1882, MECW, 46:319; MEW, 35:93.

57. Karl Marx to Friedrich Engels, 16 September 1882, MECW, 46:326; MEW, 35:95.

58. Karl Marx to Friedrich Engels, 28 September 1882, MECW, 46:337; MEW, 35:98.

59. Karl Marx to Friedrich Engels, 30 September 1882, MECW, 46:338–339; MEW, 35:99–100.

60. Friedrich Engels, "Karl Marx's Funeral," MECW, 24:468.

61. Ibid.

62. Sergei Podolinsky to Karl Marx, 30 March 1880, IISH, Amsterdam, *Marx-Engels Papers*, D 3701.

63. Sergei Podolinsky to Karl Marx, 18 April 1880, IISH Amsterdam, *Marx-Engels Papers*, D 3702. Podolinsky's two letters to Marx have been published in English in Juan Martínez-Alier, *Ecological Economics: Energy, Environment and Society* (Oxford, UK: Basil Blackwell, 1987), 62.

64. On the reasons why Engels and Marx took a renewed interest in this author, see John Bellamy Foster and Paul Burkett, *Marx and the Earth: An Anti-Critique* (Leiden: Brill, 2016), 122–123. In their opinion, for Podolinsky "socialism became merely the universalization of a system of efficient muscular labour for the benefit of all" (ibid., 117).

65. Friedrich Engels to Karl Marx, 19 December 1882, MECW, 46:410.

66. Ibid., MECW, 46:412; ibid., MEW, 35:135. Serge Latouche, *Petit traité de la décroissance sereine* (Paris: Mille et une Nuits, 2007), wrongly asserts that Podolinsky "tried in vain to sensitize Marx to ecological critique" (30). According to Martínez-Alier (*Ecological Economics*, 222): "Engels' reaction to Podolinsky's article . . . was certainly a crucial missed chance in the dialogue between Marxism and ecology." But this interpretation is opposed by Paul Burkett and John Bellamy Foster in "The Podolinsky Myth: An Obituary. Introduction to 'Human Labour and Unity Force' by Sergei Podolinsky," *Historical Materialism* 16, no. 1 (2008): 115–161. Engels—who had read

an Italian version of Podolinsky's text in *The Common People* [*La Plebe*]—added some further points in a letter he sent to Marx on 22 December 1882.

67. Marx had already copiously summarized the argument of this book in 1876: see Karl Marx, IISH Amsterdam, *Marx-Engels Papers*, B 130, B 131, B 132.

68. Karl Marx, RGASPI Moscow, f. 1, op. 1, d. 2940.

69. On Marx's relations with Lankester, see Lewis S. Feuer, "The Friendship of Edwin Ray Lankester and Karl Marx: The Last Episode in Marx's Intellectual Evolution," *Journal of the History of Ideas* 40, no. 4 (1979): 633–648.

70. Edwin Ray Lankester to Karl Marx, 25 December 1880, in ibid., 647.

71. Karl Marx to Laura Lafargue, 9 October 1882, MECW, 46:340; MEW, 35:372.

72. Friedrich Engels to Paul Lafargue, 30 October 1882, MECW, 46:352. Two days earlier, he had written to Bebel in Germany: "Marx . . . leaves the day after tomorrow for the Isle of Wight. . . . [He] is recuperating in fine style and, if there's no recurrence of his pleurisy, he'll be stronger next autumn than he has been for years. Friedrich Engels to August Bebel, 28 October 1882, MECW, 46:349, 450. Later, however, he gave a much less optimistic and more accurate reconstruction: "[Marx] was so sick of a wandering and idle life that renewed exile in southern Europe would probably have damaged his morale as much as it would have benefited his physique. With the onset of London's foggy season, he was sent to the Isle of Wight where it rained continuously and he again caught cold." Friedrich Engels to Friedrich Sorge, 15 March 1883, MECW, 46:461.

73. Karl Marx to Eleanor Marx, 10 November 1882, MECW, 46:371; MEW, 35:397.

74. Karl Marx to Friedrich Engels, 11 November 1882, MECW, 46:375; MEW, 35:110.

75. Karl Marx to Friedrich Engels, 8 November 1882, MECW, 46:366, 365; MEW, 35:106, 105.

76. Karl Marx to Eleanor Marx, 10 November 1882, MECW, 46:371; MEW, 35:398.

77. Friedrich Engels to Karl Marx, 23 November 1882, MECW, 46:385.

78. Karl Marx to Friedrich Engels, 4 December 1882, MECW, 46:392; MEW, 35:123.

79. Karl Marx to Laura Lafargue, 14 December 1882, MECW, 46:398, 399; MEW, 35:407, 408.

80. Karl Marx to Friedrich Engels, 18 December 1882, MECW, 46:409; MEW, 35:132.

81. Karl Marx to Laura Lafarge, 14 December 1882, MECW, 46:398; MEW, 35:407.

82. Marx was referring to the war of 1882, which opposed Egyptian forces under Ahmad Urabi (1841–1911) and troops from the United Kingdom. It concluded with the battle of Tell al-Kebir (13 September 1882), which ended the so-called Urabi revolt that had begun in 1879 and enabled the British to establish a protectorate over Egypt.

83. Karl Marx to Eleanor Marx, 9 January 1883, MECW, 46:422–423; MEW, 35:422.

84. Karl Marx, IISH Amsterdam, *Marx-Engels Papers*, B 168, 11–18. See David Smith, "Accumulation by Forced Migration: Insights from *Capital* and Marx's Late Manuscripts," in *Marx 201: Rethinking Alternatives*, ed. Musto, whose comments on these notes bring out their relevance for us today: "The only aspect of these events that seems surprising today is that they took place in the nineteenth century. What Marx witnessed and reported in the Egyptian case was an early template for the contemporary age of globalization" (ibid.).

85. See IISH Amsterdam, *Marx-Engels Papers*, B 167.

86. Cf. Walicki, *Controversy over Capitalism*, 120.

87. Vasily Vorontsov, *Sud'by kapitalizma v Rossii* [Destinies of capitalism in Russia] (St. Petersburg, 1882), 13–14; quoted in Walicki, *Controversy over Capitalism*, 1115–1116. It should be noted that these quotations were not in the pages on which Marx made marginal notes or underlinings. See Karl Marx and Friedrich Engels, *Die Bibliotheken von Karl Marx und Friedrich Engels*, MEGA², IV/32:667. For a critique of Vorontsov's limitations in this respect, see Rosa Luxemburg, *The Accumulation of Capital* (London: Routledge, 2014), 276–283.

88. For more on the use Marx made of these books on Russia, see Karl Marx and Friedrich Engels, *Die Bibliotheken von Karl Marx und Friedrich Engels*, MEGA², IV/32:597, 343, 463, 667, 603–604, 245–246, 186.

89. Karl Marx, *Notizen zur Reform von 1861 und der damit verbundenen Entwicklung in Rußland*, MEW, 19:407–424.

90. Karl Marx to Laura Lafargue, 14 December 1882, MECW, 46:399; MEW, 35:408.

91. Karl Marx to Friedrich Engels, 11 November 1882, MECW, 46:375; MEW, 35:110.

92. This statement to Lafargue is reported in Engels's letter of 2–3 November 1882 to Eduard Bernstein, MECW, 46:356. "Now what is known as 'Marxism' in France," Engels lamented, "is . . . an altogether peculiar product." In fact, he repeated the same idea seven years later, on 7 September 1890, in a communication to the editors of *Der Socialdemocrat*, see Friedrich Engels, "Draft of a Reply to the Editors of the 'Sachsischen Arbeit-Zeitung,'" MECW, 27:67–68; and also in two private letters: to Conrad Schmidt, on 5 August 1890, and to Paul Lafargue, on 27 August 1890, MECW, 49:7, 22. Karl Kautsky referred to the phrase incorrectly, claiming that Marx had used it in a communication to himself. see Benedikt Kautsky, *Friedrich Engels' Briefwechsel mit Karl Kautsky*, 90. Similarly, the Russian translator of *Capital*, German Lopatin, wrote in a letter of 20 September 1883 to Mariya Oshanina: "Do you remember me saying that Marx himself was never a Marxist? Engels related that, during the struggle of Brousse, Malone & Co. against the others, Marx once said with a laugh: 'All I can say is, I am not a Marxist!'" German Lopatin, in *Gespräche mit Marx und Engels*, ed. Enzensberger, 583. See also Rubel, *Marx, critique du marxisme*, 20–22.

93. Karl Marx to Eleanor Marx, 23 December 1882, MECW, 46:417–418; MEW, 35:418. Marx was referring to the chronological table of world history he had begun to prepare in autumn 1881.

94. Karl Marx to James Williamson, 6 January 1883, MECW, 46:419. This letter, written in English, did not appear in the MEW volumes and has not yet been published in MEGA².

95. Karl Marx to Friedrich Engels, 10 January 1883, MECW, 46:425; MEW, 35:140.

96. Karl Marx to Eleanor Marx, 8 January 1883, MECW, 46:420–421; MEW, 35:420.

97. Karl Marx to Friedrich Engels, 10 January 1883, MECW, 46:425; MEW, 35:141.

98. Karl Marx to Eleanor Marx, 9 January 1883, MECW, 46:423; MEW, 35:421.

99. Eleanor Marx, in *Reminiscences of Marx and Engels*, ed. Institute of Marxism-Leninism (Moscow: Foreign Languages Publishing House, 1957), 128.

100. Karl Marx to James Williamson, 13 January 1883, MECW, 46:429; MEW, 46:429.

101. Friedrich Engels to Eduard Bernstein, 18 January 1883, MECW, 46:430.

102. Friedrich Engels to Eduard Bernstein, 8 February 1883, MECW, 46:434.

103. Friedrich Engels to Laura Lafargue, 16–17 February 1883, MECW, 46:440–441; MEW, 35:436.

104. Ibid., MECW, 46:441; ibid.

105. Friedrich Engels to Eduard Bernstein, 27 February–1 March 1883, MECW, 46:450.

106. Friedrich Engels to August Bebel, 7 March 1883, MECW, 46:455.

107. Friedrich Engels to Laura Lafargue, 10 March 1883, MECW, 46:456.

108. According to Helmut Dressler, *Ärzte um Karl Marx* (Berlin: Volk und Gesundheit, 1970), Engels indicated that the cause of Marx's death was "internal bleeding as the result of a pulmonary ulcer." "We do not know," Dressler continued, "whether this was also the opinion of the doctors attending him. Given its multiple meanings, the concept of 'pulmonary ulcer' is no longer in use today. But let us suppose that Marx's death was caused by the spread of pulmonary tuberculosis. . . . In 1882, . . . Marx had had an effusion on his left side, following a wet pleurisy which in 95 per cent of cases is tuberculous in nature. There is not enough evidence to speak of hydrothorax or an accumulation of liquid matter, especially associated with cardiac insufficiency or renal blockage. On the other hand, symptoms such as a cough with 'terrible' expectoration, pain on the left side of the thorax, and a generally poor condition with insomnia and loss of appetite point to a tuberculous origin" (ibid. 145–146).

109. Friedrich Engels to Friedrich Sorge, 15 March 1883, MECW, 46:461–462; MEW, 35:460.

110. The reference is to the so-called *Letter on Happiness* that Epicurus addressed to Menoeceus.

111. Cf. Friedrich Engels to Wilhelm Liebknecht, 14 March 1883, MECW, 46:458: "In my opinion, the death, first of his wife, and then, in a most critical period, of Jenny, helped to bring on the final crisis."

112.   In a similar letter to Bernstein, Engels wrote: "The movement will continue on its way but it will miss the calm, timely, considered interventions which have hitherto saved it many a weary digression." Friedrich Engels to Eduard Bernstein, 14 March 1883, MECW, 46:459.

113.   Friedrich Engels to Friedrich Sorge, 15 March 1883, MECW, 46:462–463; MEW, 35:460–461.

BIBLIOGRAPHY

I. Writings of Karl Marx

I.1 Marx Engels Collected Works (MECW)

Marx, Karl. "A Contribution to the Critique of Hegel's Philosophy of Law." MECW, 3:3–129; "Kritik des Hegelschen Staatsrechts." MEW, 1:203–333.

———. *The Poverty of Philosophy.* MECW, 6:105–212; *Das Elend der Philosophie.* MEW, 4:63–182.

———. "The Future Results of British Rule in India." MECW, 12:217–223; "Die künftigen Ergebnisse der britischen Herrschaft in Indien." MEW, 9:220–226.

———. "Speech at the Anniversary of the People's Paper." MECW, 14:655–656; "Rede auf der Jahresfeier des People's Paper." MEW, 12:3–5.

———. "Provisional Rules of the International Working Men's Association." MECW, 20:14–16; "Provisorische Statuten der Internationalen Arbeiter-Assoziation." MEW, 16:14–16.

———. "Instructions for the Delegates of the Provisional General Council: The Different Questions." MECW, 20:185–193; "Instruktionen für die Delegierten des Provisorischen Zentral-rats zu den einzelnen Fragen." MEW, 16:190–199.

———. "Report of a Speech by Karl Marx at the Anniversary Celebration of the German Workers' Educational Society in London, February 28, 1867." MECW, 20:415; "Aufzeichnung einer Rede von Karl Marx auf dem Stiftungsfest des Deutschen Bildungsvereins für Arbeiter in Londonam" 28. Februar 1867. MEW, 16:524.

———. *The Civil War in France.* MECW, 22:307–359; *Der Bürgerkrieg in Frankreich.* MEW, 17:313–365.

———. *Critique of the Gotha Programme.* MECW, 24:75–99; *Kritik des Gothaer Programms.* MEW, 19:13–32.

———. "Workers' Questionnaire." MECW, 24:328–334; "Fragebogen für Arbeiter." MEW, 19:230–237.

———. "Letter to Otechestvenniye Zapiski." MECW, 24:196–201; Brief an die Redaktion der "Otetschestwennyje Sapiski." MEW, 19:107–112.

———. "Preamble to the Programme of the French Workers Party." MECW, 24:340; "Einleitung zum Programm der französischen Arbeiterpartei." MEW, 19:238.

———. "K. Marx. Drafts of the Letter to Vera Zasulich: First Draft." MECW, 24:346–360; "Entwürfe einer Antwort auf den Brief von V. I. Sassulitsch: Erster Entwurf." MEW, 19:384–395.

———. "K. Marx. Drafts of the Letter to Vera Zasulich: Second Draft." MECW, 24:360–364; "Brief von V. I. Sassulitsch: Zweiter Entwurf." MEW, 19:396–400.

———. "K. Marx. Drafts of the Letter to Vera Zasulich: Third Draft." MECW, 24:364–369; "Brief von V. I. Sassulitsch: Dritter Entwurf." MEW, 19:401–406.

———. "Letter to Vera Zasulich." MECW, 24:370–371; "Brief an V. I. Sassulitsch." MEW, 19:242–243.

———. "Notes on Bakunin's Book *Statehood and Anarchy*." MECW, 24:485–526; "Konspekt von Bakunins Buch *Staatlichkeit und Anarchie*." MEW, 18:597–642.

———. "Marginal Notes on Adolph Wagner's *Lehrbuch der politischen Ökonomie*." MECW, 24:531–559; "Randglossen zu A. Wagners *Lehrbuch der politischen Ökonomie*." MEW, 19:355–383.

———. "Declaration by Karl Marx on His Naturalisation in England." MECW, 24:564.

———. "[Account of Karl Marx's Interview with the *Chicago Tribune* Correspondent]." MECW, 24:568–579; "Interview mit dem Grundleger des modernen Sozialismus. Besondere Korrespondenz der Tribüne," MEW, 34:508–516.

———. "Sir Mountstuart Elphinstone Grant Duff's Account of a Talk with Karl Marx: From a Letter to Crown Princess Victoria," 1 February 1879. MECW, 24:580–583; "Sir Mountstuart Elphinstone Grant Duff, Account of a Talk with Karl Marx: Aus einem Brief an Kronprinzessin Victoria." MEGA², I/25:438–441.

———. "[Account of an Interview with John Swinton, Correspondent of *The Sun*]." MECW, 24:583–585; John Swinton. "Account of an Interview with Karl Marx: Published in the 'Sun.'" MEGA², I/25:442–443.

———. *Outlines of the Critique of Political Economy* [*Grundrisse*]. First Instalment. MECW, 28; *Grundrisse der Kritik der politischen Ökonomie*. MEW, 42.

———. *Outlines of the Critique of Political Economy* [*Grundrisse*]. Second Instalment. MECW, 29:5–253; *Grundrisse der Kritik der politischen Ökonomie*. MEW, 42.

———. *A Contribution to the Critique of Political Economy*. MECW, 29:257–417; *Zur Kritik der politischen Ökonomie*. MEW, 13:7–160.

———. *Capital, Volume I*. MECW, 35; *Das Kapital, Erster Band*. MEW, 23.

———. "Afterword to the Second German Edition." MECW, 35:17; "Nachwort zur zweiten Auflage." MEW, 23:25.

———. "Afterword to the French Edition." MECW, 35:24.

I.2 *Marx Engels Collected Works* (MECW), co-authored with
Friedrich Engels

Manifesto of the Communist Party. MECW, 6:477–519; *Manifest der Kommunistischen Partei.* MEW, 4:459–493.

———. "Preface to the Second Russian Edition of the *Manifesto of the Communist Party*." MECW, 24:425–426; "Vorrede zur zweiten russischen Ausgabe des *Manifests der Kommunistischen Partei*." MEW, 19:295–296.

———. *Letters 1856–59.* MECW, 40; *Briefe, Jan 1856–Dez 1859.* MEW, 29.

———. *Letters 1860–64.* MECW, 41; *Briefe, Jan 1860–Sep 1864.* MEW, 30.

———. *Letters 1864–68.* MECW, 42; *Briefe, Okt 1864–Dez 1867.* MEW, 31.

———. *Letters 1868–70.* MECW, 43; *Briefe, Jan 1868–Juli 1870.* MEW, 32.

———. *Letters 1870–73.* MECW, 44; *Briefe, Juli 1870–Dez 1874.* MEW, 33.

———. *Letters 1874–79.* MECW, 45; *Briefwechsel Marx und Engels, Feb 1875–Sep 1880.* MEW, 34.

———. *Letters 1880–83.* MECW, 46; *Briefwechsel Marx und Engels, Jan 1881–Mar 1883.* MEW, 35.

I.3 *Marx-Engels Gesamtausgabe* (MEGA²)

Marx, Karl. *Das Kapital. Kritik der politischen Ökonomie. Erster Band, Hamburg 1867.* MEGA², II/5.

———. *Le Capital, Paris 1872–1875.* MEGA², II/7.

———. "Das Kapital. Zweites Buch. Der Zirkulationsprozeß des Kapitals. Zu benutzende Textstellen früherer Darstellungen (Manuskript I bis IV)." MEGA², II/11:525–548.

———. "Das Kapital. Zweites Buch. Der Zirkulationsprozeß des Kapitals. Erster Abschnitt (Fragmente II)." MEGA², II/11:550–697.

———. "Das Kapital. Zweites Buch. Der Zirkulationsprozeß des Kapitals. (Manuskript VIII)." MEGA², II/11:698–828.

———. "Mehrwertrate und Profitrate mathematisch behandelt." MEGA², II/14:19–150.

———. "Exzerpte aus Georg Ludwig von Maurer: Einleitung zur Geschichte der Mark-, Hof-, Dorf- und Stadt-Verfassung und der öffentlichen Gewalt." MEGA², IV/18:542–559, 563–577, 589–600.

———. "Entstehung und Überlieferung." In *Exzerpte und Notizen: Februar 1864 bis Oktober 1868, November 1869, März, April, Juni 1870, Dezember 1872,* MEGA², IV/18:1038–1144.

———. "Exzerpte und Notizen zur Geologie, Mineralogie und Agrikulturchemie. März bis September 1878." MEGA², IV/26:3–94.

———. "Exzerpte aus Werken von Lothar Meyer, Henry Enfield Roscoe, Carl Schorlemmer, Benjamin Witzschel, Wilhelm Friedrich Kühne, Ludimar Hermann, Johannes Ranke und Joseph Beete Jukes." MEGA², IV/31.

Marx, Karl, and Friedrich Engels. *Die Bibliotheken von Karl Marx und Friedrich Engels.* MEGA², IV/32.

I.4 *Marx Engels Werke*

Marx, Karl. *Notizen zur Reform von 1861 und der damit verbundenen Entwicklung in Rußland.* MEW, 19:407–424.

1.5 Single Editions

Marx, Karl. *Œuvres. Économie I.* Paris: Gallimard, 1963.

———. *The Ethnological Notebooks of Karl Marx.* Assen: Van Gorcum, 1972; *Die ethnologischen Exzerpthefte.* Ed. Lawrence Krader. Frankfurt: Suhrkamp, 1976.

———. "Chronologische Auszüge." In Karl Marx and Friedrich Engels, *Über Deutschland und die deutsche Arbeiterbewegung,* Band 1: *Von der Frühzeit bis zum 18. Jahrhundert,* 285–516. Berlin: Dietz, 1973.

———. "Excerpts from M. M. Kovalevskij (Kovalevsky), *Obschinnoe zemlevladenie. Prichiny, khod i posledstviya ego razlozheniya* [Communal landownership: The causes, course and consequences of its decline]." In Lawrence Krader, *The Asiatic Mode of Production: Sources, Development and Critique in the Writings of Karl Marx,* 343–412. Assen: Van Gorcum, 1975; "Exzerpte aus M. M. Kovalevskij. Obschinnoe zemlevladenie (Der Gemeindelandbesitz)." In Karl Marx, *Über Formen vorkapitalistischer Produktion. Vergleichende Studien zur Geschichte des Grundeigentums 1879–80,* 21–109. Frankfurt: Campus, 1977.

———. *Mathematical Manuscripts.* London: New Park Publications, 1983; *Mathematische Manuskript.* Kronberg Taunus: Scriptor, 1974.

———. *Notes on Indian History (664–1858).* Honolulu: University Press of the Pacific, 2001.

Marx, Karl, Friedrich Engels, Vladimir Lenin, and Joseph Stalin. *Zur deutschen Geschichte.* Ed. Wolfgang Harich. Berlin: Dietz, 1953.

1.6 Unpublished Manuscripts

Marx, Karl. IISH Amsterdam, *Marx-Engels Papers,* A 167.

———. IISH Amsterdam, *Marx-Engels Papers,* B 130, B 131, B 132, B 140, B 141, B 146, B 157, B 158, B 159, B 160, B 161, B 167, B 168.

———. IISH Amsterdam, *Marx-Engels Papers,* D 3701, D 3702.

———. RGASPI Moscow, f. 1, op. 1, d. 2940.

II. Writings by Other Authors

Ahmad, Aijaz. *Theory: Classes, Nations, Literatures.* London: Verso, 1992.

Al-Azm, Sadiq Jalal. "Orientalism and Orientalism in Reverse." *Khamsin* 8 (1980): 5–26.

Alcouffe, Alain, ed. "Introduction." In *Les manuscrits mathématiques de Marx,* ed. Alain Alcouffe, 9–109. Paris: Economica, 1985.

Anderson, Kevin. *Marx at the Margins: On Nationalism, Ethnicity, and Non-Western Societies*. Chicago: University of Chicago Press, 2010.

Annales de l'Assemblée nationale. Vol. VIII, Paris, 1873.

Attali, Jacques. *Karl Marx, ou l'Esprit du monde*. Paris: Librairie Arthème-Fayard, 2005.

Badia, Gilbert. "Marx en Algérie." In Karl Marx, *Lettres d'Alger et de la Côte d'Azur*, 7–39. Paris: Le Temps des Cerises, 1997.

Baksi, Pradip, ed. *Karl Marx and Mathematics: A Collection of Texts in Three Parts*. New Delhi: Aakar Books, 2019.

Balibar, Étienne. *The Philosophy of Marx*. London: Verso, 1995.

Baron, Samuel H. "Lo sviluppo del capitalismo in Russia nel pensiero di Plechanov." In *Storia del marxismo contemporaneo*, ed. Istituto Giangiacomo Feltrinelli, 426–450. Milan: Feltrinelli, 1974.

Bax, E. Belfort. "Leaders of Modern Thought XXIII: Karl Marx." *Modern Thought* 3, no. 12 (1881): 349–354.

Beckett, James Camlin. *The Making of Modern Ireland 1603–1923*. London: Faber and Faber, 1981.

Bensaïd, Daniel. *Marx for Our Times: Adventures and Misadventures of a Critique*. London: Verso, 2002.

Bergman, Jay. *Vera Zasulich: A Biography*. Stanford, CA: Stanford University Press, 1983.

Berlin, Isaiah. *Karl Marx: His Life and Environment*. London: Oxford University Press, 1963.

Bernstein, Edward. *My Years of Exile*. London: Leonard Parsons, 1921.

Billington, James H. *Mikhailovsky and Russian Populism*. Oxford: Clarendon Press, 1958.

Bloch, Maurice. *Marxism and Anthropology: The History of a Relationship*. London: Routledge, 1983.

Bongiovanni, Bruno. *Le repliche della storia. Karl Marx tra la Rivoluzione francese e la critica della politica*. Turin: Bollati Boringhieri, 1989.

Botta, Scipione. *Vita privata di Carlo Botta. Ragguagli domestici ed aneddotici raccolti dal suo maggior figlio*. Florence: G. Barbera, 1877.

Bottigelli, Emile. "La rupture Marx-Hyndman." *Annali dell'Istituto Giangiacomo Feltrinelli* III (1961): 621–629.

Briggs, Asa, and John Callow. *Marx in London: An Illustrated Guide*. London: Lawrence and Wishart, 2008.

Brown, Heather. *Marx on Gender and the Family: A Critical Study*. Leiden: Brill, 2012.

Buber, Martin. *Paths in Utopia*. Syracuse, NY: Syracuse University Press, 1996.

Burkett, Paul, and John Bellamy Foster. "The Podolinsky Myth: An Obituary. Introduction to 'Human Labour and Unity Force' by Sergei Podolinsky." *Historical Materialism* 16, no. 1 (2008): 115–161.

Cafiero, Carlo. *"Il Capitale" di Carlo Marx brevemente compendiato da Carlo Cafiero. Libro Primo: Sviluppo della Produzione Capitalistica*. Milan: E. Bignami e C., 1879.

Casiccia, Alessandro. "La concezione materialista della società antica e della società primitiva." In Henry Morgan, *La società antica*, XVII–XXVII. Milan: Feltrinelli, 1970.

Chakrabarty, Dipesh. *Provincializing Europe: Postcolonial Thought and Historical Difference*. Princeton, NJ: Princeton University Press, 2000.

Chernyshevsky, Nikolai. "Kritika filosofskikh preubezhdenii protiv obshchinnogo vladeniya [Critique of philosophical prejudices against communal ownership of the land]." In Chernyshevsky, *Sobranie sochinenii*, 4:424–475. Moscow: Ogonyok, 1974.

———. "A Critique of Philosophical Prejudices against Communal Ownership." In *Late Marx and the Russian Road*, ed. Teodor Shanin, 182–190. London: Routledge, 1984.

Claeys, Gregory. *Marx and Marxism*. London: Penguin, 2018.

Comyn, Marian. "My Recollections of Marx." *The Nineteenth Century and After* 91 (1922): 161–169.

Dardot, Pierre, and Christian Laval. *Marx, prénom Karl*. Paris: Gallimard, 2012.

Dornemann, Luise. *Jenny Marx. Der Lebensweg einer Sozialistin*. Berlin: Dietz, 1971.

Douglas, Roy. *Land, People and Politics: A History of the Land Question in the United Kingdom, 1878–1952*. London: Allison and Busby, 1976.

Dressler, Helmut. *Ärzte um Karl Marx*. Berlin: Volk und Gesundheit, 1970.

Ducange, Jean-Numa. *Jules Guesde: The Birth of Socialism and Marxism in France*. London: Palgrave Macmillan, 2020.

Dunayevskaya, Raya. *Rosa Luxemburg, Women's Liberation, and Marx's Philosophy of Revolution*. Chicago: University of Illinois Press, 1991.

Dussel, Enrique. *El último Marx (1863–1882) y la liberación latinoamericana*. Mexico City: Siglo XXI, 1990.

Eaton, Henry. "Marx and the Russians." *Journal of the History of Ideas* 41, no. 1 (1980): 89–112.

Engels, Frederick. "On Social Relations in Russia." MECW, 24:39–40.

———. "Karl Marx's Funeral." MECW, 24:467–471.

———. *The Origin of the Family, Private Property and the State*, MECW, 26:129–276; MEW, 21:68.

———. "To the Editors of the *Severny Vestnik*." MECW, 26:311.

———. "Draft of a Reply to the Editors of the *Sachsischen Arbeit-Zeitung*," MECW, 27:67–68.

———. "Marx, Heinrich Karl," MECW, 27:341; MEW, 22:342.

———. "Preface to the English Edition" of Karl Marx, *Capital, Volume I*, MECW, 35:30–36.

———. "Preface to the First German Edition," *Capital, Volume II*, MECW, 36:5–23.

———. *Letters 1883–86*, MECW, 47.

———. *Letters 1887–90*, MECW, 48.

———. *Letters 1890–92*, MECW, 49.

———. *Letters 1892–95*, MECW, 50.

Engels, Frederick, Paul Lafargue, and Laura Lafargue. *Correspondence.* Vol. 1: 1868–1886. Moscow: Foreign Languages Publishing House, 1959.

Enzensberger, Hans Magnus, ed. *Gespräche mit Marx und Engels.* Frankfurt: Insel, 1973.

Feuchtwanger, Edgar J. *Gladstone.* London: Allen Road, 1975.

Feuer, Lewis S. "The Friendship of Edwin Ray Lankester and Karl Marx: The Last Episode in Marx's Intellectual Evolution." *Journal of the History of Ideas* 40, no. 4 (1979): 633–648.

Foner, Philip S., ed. *Karl Marx Remembered: Comments at the Time of His Death.* San Francisco: Synthesis, 1983.

Foster, John Bellamy, and Paul Burkett. *Marx and the Earth: An Anti-Critique.* Leiden: Brill, 2016.

Gabriel, Mary. *Love and Capital: Karl and Jenny Marx and the Birth of a Revolution.* New York: Little, Brown, 2011.

Gailey, Christine Ward. "Community, State, and Questions of Social Evolution in Karl Marx's *Ethnological Notebooks.*" In *The Politics of Egalitarianism*, ed. Jacqueline Solway, 31–52. New York: Berghahn Books, 2006.

Gallissot, René, ed. *Marxisme et Algérie.* Paris: Union générale d'éditions, 1976.

García Linera, Álvaro. *Forma valor y forma comunidad.* Prometeo: Buenos Aires, 2010.

Garin, Sender. *Three American Radicals: John Swinton, Charles P. Steinmetz, and William Dean Howells.* Boulder, CO: Westview Press, 1991.

George, Henry. "The Kearney Agitation in California." *The Popular Science Monthly* 17 (August 1880): 433–453.

———. *An Anthology of Henry George's Thought.* Ed. Kenneth C. Wenzer. Rochester, NY: University of Rochester Press, 1997.

———. *Progress and Poverty.* New York: Robert Schalkenbach Foundation, 2006.

Godelier, Maurice. *Perspectives in Marxist Anthropology.* London: Verso, 1977.

———. *The Mental and the Material.* London: Verso, 2012.

Gottlob, Michael. *Geschichtsschreibung zwischen Aufklärung und Historismus. Johanna von Müller und Friedrich Christoph Schlosser.* Frankfurt: Peter Lang, 1989.

Guesde, Jules, and Paul Lafargue. "Le programme du Parti ouvrier." In Jules Guesde, *Textes choisis, 1867–1882*, 117–119. Paris: Éditions sociales, 1959.

Habib, Irfan. "Marx's Perception of India." In *Karl Marx on India*, ed. Iqbal Husain, XIX–LIV. New Delhi: Tulika, 2006.

Hall, Alfred Rupert. *Philosophers at War.* Cambridge: Cambridge University Press, 1980.

Harstick, Hans-Peter. "Einführung. Karl Marx und die zeitgenössische Verfassungsgeschichtsschreibung." In Karl Marx, *Über Formen vorkapitalistischer Produktion*, 13–48. Frankfurt: Campus, 1977.

Harstick, Hans-Peter, Richard Sperl, and Hanno Strauß (1999). "Einführung," MEGA², IV/32: *Die Bibliotheken von Karl Marx und Friedrich Engels*, 7–102.

Haupt, Georges. *Aspects of International Socialism*. Cambridge: Cambridge University Press, 1986.

Heinrich, Michael. "*Capital* after the MEGA: Discontinuities, Interruptions, and New Beginnings." *Crisis & Critique* III, no. 3 (2016): 92–138.

Herzen, Alexander. *The Russian People and Socialism: An Open Letter to Jules Michelet*. London: Weidenfeld and Nicolson, 2011.

———. "Revolution in Russia." In *The Herzen Reader*, ed. Kathleen Parthe, 61–65. Evanston, IL: Northwestern University Press, 2012.

Hobsbawm, Eric. "Introduction." *Pre-Capitalist Economic Formations*, by Karl Marx. London: Lawrence & Wishart, 1964.

Holmes, Rachel. *Eleanor Marx: A Life*. London: Bloomsbury, 2014.

Hospitalier, Édouard. *La physique moderne. Les principales applications de l'électricité*. Paris: G. Masson, 1882.

Hudis, Peter. "Accumulation, Imperialism, and Pre-Capitalist Formations: Luxemburg and Marx on the Non-Western World." *Socialist Studies* VI, no. 2 (2010): 75–91.

Hyndman, Henry. *The Record of an Adventurous Life*. New York: Macmillan, 1911.

———. *England for All*. New York: Barnes & Noble, 1974.

———. IISH Amsterdam, *Marx-Engels Papers*, C 261, C 262.

Institute of Marxism-Leninism, ed. *Reminiscences of Marx and Engels*. Moscow: Foreign Languages Publishing House, 1957.

Kaiser, Bruno. *Ex libris Karl Marx und Friedrich Engels. Schicksal und Verzeichnis einer Bibliothek*. Berlin: Dietz, 1967.

Kapp, Yvonne. *Eleanor Marx: Family Life 1855–1883*. Vol. 1. London: Virago, 1979.

Kautsky, Benedikt, ed. *Friedrich Engels' Briefwechsel mit Karl Kautsky*. Vienna: Danubia, 1955.

Kisch, Egon Erwin. *Karl Marx in Karlsbad*. Berlin: Aufbau, 1953.Klein, Maury. *The Life and Legend of Jay Gould*. Baltimore: Johns Hopkins University Press, 1997.

Krader, Lawrence, ed. "Introduction." *The Ethnological Notebooks of Karl Marx*, by Karl Marx, 1–85. Assen: Van Gorcum, 1972.

———. *The Asiatic Mode of Production: Sources, Development and Critique in the Writings of Karl Marx*. Assen: Van Gorcum, 1975.

Krätke, Michael R. "Marx and World History." *International Review of Social History* 63, no. 1 (2018): 91–125.

Krysmanski, Hans Jürgen. *Die letzte Reise des Karl Marx*. Frankfurt: Westend, 2014.

Lafargue, Paul. "Frederick Engels." *The Social Democrat* 9, no. 8 (1905): 483–488.

Lanzardo, Dario. "Intervento socialista nella lotta operaia. L'inchiesta operaia di Marx." *Quaderni Rossi* 5 (April 1965): 1–24.

Latouche, Serge. *Petit traité de la décroissance sereine*. Paris: Mille et une Nuits, 2017.

Lazarus, Neil. "The Fetish of 'the West' in Postcolonial Theory." In *Marxism, Modernity and Postcolonial Studies*, ed. Crystal Bartolovich and Neil Lazarus, 43–64. Cambridge: Cambridge University Press, 2002.

Liedman, Sven-Eric. *A World to Win: The Life and Works of Karl Marx*. London: Verso, 2018.

Limmroth, Angelika. *Jenny Marx. Die Biographie*. Berlin: Karl Dietz, 2018.

Limmroth, Angelika, and Rolf Hecker. *Jenny Marx. Die Briefe*. Berlin: Karl Dietz, 2014.

Lindner, Kolja. "Marx's Eurocentrism: Postcolonial Studies and Marx's Scholarship." *Radical Philosophy*, no. 161 (2010): 27–41.

Literatura partii Narodnoi Voli. Paris: Société nouvelle de librairie et d'édition, 1905.

Lombardo Radice, Lucio. "Dai manoscritti matematici di K. Marx." *Critica Marxista-Quaderni*, no. 6 (1972): 273–286.

Luxemburg, Rosa. *The Accumulation of Capital*. London: Routledge, 2014.

Martínez-Alier, Juan. *Ecological Economics: Energy, Environment and Society*. Oxford, UK: Basil Blackwell, 1987.

Matthew, Colin. *Gladstone: 1875–1898*. Oxford: Clarendon Press, 1995.

McLellan, David. *Karl Marx: His Life and His Thought*. London: Macmillan, 1973.

Mehring, Franz. *Karl Marx: The Story of His Life*. Ann Arbor: University of Michigan Press, 1962.

Meier, Olga, ed. *The Daughters of Karl Marx: Family Correspondence 1866–1898*. New York: Harcourt Brace Jovanovich, 1982.

Melotti, Umberto. *Marx and the Third World*. London: Palgrave, 1977.

Mohri, Kenzo. "Marx and 'Underdevelopment.'" *Monthly Review* 30, no. 11 (1979): 32–42.

Morgan, Henry. *Ancient Society*. New York: Henry Holt, 1877.

Moses, Daniel. *The Promise of Progress: The Life and Work of Lewis Henry Morgan*. Columbia: University of Missouri Press, 2009.

Most, Johann. *Kapital und Arbeit. Ein populärer Auszug aus "Das Kapital" von Marx 1873*. MEGA², II/8:735–800. Chemnitz, 1873.

Mulhall, Michael George. "Egyptian Finance." *Contemporary Review* XLII (1882): 525–535.

Musto, Marcello. "The Rediscovery of Karl Marx." *International Review of Social History* 52, no. 3 (2007): 477–498.

———, ed. *Karl Marx's Grundrisse: Foundations of the Critique of Political Economy 150 Years Later*. New York: Routledge, 2008.

———, ed. *Workers Unite! The International 150 Years Later*. London: Bloomsbury, 2014.

———. "The Myth of the 'Young Marx' in the Interpretations of the *Economic* and *Philosophic Manuscripts of 1844*," *Critique* 43, no. 2 (2015): 233–260.

———. *Another Marx: Early Manuscripts to the International*. London: Bloomsbury, 2018.

———. *Karl Marx. Biografia intellettuale e politica 1857–1883*. Turin: Einaudi, 2018.

———, ed. *The Marx Revival: Essential Concepts and New Interpretations*. Cambridge: Cambridge University Press, 2020.

Natalizi, Marco. *Il caso Černyševskij*. Milan: Bruno Mondadori, 2006.

Nicolaevsky, Boris, and Otto Maenchen-Helfen. *Karl Marx: Man and Fighter*. London: Pelican Books, 1976.

Nieuwenhuis, Ferdinand Domela. *Kapitaal en Arbeid*. The Hague, 1881.

Oittinen, Vesa. *Marxism, Russia, Philosophy*. London: Palgrave, 2020.

Otani, Teinosuke, Ljudmila Vasina, and Carl-Erich Vollgraf. "Einführung," MEGA², II/11:843–905.

Payne, Robert. *Marx: A Biography*. New York: Simon & Schuster, 1968.

Pereira, Norman G. O. *The Thought and Teachings of N. G. Černyševskij*. The Hague: Mouton, 1975.

Perlman, Selig. "The Anti-Chinese Agitation in California." In *History of Labour in the United States*, vol. 2, ed. John R. Commons, David J. Saposs, Helen L. Sumner, Edward B. Mittelman, Henry E. Hoagland, John B. Andrews, and Selig Perlman, 252–268. New York: Macmillan, 1918.

Peters, Heinz Frederick. *Red Jenny: A Life with Karl Marx*. New York: St. Martin's, 1986.

Pipes, Richard. "Narodnichestvo: A Semantic Inquiry." *Slavic Review* XXIII, no. 3 (1964): 421–458.

———. *Struve: Liberal on the Left, 1870–1905*. Cambridge, MA: Harvard University Press, 1970.

Poggio, Pier Paolo. *L'Obščina. Comune contadina e rivoluzione in Russia*. Milan: Jaca Book, 1978.

Prawer, Siebert S. *Karl Marx and World Literature*. London: Verso, 2011.

Rae, John. "The Socialism of Karl Marx and the Young Hegelians." *The Contemporary Review* XL (July–December 1881): 587–607.

Renehan, Edward J. *Dark Genius of Wall Street: The Misunderstood Life of Jay Gould, King of the Robber Barons*. New York: Basic Books, 2006.

Rubel, Maximilien. *Karl Marx. Essai de biographie intellectuelle*. Paris: Rivière, 1957.

———, ed. *Karl Marx / Friedrich Engels: Die russische Kommune*. Munich: Hanser, 1972.

———. *Marx, critique du marxisme*. Paris: Payot, 1974.

———. *Marx: Life and Works*. London: Macmillan, 1980.

Rühle, Otto. *Karl Marx: His Life and Work*. New York: Routledge, 2011.

Ryazanov, David. "Neueste Mitteilungen über den literarischen Nachlaß von Karl Marx und Friedrich Engels." *Archiv für die Geschichte des Sozialismus und der Arbeiterbewegung* 11 (1925): 385–400.

———. "The Discovery of the Drafts." In Shanin, *Late Marx and the Russian Road*, 127–33.

Said, Edward. *Orientalism*. London: Routledge, 1995.

Saito, Kohei. *Karl Marx's Ecosocialism: Capital, Nature, and the Unfinished Critique of Political Economy*. New York: Monthly Review Press, 2017.

Sawer, Marian. *Marxism and the Question of the Asiatic Mode of Production*. The Hague: Martinus Nijhoff, 1977.

Shanin, Teodor. "Late Marx: Gods and Craftsmen." In Shanin, *Late Marx and the Russian Road*, 3–39.

———, ed. *Late Marx and the Russian Road*. London: Routledge, 1984.

Shannon, Richard. *Gladstone*, vol. 2: *1865–1898*. Chapel Hill: University of North Carolina Press, 1999.

Smith, Cyril. *Marx at the Millennium*. London: Pluto, 1996.

Smith, David. "Accumulation by Forced Migration: Insights from *Capital* and Marx's Late Manuscripts." In *Marx 201: Rethinking Alternatives*, ed. Marcello Musto. London: Palgrave Macmillan, 2020.

———, ed. *Marx's World: Global Society and Capital Accumulation in Marx's Late Manuscripts*. New Haven, CT: Yale University Press, forthcoming 2020.

Sofri, Gianni. *Il modo di produzione asiatico. Storia di una controversia marxista*. Turin: Einaudi, 1969.

Sperber, Jonathan. *Karl Marx: A Nineteenth-Century Life*. New York: Liveright, 2013.

Stedman Jones, Gareth. *Karl Marx: Greatness and Illusion*. Cambridge, MA: Harvard University Press, 2016.

Stenographische Berichte über die Verhandlungen des Reichstags. Vol. I. Berlin, 1882.

Tairako, Tomonaga. "Marx on Capitalist Globalization." *Hitotsubashi Journal of Social Studies* 35 (2003): 11–16.

———. "A Turning Point in Marx's Theory on Pre-Capitalist Societies—Marx's Excerpt Notebooks on Maurer in Mega IV/18–." *Hitotsubashi Journal of Social Studies* 47, no. 1 (January 2016): 1–10.

Tible, Jean. *Marx Selvagem*. São Paulo: Autonomia Literária, 2018.

Tichelman, Fritjof. *Schriften aus dem Karl-Marx-Haus*, vol. XXX: *Marx on Indonesia and India*. Trier: Karl-Marx-Haus, 1983.

Tsuzuki, Chushichi. *H. M. Hyndman and British Socialism*. London: Oxford University Press, 1961.

———. *The Life of Eleanor Marx, 1855–1898: A Socialist Tragedy*. Oxford: Clarendon Press, 1967.

Venturi, Franco. *Roots of Revolution: A History of the Populist and Socialist Movements in Nineteenth Century Russia*. New York: Alfred A. Knopf, 1960.

———. "Introduzione." In Franco Venturi, *Il populismo russo. Herzen, Bakunin, Cernysevskij*, I:VII–CXII. Turin: Einaudi, 1972.

Vesper, Marlene. *Marx in Algier*. Bonn: Pahl-Rugenstein Nachfolger, 1995.

Vollgraf, Carl-Erich. "Marx's Further Work on Capital after Publishing Volume I: On the Completion of Part II of the MEGA." In *Marx's Capital: An Unfinishable Project?* Brill: Leiden, 2018. 56–79.

Vorländer, Karl. *Karl Marx*. Leipzig: F. Meiner, 1929.

Vorontsov, Vasily. *Sud'by kapitalizma v Rossii* [Destinies of capitalism in Russia]. St. Petersburg, 1882.

Wada, Haruki. "Marx and Revolutionary Russia." In Shanin, *Late Marx and the Russian Road*, 40–76.

Wagner, Adolph. *Lehrbuch der politischen Ökonomie* (Leipzig: Winter, 1879–1899).

Walicki, Andrzej. *Controversy over Capitalism: Studies in the Social Philosophy of the Russian Populists*. Oxford: Clarendon Press, 1969.

Webb, Daren. *Marx, Marxism, and Utopia*. Aldershot, UK: Ashgate, 2000.

Weissweiler, Eva. *Tussy Marx: Das Drama der Vatertochter*. Cologne: Kiepenheuer & Witsch, 2002.

White, James. *Marx and Russia: The Fate of a Doctrine*. London: Bloomsbury, 2018.

Wurmbrand, Richard. *Was Marx a Satanist?* Glendale, CA: Diane Books, 1979.

Yanovskaya, Sofya. "Preface to the 1968 Russian Edition." In Karl Marx, *Mathematical Manuscripts*, VII–XXVI. London: New Park, 1983.

Zasulich, Vera. "A Letter to Marx." In Shanin, *Late Marx and the Russian Road*, 98–99.

INDEX

Adolphus, Gustavus, 102
Al-Azm, Sadiq Jalal, 153n101
agriculture, 27, 32, 52, 58, 66, 69, 70, 87, 165–66n147
anarchism, 44, 74–75, 95; Marx and anarchism, 59, 75, 95, 119
Anderson, Kevin, 135n40, 136n58
antisemitism, 163n112
Aristotle, 25
Australia, 23
Austria, 91

Bachofen, Johann, 29
Badia, Gilbert, 169n20
Bakunin, Mikhail, 46, 59, 62, 74, 78, 121, 145n179, 150n74; Marx on Bakunin, 59
Balsem, Nicolas, 80
Bax, Ernest Belfort, 85
Bebel, August, 123, 135n30, 145n189, 163n104, 170n32, 172n72
Belgium, 78
Bengal, 22, 32
Bennett, Richard, 23
Berlin, Isaiah, 137n73
Berlin University, 24
Berlin Wall, 4
Bernstein, Eduard, 17, 78, 97, 123, 144n171, 145–46n189, 163n104, 175n112
Black Repartition, 74, 75, 156n153
Blanqui, Auguste, 55, 78
Blanquism, 62; neo-Blanquism, 74
Bloch, Maurice, 138n77
Bonaparte, Napoleon, 100
Bongiovanni, Bruno, 157n161–62

Botta, Carlo, 100–102, 127
bourgeoisie, 3, 4, 12, 13, 21, 30, 32, 35–37, 39, 41, 45, 47, 48–49, 54, 55, 59, 62, 63, 66, 71, 73, 74, 75, 89, 99–100, 102, 119, 125, 142n143, 147n21, 156n150–51, 165n133; British, 39, 119, 142n143; French, 21, 36; Russian, 71, 73, 74, 147n21
Brezhnev, Leonid, 2
Britain, 4, 7, 9, 19–20, 23, 40, 42–43, 48–49, 50–51, 66, 77, 78, 83–85, 109, 119, 135n40, 136n58, 172n82
British East India Company, 22
British East Indies, 20, 66
British Museum, 12, 35
Brousse, Paul, 44, 78–79, 173n92
Brown, Heather, 138n77, 139n96
Brown, Willard, 38
Bull, John, 43–44, 144n167

Cafiero, Carlo, 80
Capital, 1, 4, 7, 14, 16, 26, 33, 35, 46, 53, 55–56, 58–59, 63–64, 72, 76, 77–93, 100, 101, 103, 117, 133n3, 134n9, 140–41n121, 146n6, 160n51, 162n88; *Volume I*, 16, 26, 46, 55, 56, 59, 63, 72, 88, 90, 92, 93, 101, 162n88, 169n15; *Volume II*, 16, 26, 76, 82, 85, 86, 87, 90–93 , 131n9, 160n51; *Volume III*, 76, 88, 93, 131n9, 160n51
capitalism, mode of production, 3, 4, 7, 11, 25, 39, 50, 54, 56–57, 59–60, 64, 72, 78, 88, 125, 162n102
Capponi, Gino, 102